SHERRY WITH THE BISHOP

CAROL BIEDERMAN

Word Project Press of Sonora, CA

Published in the United States by
Word Project Press
of Sonora, CA

Requests for permission to make copies of any part of this work should be submitted Online at
info@wordprojectpress.com

Credits
Front Cover Photo and Design: Melody Baker
Inside Layout: Melody Baker
Illustration: Gordon Biederman
Author Photo: Melody Baker

ISBN-10:0997034904
ISBN-13:978-0-9970349-0-5

ACKNOWLEDGEMENTS

A special thank you to Word Project Press, my editors/ critiquers/readers in the Sonoma Writers' Group of Sonoma, California and WOW writers of Sonora, California. Thank you, also, to the ever-supportive Gordon.

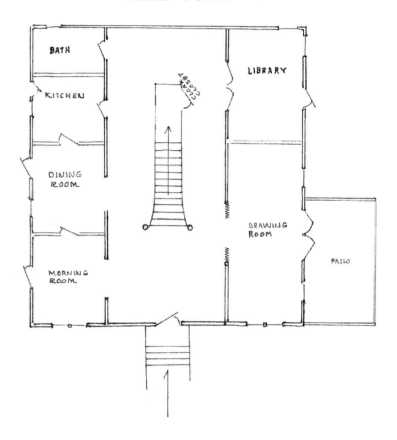

Dawson's Sketch

CONTENTS

PROLOGUE

. . . and by thy words thou shalt be condemned.
Matt. 12:37

June 6

Gwen Cunningham was dead; there could be no doubt about that. Just minutes before, she had cried out and grabbed at her throat, then struggled to her feet from the wingback chair in which she was sitting. The crystal sherry glass she had been holding fell, bouncing off a marble end table and shattering into tiny prisms, each catching the rays of the afternoon sun streaming through the windows. Her body arched, and she fell heavily to the floor, convulsing, vomiting. Then her body stiffened, and she lay still.

There was a collective gasp, a few exclamations of disbelief, from those assembled. Dr. Charles Glasco, a guest at this small gathering, dropped to his knees and felt for a pulse. He leaned over her, his face close to hers, as though to detect a fragile breath. Then he shook his head and stood.

"Heart attack?" Bishop Kindermann asked.

"Maybe." Glasco said. "Although . . . you saw how she convulsed and vomited . . . it could be . . ." He paused. "It could be poison." He turned to the hostess. "I think we should call the police, Mavis."

There was another gasp at the word 'police,' and the party exchanged glances; those who were sitting, stood,

9

and, with the exception of the bishop, moved as a body of one to the kitchen.

Kneeling beside the dead woman, the bishop took her hand and said softly, "Into Thy hands, oh Lord, we commend your servant, Gwen." As he stood, he made the sign of the cross – adding – his words measured, his face taut, "And may God have mercy on your soul." Then he followed the rest of the party.

PART ONE:

PERSONS OF INTEREST

CHAPTER ONE

The Investigators and the Guests

...that he might perform the words of the law...
2 Kings 23:24

June 6

It was less than an hour later Detective Chief Inspector Dawson and Detective Sergeant Eggleton arrived at the home of Mavis Dillon.

Bill Eggleton, thirty-seven years old, looked like an ex-football player, which, in fact, he was: two years of high school football and two of college, a sport he loathed. "It was so . . . so much . . . impact," he once said to his wife, Laura. His jackets and shirts strained across his chest and shoulders; his slacks clung to his heavy thighs. Twelve years with the police force had left his face unlined, but his heart deeply etched. At odds with his genial countenance was a dry, sardonic wit; the unwary, charmed by his benign expression – and a tendency to blush – were often surprised. He considered his best friends to be his wife and, when they were not on duty, his superior officer, Jake Dawson. When they were on duty, they were professional and sometimes brusque.

Unlike Eggleton, Jake Dawson's face, at fifty-nine, bore testimony to his profession. Although he held a degree in music from a prestigious university, reality set in when he realized his dream of performing on the great stages of the world was just that, a dream, and he faced a life in academia – performing for faculty recitals and teaching music theory and history. He returned to college for a degree in Criminal Justice. While he did not regret his decision, his life as a peace officer had taken a physical and emotional toll. A tall, thin man, his clothes sat easily on his body, lending an air of informal elegance; his hair, the color of polished silver, was worn long, covering his ears, one of which bore the results of a close call with a bullet. That event had resulted in years of cold sweats and uncontrollable night shakes, finally leading to his wife's departure with their daughter. "I can't live with the fear," she had said. He didn't know if she meant hers for him or his for himself; he didn't ask. He, too, possessed a dry wit, although he seldom found reason to use it. He rarely thought about friendships – certainly not best friends.

A young, uniformed officer opened the door for the two detectives, showing them into a large, marble-floored entry hall. Descending the massive staircase behind the young policeman was an attractive woman dressed in a blue calf-length dress that swirled gracefully about her legs. Dawson judged her to be in her late forties. She came toward them, her hand extended.

"I'm Mavis Dillon," she said. "This is my home."

Dawson shook her hand and then looked inquiringly at the officer.

"The body's in there, Sir." The young man pointed with his chin toward the large room that opened off the entry hall. Another officer stood at the door.

"The drawing room," Mrs. Dillon said. She gave her

head a quick shake, as though to rid herself of the reason for the policemen's presence in her home.

Dawson smiled. "If you would wait in another room for me," he said. "I'll be with you in a few minutes."

Although Mavis Dillon's face registered annoyance at Dawson's peremptory tone, she simply said. "I'll be in the morning room with the others," and turned toward a door on the opposite side of the hall from the drawing room.

"The others?" Dawson asked the officer when the door had closed behind Mrs. Dillon.

"Some sort of party going on here – sherry party." The officer shook his head, as if the idea of a party with sherry as the drink of choice was too foreign. "Seems the old gal dropped dead right in the middle of it. As soon as we got here, we put 'em in there – there's an officer with 'em," he said, gesturing to the door where Mrs. Dillon had disappeared. "One of 'em's a doctor: he's the one told Mrs. Dillon to call the police."

"Dr. Henchcombe and Dr. Lieberman here?"

"No, Sir. Not yet. Medical Examiner's office said they'd let Dr. Henchcombe know. Dr. Lieberman wasn't at Forensics, but I found him at home. He wasn't too happy about coming out. Said he had a dinner party to go to."

"Marty's never happy about anything," Dawson said as he walked toward the drawing room. "Besides," he whispered to Eggleton, "he wasn't going to any dinner party. He's too obnoxious to get invited any place."

Eggleton smiled. He'd heard all of this before.

The drawing room was large, furnished with upholstered chairs and sofas. Scattered on the hardwood floor were faded Oriental carpets. Small tables dotted the room, each with a vase of fresh flowers. Through the French doors, a garden, rich with green lawn and vibrantly colored blossoms, indicated the bouquets were home grown. Hanging over the mantel was a portrait of a beautiful young woman holding a violin. Gwen Cunningham's sprawled body was a jarring note in the gracious room.

Dawson knelt beside the body of the dead woman. Leaning close to her face, he sniffed. Then, sitting back on his heels, he looked at her contorted features. At last he pushed himself to his feet. "I'm going to wait for Hench and Marty" he said to Eggleton. "You go talk to the people across the hall. Find out what became of their glasses – and the sherry bottle."

Not my first rodeo, Eggleton thought.

"Get their names, and give them to Lieberman when he gets here – tell him to run them."

Eggleton flinched at the idea of telling Lieberman anything.

"What the hell's going on here?" It was the strident voice of Forensic Specialist, Dr. Martin Lieberman who had just arrived in the entry hall. He was a burly man with a pockmarked complexion, unkempt hair, and a bushy beard. His clothes were usually wrinkled and fit haphazardly – hence the department rumor he slept in them. He carried a laptop computer.

Behind Lieberman, and dwarfed by Lieberman's bulk, stood Medical Examiner/Coroner/ (and when necessary) lab technician, Dr. Steven Henchcombe. Clean shaven and neatly combed, he gave the appearance of a perfectly-formed miniature. His clothes, almost child-size, were without a wrinkle, the pants creased. His shirt collar was meticulously white; his tie coordinated exactly with his gray pinstripe suit. His black shoes reflected lights from the crystal chandelier that hung just above the foot of the stairs.

On hearing their voices, Dawson hurried out of the drawing room. "Hello Marty," he said as he crossed the hall toward the two men. "Hello Hench. Glad you're here." He gestured toward the drawing room. "Body's in there," he said. "Doctor that was here when it happened thought it might be poison. That's why he called the police. Deputies arrived, didn't like what they saw, and called Bill and me."

"Yeah. And you called us. My dinner date is going to be pretty pissed if this turns out somebody dropped dead of a heart attack."

"You don't have a dinner date, Marty. Let's go," Dawson said and led the way into the drawing room.

He watched as Dr. Henchcombe tweaked his trousers at the knee and knelt beside the body; he watched as Dr. Lieberman walked around the room, stopping occasionally to purse his lips, frown, and utter some profanity before moving on.

"Anything?" he asked finally.

"Probably poison," Henchcombe said, readjusting his position slightly to lean over the spot where she had vomited. Then he stood and gently shook his pant legs which fell without a wrinkle into their neat creases. "Either murder or suicide."

"Unlikely way to commit suicide, isn't it? Painful and messy. And why at a party?"

Henchcombe shrugged. "That'll be your job," he said. "I want to check something out before I say any more" He opened a small black leather bag with one hand and pulled his cell from his pocket with the other.

"Marty?"

Lieberman shook his head. "Just signs of a number of people drinking sherry and eating snacks. I can get the boys in to dust the room, but what you're going to find will be a million fingerprints of the people who attended the function. I think first you need to decide if you're calling this murder or suicide. Which means you're going to have to interview every person at this shindig – before they leave today."

"Plan to," Dawson said and left, closing the door to the drawing room and crossing the hall to the morning room. Drawing room. Morning room. *What kind of people name their rooms?* he wondered.

Inside the morning room, Eggleton was quietly taking names. In contrast to the white wicker furniture, the green plants, and the cheerful yellow cushions that decorated the room, an aura of gloom hovered. *Understandable,* Dawson thought – *they've lost a friend.* There was a silver coffee and tea service on a small table along with a stack of cups and saucers. A discreet bar along one wall held a display of hard liquors and mixes, and several people held glasses or cups. The murmur of conversation died when Dawson stepped in.

He surveyed them from his position near the door. Dominating the room was an imposing, dark-haired man wearing a clerical collar, a purple shirt such as he'd seen worn by the clerical hierarchy, and a large gold pectoral cross. Mavis Dillon stood by an unlit fireplace and beside her stood a man in his late sixties or early seventies. He was a small man, dressed in overalls and holding a woolen plaid tam-o'-shanter cap in one hand - in the other was a highball glass of some amber liquid. *Scotch,* thought Dawson: the old man and his drink. An attractive middle-aged woman sat in a wicker rocking chair; beside her stood a stocky, well-tanned man, his hand resting on her shoulder. Two women sat on the sofa. One had obviously been crying, the other was patting her shoulder. A younger woman, dressed in a bright blue sheath dress against which lay a string of pearls, held a cup in one hand and a saucer in the other. When she saw Dawson's eyes settle on her, her hands, which had been trembling slightly, jerked, and with a small clatter, she set the cup and saucer on a table and began twisting the pearls. The only person in the room that Dawson knew, other than Eggleton, was Charles Glasco.

Dr. Glasco had attended Dawson's father in his last illness, and Dawson had nothing but praise for the compassionate doctor. Some late evenings, as Dawson sat by the bed of his dying father, he and Glasco talked softly in the dimly lit room. In conversation, punctuated only by the murmur of the machines that monitored the ebb of the old man's life, Dawson and Glasco had found commonalities that eventually led them to a casual friendship. Each divorced for a number of years, neither had chosen to remarry. Both were fathers of daughters they saw infrequently, and both eschewed the machinery that would prolong inevitable death. "My father told me he didn't want to be hooked up to feeding machines," Dawson told Glasco. "Or respirators. He didn't believe in it."

Glasco concurred.

It was Glasco who stepped forward when Dawson

entered the room. Dawson took his arm and walked to an unoccupied corner of the room. "Any idea what happened here?" he asked, speaking softly.

"Could be poison, the way she convulsed," he said. "I guess you'll find out soon enough."

Just then the officer who had been on duty in the foyer opened the door to the morning room. "Dr. Lieberman and Dr. Henchcombe would like to speak with you, Sir," he said.

"Give me the names, Bill – I'll give them to Marty." With relief Eggleton handed the list to Dawson.

"Poison," Henchcombe said. "I'll be a hundred percent sure when I get her on the table, but I think you can go ahead and find out who in there . . ." he tipped his head toward the morning room, ". . . is carrying some poison. I'd look for a clear liquid for starters. Oily. Possibly nicotine." He patted the pocket that held his cell phone. "It's not generally available to the public, but it is used in nurseries for pest control. Diluted – but seeing this garden . . ." and he gestured toward the doors that led to the patio, "I imagine there's some pretty potent stuff around here to control pests. Get somebody to describe exactly what happened."

"Doctor says she convulsed."

"Consistent with nicotine," Henchcombe said.

"You're really serious about nicotine?"

"Uh huh. Powerful stuff. Has a slightly fishy smell when it's warm." He held up a small cigarette lighter and plastic bag with a spoon as if to explain he had done an on-the-spot science experiment with the vomit. "Like I said, I'll know more when I cut her open."

"Would she have been able to taste it?"

"Acidic, but the sherry probably covered that."

"I'll get back to the morning room," Dawson said as he walked to the door. "You going to be around for a while."

"Yes," Henchcombe said.

Lieberman scowled and muttered, "Dinner date."

"Sure," Dawson said, and closed the door.

All eyes turned to Dawson when he returned to the morning room.

"Any idea how she might have gotten hold of poison?" Dawson asked without preamble.

His question elicited little response. The crying woman on the sofa stifled a sob, the young woman twisted her pearl necklace, the older man – *probably the gardener* Dawson thought – took a swig of his drink, the clergyman cleared his throat, but no one spoke.

"Is there any poison in the house, Mrs. Dillon?"

Mavis looked at the assembled group. Finally she said, "There is some nicotine concentrate in the kitchen – on the window sill."

Dawson's eyebrows shot up. "Nicotine concentrate in the kitchen?" he repeated and motioned to Eggleton.

"Go tell Lieberman," he whispered.

Eggleton nodded.

"Isn't the kitchen an unusual place for poison?" Dawson turning back to Mavis.

The stocky man spoke up. "I put it there," he said. "On the window sill. I told Mavis where I was putting it when Dolores and I arrived. My name is George Alexander. I'm a landscape consultant with Tyler Nurseries. Mavis," he nodded toward Mrs. Dillon, "asked me for something to kill the aphids on her flowers. We use it at the nursery sometimes, so I brought her a small amount. You mix it with water and spray it. This has been an exceptionally bad year for aphids, and the nicotine is highly effective."

"Highly poisonous, too, I would imagine."

The little man standing near the fireplace spoke. "Aye, that it is, that it is. And glad I was to be havin' it. I've tried everythin' in me shed, but nowt would touch 'em, I can tell ye that." His cheeks were pink from the fortifying drink. His brogue was lilting, bringing a tone of cheer to the somber room.

"Is that what you were thinking, Charles?"

"Well, not necessarily nicotine. I thought poison was a possibility. It appears your specialists think the same, or you wouldn't be asking the question."

"Exactly what happened when she fell?"

"I didn't see it all," Charles said. "I heard her call out and then she fell – seemed to convulse." He shook his head. "Sorry. I can't be more specific."

Dawson looked around the room. "Anybody else?"

The clergyman stepped forward. "Bishop Jerry Kindermann," he said, holding out his hand. The bishop, despite his German name, had light tan skin, penetrating black eyes, and curly black hair liberally sprinkled with gray. German father, Dawson thought as he shook the bishop's hand, mother probably from one of the Mediterranean countries.

"I was standing near the chair where she was sitting.

She made a horrible sound, stood up partway and then she pitched forward. She vomited and her body – well . . . well, it was like a seizure." He paused for a moment. "Inspector," he said, "perhaps I shouldn't ask this, but these people have had a great shock. Is there any chance they could go home, or will you . . . will you be questioning us individually?" He coughed, looking embarrassed. "I'm afraid I'm a great mystery fan – reading when I should be preparing sermons, actually – and in the books the detectives question . . ." He stopped, shaking his head. "I'm sorry – I'm rambling. It's different when it really happens, isn't it? I know we would all be grateful if we could go home." He turned to Mavis. "I'm afraid our hostess is just about out on her feet. It's been a terrible experience, but for Mavis especially, I think."

"I will need a statement from each of you individually," Dawson said.

Dolores Alexander gasped; her husband patted her shoulder.

"Should we have a lawyer present?" the bishop asked.

"Premature. If it becomes necessary, you'll be advised. However, if you want to have a lawyer present, you are certainly free to call." He swept his hand – encompassing the room. "Any of you. In the meantime, I suggest you make yourselves comfortable. This will take some time – quite a bit of time. The uniformed officer is here to prevent any discussion of the incident. I trust you will give him your co-operation." He gestured to Mavis Dillon. "Is there a room where I can take these statements?"

"Of course," she said. "I'll get you settled in the library."

As they followed Mavis down the hall, Eggleton

whispered, "Given the bishop's position . . ."

"He's a suspect, just like the others," Dawson whispered back. "He can call his lawyer if he wants."

"Surely a bishop wouldn't . . ."

"Oh, come on!"

Another beautifully appointed room, Dawson thought as they entered. A large oak desk dominated the room; book shelves lined the walls. Mavis positioned two leather armchairs to face each other. "I expect your sergeant will want to use the desk to take notes," she said as she shoved a pile of papers into a drawer. "Will you need anything else? Coffee?"

"Please – and perhaps a carafe of water." Then he added, "Mrs. Dillon, it might save time if you could tell me what this gathering is about."

"Oh! Of course. You don't know, do you? Tomorrow is confirmation at Saint Francis Episcopal Church, so the bishop is here for the occasion. It's the tradition, when he visits, for a member of the vestry to entertain the bishop and vestry members for a sherry party. This year I volunteered."

"Vestry being?"

"It's the governing body of the local church," Mavis said.

"And the guests are?"

"You've met the bishop, and you obviously know Charles Glasco. The younger woman is Nancy Gifford, the Rector's wife. Father Greg was tied up this afternoon with confirmation class, so he wasn't able to attend. Linda and Sandy are vestry members. George is the treasurer. He brought his wife, Dolores. I'm a vestry member. And Gwen is . . . ," she cleared her throat and made a gesture in the direction of the drawing room, "Gwen was a vestry member as well. My gardener, Andrew, is here, too. He was working in the back garden during the party." She smiled. "We're getting the grounds ready for my daughter's wedding reception. . ." She stopped, her hand to her heart. "Dear God! I hadn't thought . . . I hope this doesn't . . ."

"There doesn't seem to be much grief about this death – unless the lady who's crying . . ."

Mavis' smile was tight and did not reach her eyes. "I don't expect you'll find many mourners, Inspector – at least not among those here. Sandy cries from shock, no more."

"What about next-of-kin?" Dawson asked. "Is there a Mr. Cunningham or any children, anyone we should contact today?"

"I don't know of any," Mavis said. "You could ask Father Greg when he arrives. I had Nancy call him."

"Did Mrs. Cunningham bring a purse with her this afternoon?"

Mavis' hand flew to her mouth. "Of course!" she exclaimed. "How stupid of me to forget. It's in the cloak room. I'll get it for you right away."

Dawson put his hand on her arm. "My sergeant will go with you," he said, holding out a pair of plastic gloves to Eggleton.

"I have some," Eggleton said.

"Get it printed."

Eggleton rolled his eyes.

"Well," Mavis said, "I'll show the sergeant to the cloak room, and then I'll get some coffee started." She glanced over her shoulder at the Inspector. "I'll send a box of tissues, too. If you're going to interview Sandy, you'll need those."

Eggleton gestured Mrs. Dillon ahead of him and closed the library door, leaving the Inspector to ponder what she had said about no one grieving Mrs. Cunningham's death. Apparently he had been wrong when he thought the people in the morning room had lost a friend. He jotted a few notes: Bishop, rector's wife, Sandy/shock, Andrew/gardener, wedding, George/treasurer. Then, slipping his notebook into his jacket pocket, he returned to the drawing room where Martin Lieberman was directing his crew with an efficiency that always impressed Dawson. He knew better than to get in Lieberman's way.

Both Dawson and Lieberman had come from Southern California precincts to the more rural jurisdiction of the wine country. Their reasons for coming were dramatically different, but each brought with him the expertise of years of service on a large metropolitan force.

Dawson came to put behind him the sadness of his divorce and to be near his elderly father. The two men, father and son, enjoyed a convivial bachelorhood for several years, and when his father died, Dawson was left with the family home, a large, rambling Victorian surrounded by beautiful grounds. In addition, there were several hundred acres of Chardonnay and Merlot grapes. Dawson sold the house – it held too many memories for him – and moved into a condominium, which he furnished with the Spartan necessities of life and his grand piano which took up most of the space in his living room. He leased the vineyards to a large local winery, providing him with a significant supplemental income. The sadness of the divorce remained with him.

Lieberman came because, although he was a renowned forensic specialist, he wanted a place where he could meditate, write poetry, and walk in the country. Shy about his avocation, Lieberman had adopted an abrasive and crude persona, which he honed to authenticity. He told no one except Dawson of his reasons for the move – and then only after a considerable amount of Wild Turkey. Dawson had agreed to help Lieberman maintain his fiction.

Over the years of working together, Dawson had come to recognize Lieberman's forensic genius: hairs, skin scrapings, a fleck of ash or a strand of tobacco, a thread, a book open to a significant page, a telephone positioned to accommodate a left-handed dialer, a spot of mud, a chip of paint, a drop of blood inside a coat pocket, a cotton ball, all these and more figured in the cases handled by Dawson and Lieberman, and Dawson knew to leave Lieberman to his work.

A story, part of the department folklore, told of one incident– about a year after Lieberman joined the force at Castlemont– when the Chief of Police reprimanded him for his language. Lieberman, who also enjoyed an additional income left him by a wealthy aunt who liked his poetry, was reported to have said, "Fine. You know where to send my check," and walked out of the building. Remembering the number of cases closed since Lieberman had joined the force, and knowing skills like Lieberman's would be impossible to replace, the chief had followed Lieberman out to his car and begged him to reconsider. Rumor went on to say Lieberman said 'asshole' and walked back into the building– to which the chief responded, "Thank you."

Now Lieberman was haranguing the photographer,

his words jarring in Mavis Dillon's beautiful room.

"Get your butt over here!" He whirled around and glared at Dawson. "What the hell are you looking at?"

"Just always a pleasure to see the quiet, professional way you work, Marty." Dawson said, smiling. He started to leave the room. "Always such a pleasure," he said over his shoulder.

"Your goddamn sergeant has one of my photographers taking pictures of the effin' cloak room!" Lieberman roared. "How the hell am I supposed to do anything around here if my crew is off taking pictures for House-goddamn-Beautiful?"

Dawson shook his head.

"What?"

"Your limited vocabulary, Marty," Dawson said. "I would think an educated man like yourself would have a broader vocabulary. By the way, Marty," Dawson said with a small, tight smile. "There's a lot of people in the morning room." He tipped his head in the direction of the closed door. "One of them's a bishop."

Lieberman turned pale. Perhaps the one thing in the world Lieberman respected was the hierarchy of faith: Catholic, Protestant, Evangelical, Jewish, Muslim —any and all; his father had been a rabbi. He swallowed deeply.

"You got the nicotine?"

Lieberman just nodded.

Eggleton was seated at the huge desk when Dawson walked in, the purse on the desk beside him. The outside of the purse was dusty with fingerprint powder.

"Would you look at the size of this desk?" Eggleton

said, running his hands across the expanse of it. "I bet something like this cost more than you and I take home in a month combined!"

"Probably so, Sergeant," Dawson said. "Probably so. But would having a desk this size make you happy?" He raised his eyebrows at his sergeant.

"Probably so, Inspector. Probably so."

Dawson made a small sound Eggleton thought might be a laugh. "Let's take a quick look inside this purse before we start questioning anyone. Did the contents get printed?"

"Not yet."

Taking the plastic gloves from his pocket a second time, Dawson slipped them on and carried the purse to a long library table beneath the windows. Eggleton followed.

"Wow!" Eggleton exclaimed as Dawson spilled the contents onto the table. "Look at all that stuff!"

"At the risk of being labeled a sexist, I think most women's purses are much the same," Dawson said, grabbing two plastic bottles of pills and a lipstick as they rolled toward the edge of the table.

"Two different prescriptions," Eggleton observed, rolling the bottles with the eraser of his pencil. "Different doctors – different pharmacies. Ambien and Ativan."

"Huh? Oh yeah," Dawson, distracted by a small daily planner he was leafing through, said. "Write those down." He read for several more minutes and then slid the planner toward Eggleton. "Look at today's date."

"Sherry with Bish., Nancy/Myersons?, Geo./Acct.? - I assume that's account or accountant - Bish./sec./son?, Mavis/bkgd.?, Linda/Sandra, rlnsp.?" Eggleton looked up from the page as he stumbled over the abbreviations.

"Whatever the hell that's supposed to mean?" He continued reading. "Chas./Dan./Marg.?" He handed the book to Dawson. "What do you make of it?"

"I don't make anything of it yet, Bill. But it certainly is the entire guest list, isn't it. Except Mrs. Alexander. Maybe Mrs. Cunningham didn't know Mrs. Alexander was coming." Taking his notebook from his pocket, Dawson wrote down Mrs. Cunningham's notations, then slid the contents back into the purse and handed it to Eggleton. "Go tell Marty I'll want the pill bottles printed, too," he said, slipping off the plastic gloves.

Eggleton winced.

"He's calmed down," Dawson said with a tiny grin. "And have Hench look at the prescriptions. Then get the woman who was crying. We'll question her first."

CHAPTER TWO

Interview: Sandy Liske and Linda Gentry

For they have cast their heads together with one consent . . .
Psalm 83:5

SANDY

Sandy Liske twisted her handkerchief mercilessly between dabs at her swollen eyes and red nose.

"Sergeant, pour Mrs. Liske a cup of coffee," Dawson said. "Or, there's tea here. . ."

"Yes, tea," she said, blowing her nose. "Lots of sugar."

Eggleton rose and went to the sideboard. The room was silent save for Sandy's sniffles and the clink of pot, cup and saucer.

"Now, suppose you tell me what happened this afternoon," Dawson said when she was settled with her tea.

"Why am I first, Inspector?" she asked, her cup clattering against her saucer.

"You looked especially distraught there in the morning room, and I thought the sooner we were able to get you home, the better you'd be." Then, flashing back on what Mavis Dillon had said about there being few mourners, he continued, "Was Mrs. Cunningham a close friend of yours?"

"It's nice of you to be concerned, but I'll have to wait

until you finish with Linda. We came together."

"About Mrs. Cunningham; was she a particularly close friend?"

Sandy balled her wet handkerchief and shoved it in her pocket. "No, not especially."

"But she was a friend?" Dawson persisted.

"No. I knew her is all. We were both on the vestry at church."

"How long have you known Mrs. Cunningham?"

"About twelve years, I guess."

"But you didn't consider her a friend?"

"I said I didn't, Inspector." The hand holding the cup shook, and she set the cup and saucer on the small table by her chair.

shaky, Eggleton wrote in his notebook.

"Was she an enemy?"

Sandy looked at Dawson sharply. "I don't know what you mean. I just knew her, is all. She wasn't anything to me."

Dawson leaned forward, his elbows on his knees, his hands folded, his eyes narrowed. Again he was remembering Mavis Dillon's words. "Did you dislike Mrs. Cunningham?"

"Everybody disliked her!" Sandy's words erupted, and fresh tears ran down her cheeks. "I don't know of anybody who liked her!"

"Then you're glad she's dead?"

"That's not true! At least . . ." She hesitated. "Anyway, I didn't kill her, if that's what you're getting at."

"I'm just trying to get a picture of Mrs. Cunningham. You tell me nobody liked her, and it looks to me as if somebody may have *not liked* her enough to kill her." He leaned back in his chair. "Now, it's my job to find out who killed her, and you can help me. Tell me what happened this afternoon."

"You mean when she died?" Sandy asked and plunged on without waiting for an answer. "We were all in the drawing room – just talking. The party was pretty much winding down. People were talking about going home. Anyway, Gwen was sitting in one of the chairs, and all of a sudden she made this horrible sound and sort of rose up, like she was going to stand or something." Sandy raised herself partway out of the chair, demonstrating. "Then her back arched and she fell backwards. She hit the edge of the chair and then just slid to the floor." Sandy shuddered. "It was awful!"

"What was happening at the party earlier in the afternoon?"

"We wandered around, talking to people. Some of us went out into the garden." She paused as she picked up the cup and took a sip. "Actually, I guess we all went into the garden at one time or another. Mavis had the French doors open, and it was just natural to go in and out."

"Did you talk specifically to Mrs. Cunningham?"

"I guess."

"You guess? You don't know?"

"All right, yes. We talked to Gwen. She sort of made the rounds of everybody, and she stopped and talked to Linda and me for a while. She'd been talking with the bishop, and then she came over to us."

"And what did you talk about?"

Sandy shrugged. "I don't really remember," she said,

looking down at her tea cup.

Eggleton made a note: *lying!*

"Oh, surely, Mrs. Liske. You must remember something."

"Maybe something about us being teachers, I guess." She was still staring at her tea cup.

"So you and Mrs. Gentry are both teachers?"

Sandy raised her eyes from her study of the tea. "We teach at the high school."

"And you came to the party together?"

"Yes."

"You live near each other?"

"We live together," she said. There was a defiant edge to her voice. "Linda is widowed, and I'm divorced, so we decided the most economical thing would be to share expenses. This way it gives us something to travel on."

rlnsp? Eggleton jotted .

"Seems a wise plan," Dawson said, nodding. "So Mrs. Cunningham mentioned you both being teachers? What specifically did she say about you being teachers?"

"Inspector, this is feeling more like interrogation than interview."

"I'm trying to kill two birds, you might say. Although that may not be the best choice of words." Dawson smiled.

Eggleton drew a happy face in his notebook. *joke!* he wrote.

"But," Dawson continued, "whatever you can tell me about this afternoon means I may not have to speak to you again. I'm sure you understand."

Sandy looked as though she didn't, but she nodded.

"So again, can you tell me what she said about you

being teachers?"

Sandy shrugged. "She said it was hard to always be in the public eye."

"Those were her exact words?"

"Well no, not exact. But it's what she meant."

"You can't remember her exact words?"

Sandy shook her head. "Then she said she wanted to talk to Nancy, so she left us and went over to the bookcase where Nancy was."

"What did you do after Mrs. Cunningham collapsed?" Dawson asked abruptly.

Startled by the change of direction, Sandy looked at Dawson. "Well . . ." She stopped and her eyes filled with tears.

"Mrs. Liske?"

"We . . . We . . . Charles, that's Doctor Glasco, got down beside her and checked for a pulse. Then the bishop . . ." her voice broke. Dawson waited. "The bishop asked if it was a heart attack, and Charles said we should call the police."

Her hands began to shake again, and Dawson stood. He took the cup from her, placed it on the table beside her chair, and handed her a tissue. "Go on, Mrs. Liske," he said as he sat back down.

Sandy blew her nose loudly and stuffed the tissue in her pocket and then straightened her shoulders and raised her chin. "We decided . . ." she paused, taking a deep breath. "We decided the first one in here had to . . . had to tell you," she said.

Dawson leaned close the Sandy Liske. "Tell me what, Mrs. Liske?" he asked softly.

"We all . . ." Her voice caught again, and she started over. "We all went out to the kitchen and we all . . ."

"Yes?"

She took a deep breath and her words came in a rush. "We all handled the nicotine bottle."

Eggleton's pencil slipped from his fingers. It rolled under the desk, and he scrambled to retrieve it.

Dawson sent him a quick frown and turned back to Sandy, his voice deadly calm. "Let me get this straight, Mrs. Liske. After Doctor Glasco asked Mrs. Dillon to call the police, you all went into the kitchen and passed the nicotine bottle around? Am I getting this right?"

Eggleton's pencil raced across the page.

"Yes, Inspector." She gripped the arms of the chair.

"May I ask why?"

"Because, if she was poisoned – and you have to think that's what Doctor Glasco was getting at when he said to call the police – it would mean one of us had done it, and we didn't want any one of us to be blamed."

"And did you discuss this plan before you went out into the kitchen?"

"No."

"You all just thought of it at the same time?"

"I guess," Sandy said, shrugging.

"Before or after Mrs. Dillon phoned the police?"

"Before."

"And why would you not want any one of you to be blamed? If someone murdered her, wouldn't you want that person found?"

"No!"

"No?"

"No, Inspector!" Her eyes were damp but blazing. "She was a hateful woman. People didn't just dislike her, they despised her. She was cruel, vicious, unfeeling. She destroyed lives."

"In what way did she destroy lives, Mrs. Liske?"

"The things she said about people, implying things, gossiping, innuendos. She pried into people's affairs and then talked about what she'd learned." Sandy brought her tea cup to her lips; her hands were steady. "It was uncanny how she could ferret out someone's secrets, but she couldn't keep quiet about it. She blabbed it all over town. And much of what she said wasn't even true, or at least not entirely true. But people lost their jobs, their marriages, several even committed suicide – one of our teachers in fact. She was . . ." Sandy shook her head. "Perhaps after you've talked with the others, you'll understand." She laughed uneasily. "I was the wrong person to have to tell you about handling the nicotine bottle," she said. "I'm not terribly articulate when I'm upset. Any one of the others could have done better."

"You've done just fine, Mrs. Liske," Dawson said. "Although, I am taken aback by your information. You realize you've all tampered with what may prove to be evidence."

"Yes," she said. "But I expect you'll understand better after you've had a chance to talk to the others. May I go now?"

"Not yet," Dawson said, standing.

There was a knock on the door. Frowning, Dawson called, "Yes?"

Henchcombe stuck his head in. "There's a memo for you," he said and handed Dawson a small piece of paper.

"Hold up, Doctor," Dawson said as Henchcombe started to pull the door shut behind him. "I'm coming with you." He glanced at the note and passed it to Eggleton. Then, turning back to Sandy Liske, he said, "I'm going to share this information about the nicotine bottle with Doctor Lieberman and Doctor Henchcombe, and then I'll be back, and we will continue this conversation." He gestured to Eggleton. "Sergeant Eggleton will stay with you," he said as he left the library.

Sandy put her head in her hands. Her shoulders shook. Eggleton spent the time adding to his notes. He hated it when women cried.

"They did what?" Lieberman bellowed when Dawson finished telling him and Henchcombe about the much-handled nicotine bottle.

It was a rhetorical question; Dawson didn't bother to respond. "Is it going to do any good to print 'em?" he asked.

"Nicotine bottle's no use now. Glasses they used are so facetted they won't take a print. Shit!"

"What about sherry bottles?"

"All decanted – into facetted crystal containers," Lieberman said, wiping his hand across his forehead. "Everything's so fuckin' fancy around here. Silver, crystal, fuckin' Orientals older than God."

Dawson, who had been to Lieberman's home a number of times, resisted the opportunity to point out Lieberman was no stranger to nice furnishings.

"Nothing I can print, but the poison wouldn't have been in the decanters anyway. Unless whoever did this didn't care who or how many he – or she – killed. I checked the recycle for empties, but recycle and garbage were collected about noon today. We'll check the decanters for residue to be sure, but . . ." He raised his hands in a hopeless gesture.

"Dead end. Did you pick up anything on Cunningham's purse?"

"Eyeballing it, it looks like just her prints. I'll take 'em in and have a closer look. But if this was nicotine . . ." he paused, looking at Henchcombe.

"I'm pretty sure – ninety percent."

Lieberman shrugged. "Then the purse wasn't involved, even if someone else handled it."

"Well – check it anyway – see if there's any prints other than Cunningham's. Damn!" Dawson looked at his watch and headed toward the door. "I've got a lot of people to interview and, if the first one is any example, I'm going to be here a very long time."

"Before you leave, I want you to look at something," Henchcombe said and led Dawson to where the body of Gwen Cunningham still lay. Pinching his pant legs at the knee, he knelt beside the body and pulled a heavy metal bracelet down over Gwen's hand, revealing a scar. "Other arm's the same."

"Looks like an old scar. You're thinking a suicide attempt?"

Henchcombe nodded and pushed the bracelet back into place. "Long time ago," he said as he stood. "But . . ." He left any further thoughts hanging.

"More to think about."

"Uh huh.

"Thanks, Hench – I guess." Dawson walked to the

door. "I'm back to my interviews. See ya."

"Like hell you will," Lieberman said. "I've got a date – a dinner party."

"No you don't," Dawson said, and closed the door to the drawing room behind him.

Henchcombe smiled. A very small smile – very discreet.

When Dawson got back to the library, he found Sandy Liske, red-eyed, but calm, holding a fresh cup of tea.

"Did Mrs. Cunningham leave the room at all?" he asked as he returned to his chair.

"You mean other than to go out to the patio?"

"Yes."

"I don't know. If she did, I didn't notice."

"Just one more question, Mrs. Liske. Did Mrs. Cunningham imply anything when she was talking to you and Mrs. Gentry?"

"Imply?"

"That was your word – imply."

"About what?"

"I was hoping you could tell me, Mrs. Liske."

Sandy Liske pursed her lips, recalling the conversation she and Linda had with Gwen Cunningham that afternoon.

They had been seated on a wicker sofa on the patio, admiring Mavis's garden and discussing how they might do something similar, when Gwen, with a great clanking of bracelets and billow of chiffon, lowered herself into a nearby chair. "Well, you two!" she said. "Didn't I see you last week at Gino's? You had a bottle of champagne and spent the evening toasting each other. You were so absorbed, you never even saw me." She glanced around, as if checking to make sure none of the guests could overhear, then leaned toward them and lowered her voice conspiratorially. "But seriously, you must be careful. People might misinterpret your relationship, especially since you're living together, and it would never do to have two of our teachers sullied with gossip, now would it?"

The bishop's hearty laugh carried to them from across the garden, and Sandy thought then how incongruous it sounded against Gwen's menacing monologue. Gwen scrunched her eyes. "They call policemen 'our finest' but I think it's really teachers, don't you? But, of course you must be above reproach. A terrible burden, I should imagine."

"Really, Gwen. What are you implying?" Linda asked, but Gwen Cunningham plunged on.

"Of course, I would never suggest such a thing, but not all people are as sensitive as I. Especially school boards. Of course, they have to be so careful. I served one term, you know."

"I remember," Sandy said, remembering also a particularly tragic incident several years before when the board had not rehired Mark, a young math teacher at the high school, because of allegations regarding his sexual orientation. And the horrible aftermath. Gwen Cunningham had been on the board then.

"Things could get so unpleasant," Gwen continued. She patted Linda on the knee, as though to underscore her meaning. Linda pulled her knee aside, but Gwen appeared not to notice. "Well," she said, "I'm going to get myself one of Mavis's delicious cookies. I just wanted to give you a word of warning, dears," she said. "Tongues are wagging." She stood, tossing back her sherry as she did so.

"And both of them are yours, Gwen," Linda retorted, her face red with anger.

Gwen Cunningham's eyes narrowed. "I'll remember that," she said.

"Yikes!" Linda's whisper was full of sarcasm.

As Sandy and Linda watched her walk away, Sandy sputtered, "What an abomination!"

"What?" Linda asked. "Cunningham, or the way she treats good sherry?"

Sandy smiled as she remembered Linda's comment.

"You're smiling, Mrs. Liske," Dawson said. "You've remembered something amusing?"

Sandy jerked herself back to the present, shaking her head. "No, No, not really. I'm just remembering Linda's comment about Gwen not treating good sherry any better than she treated people."

Dawson raised his eyebrows.

"Usually she'd just toss it back – like a shot of whiskey."

tossed Eggleton wrote.

"Tossed?"

"Most of the time. I rarely saw her sip. She'd carry the glass for a while, then all of a sudden it was gone –the sherry, not the glass."

didn't sip–tell hench

"Oh," Dawson said, and brought the conversation back. "I was asking if anything Mrs. Cunningham implied made you uncomfortable . . . perhaps a reference to you and Mrs. Gentry living together," he added remembering the notation in Mrs. Cunningham's daily planner.

"No!" Sandy's hand shook, and she set the cup and saucer on the table beside her chair. The cup clattered in the saucer. "Linda and I have been friends for many years," she said softly. "We began our teaching careers the same semester at Hamilton Doyle High School. Being new to the school, I guess we just gravitated toward one another for companionship. I think we both felt left out of things. The older, more seasoned teachers, regarded our youthful idealism rather cynically, so we got together and spouted high-sounding educational theories to one another." She smiled. "I fear we've become a bit jaded over the years. Reality will do that to you."

Dawson smiled, remembering his days as a young policeman.

"Anyway, we introduced our husbands to each other, and pretty soon we were a foursome. Money was short and it seemed one or the other of us was always pregnant – I have four children, Linda has three – so most of the time we just barbecued in each other's back yard for entertainment.

Her face grew sad. "Just as we were beginning to get a little comfortable – you know, the money situation was a little easier, and the kids were nearly grown – Linda's husband had a massive heart attack and died. His funeral was no sooner over when my husband announced he wanted a divorce. So," she shrugged, "there we were, at middle age with kids in their late teens to finish raising, and the struggles began again. This time we weren't so young." She half-stood, reaching to pull a tissue from the box on the desk, and blew her nose. "I can't imagine this can be of any interest to you, Inspector," she said.

"But you are living together now?" Dawson persisted.

"Yes. Just last month I sold my house and moved in with Linda – to save expenses. We had finally gotten the kids grown, so we thought we might like to travel in a few years. When we retire, I mean."

"And Mrs. Cunningham had something to say about that?" Dawson asked.

"No!" Sandy's face flushed red. "I already said she didn't!"

me thinks the lady Eggleton doodled in his notebook.

Dawson stood up and walked to the window. A sliver of moon had appeared in a sky not yet dark. Dawson's back was to the room, and the room was quiet.

Sandy reflected on what she would never tell Dawson.

* * *

It had been just three months before, while Linda cried softly over her daughter's latest marital difficulties, and Sandy patted her shoulder, they had turned to one another and found a different kind of comfort.

* * *

At last Dawson said. "Thank you for your help, Mrs. Liske. I think we'll talk with your friend next, so you can get on home."

"Thank you, Inspector." Sandy started for the door – and stopped. "Inspector, do you think it might have been suicide?" she asked.

"Suicide?" Dawson asked, thinking about Henchcombe's discovery under the bracelets.

"All those bracelets she wore . . . I mean . . . well, everybody thought . . ."

"We'll see," Dawson said. "It's early times yet. Sergeant, would you take Mrs. Liske back to the morning room and bring Mrs. Gentry in?"

"I thought Early Times was a whiskey," Eggleton whispered as he passed Dawson.

"Huh?"

LINDA

"Mrs. Gentry," Dawson asked as he motioned Linda Gentry to a seat and took one himself, "what can you tell us about what happened this afternoon.?"

"Probably not much Sandy didn't already tell you," she said, nodding to Eggleton who was holding up the coffee pot and a cup and saucer, a question on his face. "Yes, thank you, Sergeant. Black."

"Maybe not. But why don't we start with Mrs. Cunningham's death. Can you describe what you saw happen?"

Eggleton handed the coffee to Linda as she related the scene to Dawson. Her account did not differ significantly from Sandy's, and Dawson moved on. "Did you speak directly with Mrs. Cunningham this afternoon?" he asked.

Linda looked at him over her coffee cup. "I'm sure Sandy has already told you we did," she said. "Gwen came over and talked to us for a while, said something about seeing us out for dinner at Gino's recently."

47

Eggleton cast a quick glance at Dawson, but the Inspector's face was impassive. Eggleton returned to his notebook. *gino's* he wrote.

"And what did she have to say about you having dinner at Gino's?"

Linda shrugged her shoulders. "Just that, Inspector," she said. "She saw us."

"Mrs. Liske tells me you all went into the kitchen and handled the nicotine bottle," the Inspector said.

"Yes," she said, apparently startled by his change of subject.

"Why?"

"A collective conscience, I guess. Or collective guilt. I don't think any one of us would want one of the others found guilty if this proves to be murder."

"And you all handled the bottle?"

"Yes. We all handled it," she said, placing her cup and saucer on the small table beside her chair. Eggleton noted, unlike Sandy Liske, Mrs. Gentry's hands were steady. He wondered if it was significant. He would talk to Dawson about it.

"The bishop?"

"Well, since you mention it, I don't know. He came into the kitchen a little after the rest of us did. And we were passing it around. It was sort of an in-house kind of thing, so I can't tell you either way."

"Who handled it first?"

"I don't remember for sure," Linda said. She closed her eyes as though picturing the scene. "I think it might have been George; he was the one who brought it in the first place." She opened her eyes. "Yes, George. He took it off the window sill. Then Dolores took it out of his hand if I remember correctly. I was next. I took it from Dolores."

"Who took it from you?"

"Sandy."

"And from her?"

"I don't know. It would have to be either Mavis or Charles. Or Nancy. It could have been Nancy. You'd have to ask Sandy."

"What about the bishop."

"Like I said, he came in late. He took it from . . ." she paused, frowning. " . . . Nancy. He took it from Nancy and put it back on the window sill."

"He knew where to put it?"

"Oh, yes. We all did. When George came in this afternoon – to the party – he told Mavis he was going to put it on the sill in the kitchen. We all heard him."

"What else did Mrs. Cunningham talk to you about?" asked Dawson, switching the topic again. "Anything about church business, or your jobs, anything you can remember?"

"Nothing about the church. She talked about us being teachers, and we get close scrutiny from the public. She was on the School Board for one term. Appointed rather than elected, I might add. One of the elected members quit rather suddenly. Gwen had run for the board, but was the only one not elected. Then, when the other member quit, they appointed Gwen. Much less costly than having an election for one seat." Linda shook her head. "However, the cost proved to be extremely high."

"In what way, Mrs. Gentry?"

"She was . . ." Linda stopped abruptly. "It's really not relevant," she said, her voice strained.

"Perhaps you'll let me decide what's relevant," Dawson said.

"I was about to say she was instrumental in getting a teacher fired."

"Oh" He paused for a moment.

'That was her word, Mrs. Gentry? Scrutiny?"

Linda, with an imperceptible sigh of relief, hastened to answer this change of subject. "Maybe not her exact word, but that was the implication."

Her relief was short-lived. "Why was the teacher fired?" Dawson asked.

The Inspector's habit of switching from one topic to another was wearing on Linda. She sighed. "His sexuality was really the issue, but the Board would never admit it. They just said his performance hadn't been satisfactory." She made a face. "Which was nonsense! There wasn't a teacher at the high school who worked harder than Mike, and the kids loved his classes. Gwen Cunningham was the one who brought the issue to the Board." Again, Linda wished her words back. Dawson' style of switching subjects was putting her off guard. Obviously he meant to, she thought.

"I thought personnel issues were discussed behind closed doors," Dawson said.

Linda Gentry looked at Dawson as one might look at a naïve child. If Dawson noticed, he made no mention.

"My neighbor was on the Board at the time. She said Gwen pushed for dismissal, and the Board didn't have much choice."

"Your neighbor was talking out of school," Dawson said, smiling.

Linda smiled back. "She was, indeed. She thought the

whole thing was a travesty – said she wouldn't run for the Board again if Gwen was going to be on it."

"What happened to the young man?"

Linda looked away. "He took his own life," she said, matter-of-factly. When she turned back to Dawson, her face was scarlet and her eyes brimmed with tears. She picked up her coffee cup.

"I'm sorry," Dawson said. "I do remember the case. I didn't make the connection." He paused, letting Mrs. Gentry compose herself. "I know this is difficult for you," he continued. "I'm hoping we can finish here soon. Did Mrs. Cunningham stay on the Board?"

"No. She decided not to run for another term –probably because she knew she would lose the election again."

"So she ran for a position on the Vestry of St. Francis instead?"

"No, that was another appointment. Well, actually, she did run, but, like the School Board, she wasn't elected. Then when one of the members of the Vestry moved, Gwen just sort of slid into the spot. I remember we were all shocked when she showed up at a meeting. Father Greg just shrugged when we asked him 'how come?'" Linda shrugged as if demonstrating. "Gwen is a huge contributor . . . was . . . Gwen was a huge contributor."

"Ah."

Eggleton scribbled *huge contributor*.

Dawson leaned forward. "Was Mrs. Cunningham suggesting either you or Mrs. Liske might suffer from close scrutiny by the School Board?"

Linda set the coffee cup down, her hands shaking. "Of course not."

51

"You used the word 'implication.' It's a word I've heard before in conjunction with Mrs. Cunningham," Dawson said. "Did she imply anything about either you or Mrs. Liske?"

"I've already answered that, Inspector," she said, looking down at her hands as though to quiet them.

"Or the two of you?"

Linda gave him a quick glance. She shook her head.

lying! Eggleton wrote in his margin.

"But she would imply she had information on someone," Dawson persisted. "And she wasn't afraid to let that person know she had it. Am I understanding you correctly?"

"I don't expect you'll find many mourners at her funeral, Inspector."

"Do you know if she has any family?"

"I don't know of any, but you might ask Marjorie Meyerson. She went to school with Gwen, and Gwen seemed to feel they were friends. To be quite honest, I doubt Marjorie felt the same way, but at least she would know if there is any family."

"Meyerson?" Dawson said, remembering the notation in Gwen Cunningham's daily planner.

"Jeweler," Linda said.

"Did you notice if Mrs. Cunningham left the room at all during the party? To use the bathroom or to go into the kitchen?"

"We were all in and out between the drawing room and the patio, Inspector, so no, I can't tell you. She may have, and I wouldn't have noticed."

Dawson stood up. "That will be all, Mrs. Gentry. You may take Mrs. Liske and go home now."

Linda stood. "Thank you."

"Just one more question," Dawson said as she reached the library door.

columbo Eggleton scribbled.

"Yes?"

"Do you know anyone who benefits from Mrs. Cunningham's death?"

"We all do, Inspector," she said, closing the door softly behind her.

Dawson pointed to the memo on the desk by Eggleton's notebook. "Looks like one of our suspects has a record," he said.

"Yep. The landscape guy – brought the nicotine."

"The same. Do you think Cunningham getting teachers fired for their sexual orientation was on Mrs. Gentry's mind?" Dawson asked as he walked to the library shelves, tilting his head to read the titles.

"The information about Gino's and about teachers being under scrutiny was interesting," he said.

"It was. Did you think they were being truthful? The two ladies."

"Not entirely. No."

"Well, they didn't contradict one another, so, I think what they did tell us was mostly true. But I did see they responded strongly – body language . . ."

"And coffee cups," Eggleton interrupted.

"And coffee cups," Dawson said. "when I asked about their relationship. I suspect they didn't tell us everything."

"These days 'relationship' means . . ."

"I know what it means, Bill," Dawson said, pulling

one of the books off the shelf, glanced at it, and put it back.

"You think those two ladies . . . ?"

"I do."

Eggleton shook his head. "Hard to believe," he said.

"Why?"

"Well . . . because they remind me of my Aunt Sarah, and she . . ." Eggleton said, still shaking his head.

"Oh," Dawson said. "Aunt Sarah. That certainly changes my mind." He pulled out another book. "Let's talk to the bishop. While you're collecting him, I'm going to see if Hench is still here and tell him about sometimes sipping– usually tossing. Although, he did say it has a slightly acidic taste, but the sherry would likely cover that – if she did sip."

"But if she sipped, wouldn't she have started to get sick slowly, instead of *whammo* – all of a sudden dropping dead?"

"Good point, Bill. I'll ask Hench."

"If whoever poisoned her – assuming someone did – they'd probably been at this type of function before and knew how she drank. They'd know she'd get the full dose at one time."

"It sounds like that would be most of the people here. Seems they had a number of these gatherings."

"But was Cunningham at all of them?"

"Don't know."

"Or maybe it was just from watching her today."

"We might be overworking this. I'll go see Hench; you get the bishop."

CHAPTER THREE

Interview: The Bishop

then are ye bastards, and not sons
Hebrews 12:8

The Right Reverend Gerald Kindermann's face, with chiseled features and a strong square jaw, hinted at fatigue, but his presence filled the library. Dawson thought he could understand why this man had achieved the position he held.

Eggleton thought how interesting the next half hour was going to be.

"I'm sure you're tired, Bishop," Dawson said as the two men shook hands. "I'll be as brief as possible. Have a seat."

"Thank you. Mavis mentioned laying out a cold supper for those of us still here. The woman is ready to drop in her tracks, but she remains the quintessential hostess." The bishop sighed. "It's not as though any of us are hungry. But, if we go through the motions . . ." He paused. "She's even been on the phone to the gardener's wife, saying she's putting him up here for the night." He smiled, and his face lit up, erasing the earlier signs of fatigue that had been there. "He was worrying about his 'wee wifey.' After several Scotches, she became his 'sainted wee wifey.' "

Eggleton jotted *sainted wee wifey* in his notebook.

"Just between us, I imagine much of his act is a

diversionary tactic. You can tell he thinks the world of Mavis, and he's worried about her. I suspect he doesn't want her to be here alone tonight." The bishop leaned back in his chair. "At least he has lightened our evening somewhat," he said, pressing his hands together. "Now, how can I help you, Inspector?"

bish/control Eggleton wrote.

"Perhaps you could start by telling me a bit about the hierarchy of your church," Dawson said. "I'm somewhat familiar with the hierarchy of the Catholic Church but not with the Episcopal Church."

"Are you Catholic yourself?" the bishop asked.

"I'm a recovering Catholic," Dawson said.

The bishop laughed. "I love it – a recovering Catholic."

Eggleton, knowing Dawson as well as he did, figured it might well be the bishop's last laugh of the day.

"As I was saying," Dawson continued, "I'm unfamiliar with the Episcopal – chain of command – you might say."

"Yes, of course," the bishop said, clearing his throat. "The Archbishop of Canterbury, the Presiding Bishop here in the U.S., then the Bishops, Canons, Priests, Deacons," he said, ticking them off on his fingers. "I'm someplace in the middle of the pie."

Dawson squinted and pursed his lips. "Do you have a son?" he asked.

Eggleton, who had been watching the bishop's face closely, saw him clench his jaw briefly. Because of Dawson's abrupt change of direction? Or the question? He noted *jaw.*

"We have two teenage daughters," the bishop said.

didn't answer question Eggleton wrote.

"Ah," Dawson said.

"I'm wondering what my children might have to do with your investigation."

"Perhaps later. Right now I would like to know what happened this afternoon. Beginning with your arrival."

Eggleton thought the bishop looked a bit put out, perhaps because the reins of control had changed hands, but he said, "Well, let me think. Almost everyone was here when I arrived with Nancy. I'm staying with them – Nancy and Father Greg – so Nancy and I came together – Father Greg wasn't able to attend – confirmation class, I think. We were a bit late, because Nancy's sitter . . ."

"Almost everyone?" Dawson interrupted.

"Almost. George Alexander and his wife arrived after Nancy and I did." The fact he had been talking with Mrs. Cunningham when the Alexanders arrived was something he wouldn't be mentioning.

He recalled how they had exchanged the usual trivia of *how are you?* And *lovely day isn't it?* when Mrs. Cunningham said, "I stopped by your office last week, but you were out. I expect your secretary told you." He had a vague recollection of a note about the visit, but before he could acknowledge, she lowered her voice to a whisper and, rolling her eyes in the direction of George Alexander who had just entered the room with his wife, continued. "I wanted a word with you on some . . . St. Francis business." He had followed her gaze. *She's got something she wants to tell me about Alexander,* he thought. He wondered why she didn't take it up with Father Greg. He didn't envy Greg having Mrs. Cunningham in his parish.

"When George Alexander came in," the bishop continued, "he called across the room to Mavis that he had brought the poison to kill the aphids. He held up this little bottle, and she thanked him. He said he'd put it on the window sill in the kitchen. She said something about him showing her gardener – the little man with the *wee wifey* – how to use it after the party."

The bishop paused for a moment, as though trying to remember something. "Oh, yes! Then one of the women – I think her name is Linda – asked him to get some for her. She apparently was having trouble with aphids, too. And George said if Mavis would give him a small bottle, he'd just give her some of what he brought because there would be plenty." He frowned. "He said something about it being nicotine concentrate and to add a few drops to water and spray. He said it was deadly stuff so be very careful with it. Then he walked out to the kitchen with the bottle."

"Did you know any of them before you arrived this afternoon?" Dawson asked.

The bishop nodded. "I'd met most of them. I knew Mrs. Cunningham from various committees and boards. And of course, I've been entertained here at Mavis's several times in the past." He smiled. "I may not have remembered all their names, but then I'm not too good with names. Although I should be – good with names – it's good politics."

"That's what your job is? Politics?"

"Indeed. The bishopric is a long way from the parish and the pulpit. Although I do give my share of sermons. But, I have to confess, I tend to give the same sermon more than once since I'm in a different church each Sunday."

"Allows time for reading the mystery stories, I expect."

"Ah, yes. The mysteries," The bishop smiled. "I like the tidy way in which good triumphs over evil in the novels. Unlike the real world of murder, I imagine." His voice held a question but when Dawson didn't respond, he continued. "So, yes. Mysteries are my weakness. Well, one of them."

"I should think you would need to keep any weaknesses pretty well under cover," Dawson said. He was smiling, but his eyes were hard. "Given your position."

yikes! Eggleton scribbled. *weaknesses?*

Dawson's comment was such a direct hit the bishop was taken aback, recalling again his conversation with Mrs. Cunningham.

She had turned back to the bishop after her appraisal of George Alexander and continued with the story of her visit to the bishop's office. "Your secretary - or is the correct word *assistant*? Susan, is it – lovely girl – her husband came in with their little boy while I was there. He's a beautiful child, isn't he? Although, I must say, he looks nothing like either of them – those dark eyes . . . and those dark curls – and they're both rather fair." She looked closely at the bishop. "One sometimes questions the theory of dominant and recessive genes." She shrugged. "Well, perhaps they adopted him, although I suspect you'd know . . ." She paused for an answer from the bishop.

It was not forthcoming. "I'm sorry I missed you," he lied, "but I'm frequently out of the office. You might call for an appointment," he added, hoping she wouldn't.

"Oh, yes . . . yes, of course, but since I was in the area, I just thought I'd take a chance – we certainly can't discuss things here, can we?" Again, she glanced in the direction of George Alexander, then turned back to peer closely at the bishop." Yes, I will call," she said. "I definitely will call." And with a swirl of brightly flowered chiffon, as inappropriate for her large body as a checkered tablecloth would be at a White House State Dinner, she made her way out to the patio, leaving the Bishop to ponder as he sipped the excellent sherry: did Gwen Cunningham actually know about Susan or was she just guessing?

* * *

Years of working together had formed a bond between Jerry Kindermann and Susan Gardener which reached across the titles of Bishop and Administrative Assistant. Like a long married couple, each sensed the other's needs or response to a situation before words were even spoken. And he liked her. He liked the way her dark red hair fell out of its bun by the end of the day. He liked the fact she sometimes rubbed her eyes and her makeup smudged a bit. He liked her sense of humor, her readiness to laugh, either at her own mistakes or even his, her quick intelligence. He liked that, although she wore tailored clothes for the workplace, there was always some tiny hint of frivolity —usually a small piece of funky jewelry or hair clip. He liked that her manicure was short and sensible and her shoes were low and serviceable. He liked the fact she spent her lunch hours studying Ancient Civilizations or Modern Art, Creative Writing or U. S. History. The bishop found Susan indispensable to his work. And his life.

Was he in love with Susan? Of course he was. Would

he act on it? Of course he wouldn't.

But he did. Just once.

A tiny hotel in a parish at the far corner of the Diocese: adjoining rooms– he there for a Service of Confirmation, she there to assist with a new Diocesan computer system.

Susan never actually said the child was his. But when he baptized the baby, holding him in his arms, pouring a small stream of holy water on the black curls, when he felt the tiny fist curl around his finger as he wiped away the water with the baptismal cloth, when his heart gave an almost unbearable lurch as he handed the baby to the man who would raise him – he knew.

* * *

Dawson seemed to be waiting for a response to his comment about the bishop's weaknesses, and, with narrowed eyes and a thin smile, the bishop accommodated him. "What are you implying, Inspector?"

"Implying," Dawson repeated, raising his eyebrows. "You know, implying seems to be a word used about Mrs. Cunningham. I've heard it said she was quick to 'imply' things, although no one has been specific about just what it was she implied. Perhaps you can enlighten me."

"I used the word in conjunction with what you said about me and my weaknesses, Inspector. I was not talking about Mrs. Cunningham." The bishop lowered his head, watching Dawson from beneath his eyebrows, stroking his chin with his hand as he watched.

Dawson, remembering the saying *the best defense was a good offense,* thought the bishop might have missed his calling – the law perhaps.

The bishop continued. "We're not in an adversarial position here, Inspector. I'm just as anxious as you, perhaps more so, to have this matter set straight. These people have had a shock, and the sooner it can be put behind them, the better."

Dawson let a few seconds pass before he spoke. When he did, his voice was steely cold. "You participated in obscuring evidence, Bishop," he said. "If you are so anxious to put the matter to rest, how do you explain your action?"

"I expect you're referring to my handling of the nicotine bottle."

bingo! Eggleton wrote.

Dawson nodded.

"A fair question. I took it from Nancy and returned it to the window sill. It was a gesture of support, no more."

"Support?"

"Inspector, Father Greg has spoken to me several times about Gwen Cunningham. In fact, before Father Greg took St. Francis, it was in Father Malcom Donnelly's hands, and he, too, spoke to me about Gwen Cunningham. She's been a problem for many years."

"In what way?"

"Her money and her meddling – and her bouts of . . . The bishop paused for a moment, frowning. "Do you suppose she might have committed suicide?" he asked finally.

"Suicide?" Dawson asked, remembering what Henchcombe had shown him.

"Yes. According to both Father Malcolm and Father Greg, she apparently suffered from some form of depression." He put his hand up as though to forestall any protest Dawson might make. "I know what you're going to say, and I concur; neither of those men are medical doctors. However, I submit to you it does not necessarily take a doctor to recognize the symptoms of depression. Anyway, Greg is a well-trained counselor with a background in Psychology. I think he can be trusted with that observation." He leaned toward Dawson. "What do you think? About suicide, I mean?"

"Did she seem depressed this afternoon?"

"Well, no, but I only spoke to her as a greeting." He clenched his jaw as he said it.

jaw again, Eggleton wrote.

"Regarding suicide, at this point we can't eliminate any possibility. The Coroner's report will give us more information. But I do find it interesting as Bishop of the entire diocese you would know so much about a specific parishioner."

"Your point is well taken, Inspector. However, Gwen Cunningham is – was, an enigma. And I must be honest with you; my information is largely second hand, coming to me from Father Malcom and Father Greg." He leaned back in his chair and folded his hands in his lap. "Perhaps you would do better to talk to Father Greg. He's here. He was just coming in as your Sergeant collected me from the morning room."

"Actually," Dawson said, "I'm quite interested in what you have to tell me. After all, this is not a court of law." He smiled. "Hearsay evidence is quite admissible under the circumstances. In what way was Mrs. Cunningham an 'enigma?'"

"Valuable to have around, but nobody wanted to be around her. She was a highly intelligent woman and of great merit on any committee. She also served at the diocesan level on several projects." The bishop paused, weighing his next statement. "I will be frank with you, Inspector. I found her to be a most unpleasant person, but she was an excellent resource for any board. She offered a great deal of expertise."

"How so?"

"For one thing, she was a very wealthy woman and absolutely brilliant in the field of investment and finance. This, naturally, is a skill to be highly valued in the fiscal domain of the church. If she offered nothing more, that alone would have made her an asset. Which leads me back to your insightful question as to why I should know such specifics about an individual member of the diocese. She has, for all the years she's been a member of St. Francis, been a heavy contributor to the church – extremely generous with both talent and treasure." His face took on a wry expression. "But, as such, she felt entitled to pull a few strings – actually, quite a few. It was in this light both Father Malcolm and Father Greg sought my advice. I remember Father Malcolm saying once, 'Sometimes I feel as though I'm prostituting myself for her money.'"

"And your advice to Father Malcolm?"

"I told him it wasn't worth it," the bishop said. Then, with a small smile, he added, "At which point Father Malcolm reminded me of the leaky roof."

"I'm still not clear on how you became aware of her mental condition."

The bishop stood, rolled his shoulders, and rubbed

the small of his back. "I get tired if I sit too long in one position," he said, walking over to the silver service where it sat on the table. He gestured with the pot toward the police officers. "May I pour either of you a cup?" Dawson and Eggleton shook their heads.

control again Eggleton wrote.

Carrying his cup, the bishop returned to his chair. "Mrs. Cunningham's mental condition," he mused. "As I mentioned before, my information is largely second hand."

"Nevertheless . . ."

The bishop shrugged. "Very well," he said. "From what I've heard, she would confine herself to her house for long periods of time, refusing to come out or answer her phone. Both Greg and Malcolm said they tried to call on her. They said, even when they identified themselves, she just told them to go away. Then, after a few weeks with no sign of her, she would reappear and take up where she left off. "

"Which may or may not indicate a mental condition," Dawson pointed out.

"Perhaps, Inspector," the bishop said. "But given the degree of her involvement in community affairs, I would call it a fair indicator. After all, her absence from committee meetings could only weaken her position of power, so I can't imagine she willingly absented herself. Also, there was her subsequent reaction to both Father Malcolm and Father Greg." He paused to sip his coffee. "Apparently, after one of these episodes, they each, on separate occasions of course, suggested she seek psychiatric help. Father Greg told me she blew up and actually left the church for a while when he suggested help. She told each of them they had no right to interfere in her private life – which was when they told me they had jeopardized a significant source of parish income."

"Did she leave the church each time professional help was suggested?"

"Just the second time. As I understood from Father Malcolm, the first time she threatened to leave but didn't actually go."

"And both confided in you after it happened?" Dawson asked.

"Yes," the bishop said, setting down the coffee cup. "Despite any agenda, Inspector – and you will pardon my cynicism – from where I sit, the bottom line with the church is money. Therefore, any significant drop in revenue, either at the local or the diocesan level, comes to my attention." The bishop frowned. "It's sad, isn't it, when you stop to think about the supposed mission of the church – the spread of Christianity – sad for raw, hard cash to carry such weight." He paused, staring off into space, perhaps picturing the idyllic Christian community, free of purse strings and contributors. "Could be why you're recovering," he added, almost as an afterthought.

"You were saying . . .?"

The bishop shook his head slightly. "I digress," he said.

Duh! Eggleton thought.

"Anyway, Father Greg called to tell me his golden goose had flown the coop. Apparently her golden egg covered a lot of the church expenses and of course, she was a heavy contributor to diocesan projects."

"But she returned to the church," Dawson said.

"Eventually, yes. Frankly, knowing what I do about

her, I think the church might have been a cloak of righteousness she felt compelled to wear, given her penchant for making lives miserable." Again he picked up the cup and sipped his coffee.

hands steady, Eggleton noted.

"It's been my experience some of the greatest sinners are those who carry God's banner the highest. You will remember Jesus's parable about those who exalt themselves."

Dawson looked blank.

"Gospel of Luke," the bishop said, as though that explained everything. "In her case, I don't believe anyone was fooled." He paused. "Unless it was Mrs. Cunningham herself," he added.

"A moment ago you mentioned meddling," Dawson said. His manner was mild, casual almost, but Eggleton recognized the approach to a significant question. "Did she meddle in your affairs, too, Bishop?"

The bishop met Dawson's gaze – and bit down hard; his hand went to his cross.

jaw, Eggleton wrote.

"My affairs?"

"Yes. Church business or your personal life?"

"May I remind you again I didn't know her personally?"

"Come now, Bishop. That doesn't answer my question. What about those weaknesses you spoke of?"

"We're back to weaknesses, are we? And what would my weaknesses have to do with your investigation?"

"You brought them up –of course, you're under no obligation to answer my question."

The bishop made a sound that might have been

interpreted as a short laugh. "That's not a problem. Let me see." He held up his hands, ticking off on his fingers as he spoke. "Mysteries as I said, a fondness for cognac, a tendency to be short tempered with my teenage daughters, an inordinate desire for chocolate, and a great distaste for meetings of any kind. Especially meetings. I do hate meetings. Not good in my business; I attend a lot of them. Which, I believe, covers my list of weaknesses." He didn't mention Susan.

"Thank you," Dawson said, dipping his head as though to underscore his gratitude. "That we should all be blessed with so benign a list."

The bishop looked sharply at Dawson, but Dawson's face revealed nothing. Eggleton covered a laugh with a cough.

"Can you give me any more insight into a reason for Mrs. Cunningham to be murdered?" Dawson asked. "Beyond what you've already shared with me, I mean."

"No," the bishop said. "But if – and I say 'if' because I think suicide is a real possibility – if someone did murder her, I would have compassion for the person who did it. I am sure, knowing what I do of Mrs. Cunningham, the provocation was great."

"You would want the murderer to go unpunished?" Dawson's voice was cold.

"Punishment." The bishop said. "You pose an ethical dilemma, Inspector."

"Certainly something you would be familiar with," Dawson said.

"Ah, yes. Well, if it was murder, I guess punishment is called for. Although, I think guilt would provide significant punishment." He looked at Dawson. "Not sufficient in your eyes, Inspector, but real nonetheless. I believe every one of the people here today has a deep sense of conscience."

"Including you, Bishop?"

"Am I a suspect?"

"You made yourself one when you chose to handle the nicotine bottle."

touche! Eggleton suppressed a smile as he jotted.

"I see. Yes, including me."

Dawson wrote something on a piece of paper. He handed it to the bishop. "Does this mean anything to you?" he asked.

!!!! Eggleton scratched.

Looking at the paper in his hand, the bishop's face turned ashen.

pale was Eggleton's next entry. *The gloves are off,* he thought.

"Bish. sec./son?" the bishop read aloud. "No, I can't say it means anything." He handed the paper back to Dawson, his hand shook slightly; Eggleton made a note.

"You mentioned two daughters. Do you have a son, perhaps?"

"I think I already answered that, Inspector," the bishop said, not about to confess to the Inspector about the beautiful Michael Junior, with his dark eyes and hair, now eighteen months old. 'Our little throw-back,' Michael Senior called him. 'To my Armenian grandfather.'

did not answer again, Eggleton noted.

"Inspector, what does this line of questioning have to do with Mrs. Cunningham?"

"We found a note in her date book, Bishop. Under

today's date. It says, Bish period, Sec period, slash son? What I just handed you. I can only assume 'Bish.' refers to you, and she was making some reference to a son."

"Perhaps 'son' in this case is an abbreviation for a longer word. After all, 'Bish' is certainly an abbreviation for Bishop. I'm referred to as 'The Bish' all the time. Not in my hearing, of course."

"You see, sir, the problem with that idea – that 'son' is an abbreviation – is there is no period after the word. Now, your title is obviously abbreviated; it has a period. As does 'sec.' But 'son' doesn't. So I have to assume Bish stands for Bishop, sec is an abbreviation for some word beginning with s-e-c, and son means son. He nodded his head toward the bishop. "Would I be correct in making those assumptions, do you think?"

"As I said before, Bish probably refers to me. As to the rest of your hypothesis, I really can't say." His jaw clamped tight; his eyes turned steely; he fingered his cross.

Eggleton's pencil flew.

"After we found her notebook, I checked the dictionary for words beginning with sec," Dawson said, gesturing to where a large dictionary rested on a stand. He pulled another piece of paper from his pocket. "This is what I came up with: seclude, Seconal, second." He turned to the bishop. "Does any of that ring a bell?"

The bishop shook his head.

"There were several columns with forms of second," Dawson continued. "Then it goes on to: secret, secretary, section, secular, secure. Those seem to be the only ones that might make sense." He looked at the bishop. "Does it jog your memory in any way? Anything Mrs. Cunningham might have mentioned?"

"No."

"But she did talk to you?"

"Briefly."

bish.not talking as much now Eggleton noted.

"About?"

"She said she had been in my office to talk to me – she didn't say about what – and I wasn't in at the time. I suggested she make an appointment."

"Anything else?"

The bishop's shoulders slumped, and he appeared to sit smaller in his chair. Gone was the vitality he had brought into the room. His face was still ashen and his eyes drooped with fatigue. His tone was flat. "No," he said.

Like a balloon with the air leaked out, Eggleton thought.

"Tell me," Dawson said. "Will the church benefit from Mrs. Cunningham's will?

"I don't know."

"At any time during the afternoon did you leave the party? To use the bathroom, perhaps?"

"No."

"Did you see anyone else leave and go into the hall or toward the kitchen?"

"I didn't notice."

Dawson stood. "Thank you, Bishop. If we have more questions, we'll contact you."

"Yes. Yes. I suppose you will," the bishop said as he left the room.

Minutes passed before either policeman spoke.

Dawson stood looking out the window again; Eggleton was leaning back in the desk chair, his legs sprawled.

It was Dawson who broke the silence. "Holy shit." It was merely a statement.

"Yes, Sir. I think that's exactly what it was," Eggleton said and then paused for a moment before he continued. "There was no love lost between the two of you, was there?"

"Quaintly phrased, Bill, but no. I think you and I may end up visiting the bishop at a later date."

"I thought as much."

"What did you think of him?" Dawson asked.

"Well, I don't think the gardener is the only one with diversionary tactics. And I don't think the bishop was being entirely truthful."

"How so?"

"For one thing, I hope the man never plays poker, he'd lose his purple shirt. His jaw is a sure 'tell.' You can read when he's been put off center by the way he does a quick clench of his teeth. Makes his jawbone pop."

"Show me."

"Well, I don't have the type of jawbone he has, but something like this." Eggleton clenched his teeth, making his jawbone move slightly. "It's more noticeable with a facial structure like he has – square jaw."

"Anything else?"

"Fingered his cross a few times."

"I noticed that."

"Also, he didn't answer your questions about having a son – either time."

"No, he didn't. He just said, 'I have two daughters.' "

"And, 'I think I've already answered that, Inspector' "

Dawson nodded. " So, when I was asking about the note in Mrs. Cunningham's book, what did you observe?"

"The cross. A lot of jaw work. And pale. I thought he might pass out."

"Yeah. Me, too. Anyway, good work, Bill. I was so caught up in playing 'who's in charge here' I missed the jaw."

Eggleton made a small nod of acknowledgement.

Dawson pursed his lips. "Actually, with what you've just pointed out, I think we may have learned a great deal."

There was a tap on the door. Eggleton opened it to find a deputy.

"Mrs. Dillon wants to know if she can make a cold supper for people still here," the deputy said.

"Where does she plan to serve this?"

"Kitchen."

"I don't see why not – if Doctor Lieberman's finished in the kitchen."

"He and Dr. Henchcombe have left, Sir."

"Fine. Be sure you stay with them all the time."

As the door closed, Dawson said. "Maybe we'll get lucky and have someone confess to the dirty deed to-night."

Sure," Eggleton said. "In your dreams," he added under his breath.

"I heard that."

"I'll call Laura – tell her I won't be home until late."

Dawson pointed to the note on the desk. "I think we'll see the Alexanders next. Let's start with Mrs. Alexander."

CHAPTER FOUR

Reflection: Gwen and Marjorie

I behaved myself as though he had been my friend...
Ps. 35:14

Marjorie Meyerson preferred to be called by her full name: Marjorie. She hated the diminutive, Marge – considered it a harsh, incomplete sound – and gently corrected people when they used it.

So she was a bit put out the first word Sandy Liske said when she called was "Marge!" Sandy knew she preferred Marjorie. They were friends, having served on the Historical Society Board for many years. She was about to say 'Marjorie,' but Sandy plunged on. "Don't you dare tell anyone I called, or I could end up in jail or something, but I think you should know Gwen is dead, and the police will be contacting you, because you seemed to be her friend."

"What?"

"I'm telling you, Gwen Cunningham is dead. Police think she was poisoned."

Marjorie sat down in the recliner chair that had been her husband's. "Go on," she said.

"That's just it, Marge. Poison."

"Marjorie," Marjorie said automatically.

"Oops. Sorry."

"Never mind." Marjorie said. "Gwen is dead; the police think it's poison. When did this happen?"

"This afternoon. The vestry from St. Francis was having a sherry party at Mavis Dillon's house, and all of a sudden Gwen collapsed on the floor."

Marjorie was surprised she didn't feel anything – except maybe a bit of relief. No, actually, more than a bit. She was ashamed of herself.

"Do the police think someone at the party poisoned her?"

"Uh huh. Marjorie, I'm so sorry. I just thought you ought to know. They asked Linda . . ."

"Sandy, slow down. I'm getting lost."

"Sorry. They . . ."

"Who are *they?*"

"The police! They already interviewed Linda and me – actually, I was first – and then they said we could go home. So I called you right away, because Linda said they asked her if she knew anyone who was a friend, and Linda said you and Gwen were – well, at least you were more acquainted with her than any of the rest of us. Close, maybe?"

"Hardly, Sandy," Marjorie said. "I went to school with her – college – and we saw each other occasionally for lunch since she moved here, but we weren't *close.*" Then, with a little catch in her voice, she added, "I don't know anyone who was."

"Perhaps she thought of you as her friend."

"How sad," Marjorie murmured, more to herself than Sandy.

"Yes," Sandy replied, wondering briefly if Marjorie meant 'sad' because Gwen was dead or because she didn't consider herself Gwen's friend.

"Marjorie, would she have committed suicide?"

"I don't know, Sandy."

But she did know.

Marjorie and Gwen met as college freshman: Gwen a Business Administration major and Marjorie a Psych major. The college was a small Methodist institution in the Pacific Northwest, and, since it was before the 'Greeks' came to the college, no one rushed or pledged. Gwen and Marjorie were assigned to Sinclair Dormitory: Gwen in a private room, Marjorie next door in a room for two. At the time, Gwen had been a chubby, round-faced girl without style, either in clothes or grooming: brilliant, but shy and socially inept. While the other girls in the dorm dated and partied, Gwen spent evenings and weekends in her room. Marjorie had tried to befriend her: walking with her to classes, sitting with her at the cafeteria occasionally, collecting her from her room for dorm meetings, and Gwen had seemed grateful for the attention. But there was something about Gwen Marjorie couldn't put her finger on, except she never felt quite at ease with her.

It all came to a head in the spring of their freshman year when the college held its annual Mothers' Day weekend. One night an excited Gwen burst into Marjorie's room. Marjorie could still remember the conversation, almost to the word.

"My parents are coming for the family weekend," Gwen said. "I've got plans to fix my room up so it will look like yours." She gestured around the room Marjorie shared with her roommate. "Are your parents coming?"

"No," Marjorie said. "They're in Europe, so I'll enjoy watching you get ready for yours."

"I'm going to get a poster – Michael Jackson maybe. And I'm going to get a Chianti bottle and drip some candles on it." Then she stopped, frowning. "Do you know where I can get an empty Chianti bottle?"

"The Italian restaurant on Cedar," Marjorie said. "I'll go with you. Would you like me to fix your hair a little? And maybe some make-up?"

"I'd like you to go with me," Gwen said. "But. . ." she shook her head ". . . I don't know about make-up."

"Just a touch," Marjorie urged. "A tiny bit of color on your cheeks is all. Maybe some lipstick."

And that was what Marjorie remembered: she had urged.

By Friday afternoon, Gwen's room was much like any college girl's room: a Michael Jackson poster, the dripped Chianti bottle, a tie-dyed bedspread, a stuffed bear on the bed. Marjorie assured Gwen her room looked great. But Marjorie had never met Gwen's parents; later she would wonder why Gwen had thought her parents would approve of any of those items.

When the big day came, Gwen had been beyond excitement. Marjorie had set Gwen's hair in big rollers, teased it a bit, and shaped it to a soft, flattering style. Then she lightly applied a blush across Gwen's cheek bones and handed her a lipstick which Gwen ran over her lips. A bit too much, but Marjorie gave her a tissue to blot and said, "You look amazing, Gwen," as they stood in front of the mirror in Marjorie's room. And Marjorie was speaking the truth – even Gwen seemed pleased with her reflection.

"You there, Marjorie?" Sandy asked.

"Sorry. Just thinking. Listen, are you home, Sandy? Could I call you back? I have more questions, but right now, I just need to sit with this a few minutes."

"I'll be here. We're not going anyplace."

Gwen ran to the window in Marjorie's room every five minutes, until, at last, a long, black Cadillac pulled up to the dorm. "They're here! They're here," Gwen squealed and ran downstairs.

Marjorie watched from the window as a short, rotund man with soft features and a shiny bald head, exited the driver's side. His lips were thick and shiny; Marjorie scrunched her face in distaste. A tall, thin woman stepped from the passenger's side of the car. She wore a brown tweed suit, gloves and a velvet pill-box hat – and a scowl. Although Marjorie couldn't see anything that might account for the scowl, she would later realize the woman had seen Gwen, with her new hairstyle and makeup, at the door of the dormitory. Gwen and her parents disappeared into the dorm, and Marjorie settled on her bed, her pillows piled against the headboard, propping herself to read her Psych text, when she heard crashing and yelling from the other side of the common wall between her room and Gwen's. She jumped off the bed and ran to the door.

The scene in Gwen's room was something she would never forget. Gwen was scrubbing her face with a wet washcloth; Gwen's mother was screaming, "Slut," and smashing the Chianti bottle against the side of Gwen's desk; Gwen's father was sitting on the bed, his tongue running over his fat lips, his eyes bright with excitement, his hands trembling on his thighs. Marjorie turned and ran down the hall to the dorm mother's office.

By the time Marjorie and Mrs. Starkley got back to Gwen's room, the door was standing open, and the room was empty.

"Oh, dear Heaven," Mrs. Starkley gasped when she saw the condition of Gwen's room with the smashed Chianti bottle on the desk, its shards of glass and globs of candle wax held together in places with torn shreds of raffia wrap. More glass and wax lay across the floor; the desk chair was overturned, the Michael Jackson poster torn in half lay on the bed. From the window, they could see the black Cadillac pulling out of the parking lot. There were two people in it.

"Where's Gwen," Mrs. Starkley and Marjorie asked simultaneously.

"You check downstairs," Mrs. Starkley directed Marjorie. "I'll check the bathroom."

It was Mrs. Starkley who found Gwen in the tub of bloody water.

"If only I hadn't put the makeup on her," Marjorie wept as she and Mrs. Starkley waited for the ambulance to arrive. Gwen's quiet form, wrapped in a cocoon of blankets, lay on Marjorie's bed.

"I don't understand," Mrs. Starkley said as she folded her arms around Marjorie, and, between sobs, Marjorie told the story of Gwen and the transformed dorm room, the make-up.

The dorm, usually a living thing, buzzing with talking

and laughter, running footsteps, doors closing, phones ringing, was thickly silent as news and shock whispered in the halls. Then there was the screaming siren and the sound of footsteps running up the stairs.

"Don't call her parents," Marjorie pleaded as Mrs. Starkley climbed into the ambulance with Gwen. "Please don't call her parents."

"You know I have to," Mrs. Starkley said, her face heavy with the sadness of this responsibility.

"Hi Sandy. It's Marjorie. Tell me about this afternoon."

CHAPTER FIVE

Interview: Dolores and George Alexander

Forsake her not, and she shall preserve thee:
love her, and she shall keep thee.
Prov. 4:6

DOLORES

The woman Eggleton brought into the library was a well-dressed, attractive woman of middle age. The strain of the afternoon had taken a toll, and her face was drawn.

Dawson motioned her to the chair opposite his; she began speaking before he could say anything. "I've been thinking about the events of this afternoon, and I realize I may have done a very foolish thing. I know Sandy told you about us all handling the nicotine bottle."

"She wasn't supposed to be talking about the interview," Dawson said, frowning. "That's why the officer is in the room with you."

"She didn't talk to us," Dolores said. "She just nodded. We had agreed the first one in would tell you about the bottle, and she was the first one. She was just affirming she had."

Dawson sighed. "And what is this foolish thing you've done?"

"I'm the one who took the bottle out of my husband's

hand. I probably shouldn't have."

"Why *did* you take it out of your husband's hand?"

She took a deep breath. "I didn't want his fingerprints on it," she said at last.

"His fingerprints should have been on it, Mrs. Alexander. He's the one who brought it."

"Which is what I've been thinking about. However, I wasn't thinking at the time. I was so rattled with Gwen's collapse and then Charles saying she was dead, I . . ." She paused, shaking her head. "I'm sorry. I guess I've messed up your investigation."

"Well, you haven't helped. Why do you suppose Mrs. Gentry took it out of your hand?"

She pursed her lips. "We were tossing that around before you came, Inspector. Before we were told we couldn't discuss anything. Anyway, I think you could call it a 'consortium of guilt.'"

"Consortium of guilt," Dawson said slowly, as though trying to make sense of what she had said. "Can you explain exactly what that might mean?"

consorshum Eggleton wrote, scratched it out and tried *consorshim.* He crossed that out, too.

"Well, I don't want to speak for everybody, but I think probably not one of us is sorry she's dead. I know it sounds terrible, Inspector, especially since we're all supposed to be Christian people here." She leaned forward, as if proximity to Dawson would emphasize her point. "That's the problem. We are Christian people, and yet we're glad she's dead. I think we all feel guilty about that."

"Which doesn't tell me why Mrs. Gentry took it out of your hand. The bottle."

"I can't speak for anyone else."

"What do you *think* was in her mind, Mrs. Alexander?"

Eggleton could hear the tension in Dawson's voice and felt sorry for him. For Mrs. Alexander, this was her opportunity to talk; for Dawson it was just one more interview in a long afternoon and evening of interviews, and they weren't close to being through.

"Well . . ." she paused. "Let me back up a bit. I *think* George took it off the window sill to be sure his prints were on it. You'd have to ask him."

He will, Eggleton thought.

"I will," Dawson said. "Later. Now tell me why would your husband think his prints might not be on it?"

"I think . . . I think he wanted his prints on because they belonged there. Any other prints would be suspect, and he might have wanted to obliterate them. Or maybe he thought someone had wiped the bottle clean. If there were no prints, it would mean Gwen was murdered, wouldn't it? I mean, if someone deliberately put nicotine in her drink, they would wipe the bottle, wouldn't they?"

"It's possible," Dawson said with a slow nod of his head. "Might he have thought yours would be on there?"

"Oh, Inspector. I don't think George would think that! Surely not!"

"But someone else's might be? Someone else's prints?"

"He wouldn't want anyone to be held responsible."

"Not even a murderer?"

Dolores took a long time answering. "Not in this case." she finally answered.

"I see," Dawson said.

85

Eggleton was glad Dawson saw, because he saw nothing. The reasoning was beyond him.

"Let's get back to Mrs. Gentry, Mrs. Alexander. Why did she take it from you?"

"I expect her move was as impulsive as mine, although for a different reason." She pointed at a pitcher of ice water on the desk. "Might I have a glass?"

"Of course. Sergeant?"

She drank greedily and handed the glass back to Eggleton. "Thank you. Now, let me begin again. Have you read *Murder on the Orient Express?*"

Dawson looked at her quizzically but nodded.

"All those people wanted that wicked man dead. Each person had a different reason, and so they all conspired to murder him. Each of them plunged the knife into him."

The room was silent for a time. When Dawson finally spoke, his voice brought shivers to Eggleton's neck. "Are you telling me all of you at this sherry party conspired to kill Mrs. Cunningham?"

"No! Not at all. What I am saying is, since she was dead anyway, and the possibility existed one of us might have killed her, that . . . well . . .," her voice trembled, ". . . that everybody decided to take a share of the responsibility, since it would be terrible for one person to pay for this crime when, in our hearts, we are all glad she's dead." She began to cry. "That sounds pretty awful, doesn't it?"

Dawson stood and walked to the window. He said nothing.

jesus!!! Eggleton wrote, his hand shaking.

Finally Dawson spoke. "All right," he said, speaking over his shoulder. "For the moment let's use your *Orient*

Express analogy. In that story, as you say, each individual, for whatever his or her personal reason, wished – I forget his name – dead."

"Ratchett," Eggleton supplied.

"Thank you, Sergeant. Each individual wished Ratchett dead." He turned back to Dolores. "Now to carry the analogy to this situation, are you saying each person here had a reason for wanting Mrs. Cunningham dead?"

"I don't know about a specific reason, Inspector. I do know everyone was a little frightened of her. If not because of something she had done to them specifically, we all know of someone who has suffered terribly because of her. You just never knew when it would be your turn." She paused, looking down at her hands folded in her lap. "Actually, I'd have to say more than a little frightened. We were very frightened of her."

"Were *you* frightened because of information she might have about you?"

"Gwen didn't always need information, Inspector. Sometimes she surmised something that wasn't even true . . .

didn't answer the ? Eggleton wrote.

. . . I'm remembering Jack Rosenquist. He had to re-tire early from teaching due to his health. He had arthritis and couldn't get around well. After he retired, he spent a lot of time in the park. His wife would drive him there and leave him for a couple hours each day, just watching the children play, talking to them – occasionally telling them stories. He had loved teaching and missed the children dreadfully. Well, Gwen saw him in the park and began to contact mothers all over town– saying Jack was watching their children. Of course, the mothers called the police. The police talked to Jack, heard his story, and let him go." She sighed, shaking her head. "He was tarred by Gwen's insinuations, and he never went back to the park. His wife told me later he was so devastated he just holed up watching TV. One day she found him dead in his recliner. He'd given up all will to live. That's the kind of thing Gwen could do."

"Didn't people have her number after a while?"

"Not really. Because some of what she came up with was real. For instance, she noticed Father Ian – he was a priest at St. Ignatius Catholic Church – making an unwarranted number of house calls to Mary Francis Kelly. Gwen reported that to Father Ian's bishop and the next thing you know, Father Ian was transferred to another parish – in Southern California. Mary Francis broke down completely and admitted the whole affair." Dolores shrugged her shoulders and spread her hands. "So you see, Gwen didn't make up everything. Some of her gossip was the truth or held an element of truth. That's why people were so afraid of her. You couldn't just say, 'Oh well, that's Gwen Cunningham talking. Take no notice.'"

Dawson returned to his chair. "Let me see if I understand what you're saying," he said, ticking off the items on his fingers. "First off, your husband picked up the bottle to assure his prints being on it."

"Yes."

"Secondly," Dawson continued, "you took the bottle from him to eliminate his prints."

"Or obscure them, yes."

"Thirdly, Mrs. Gentry took the bottle from you and thus began your 'consortium of guilt.' Am I correct?"

"Which is not to say had my husband and I been further down the line, and someone else had been the first to pick up the bottle, we wouldn't have been part of the 'consortium' as well."

"Uh, huh," Dawson said, turning to Eggleton. "Did you get that, Sergeant?"

"Sure," Eggleton responded, pointing to his notebook. He'd written it down; he didn't understand a word of it.

"All right, Mrs. Alexander. Suppose you tell me just why you didn't want your husband's prints to be found on the bottle."

She lifted her head high. "George has a prison record, Inspector. But I expect you have run all our names through your data base and already know about it."

Eggleton smiled.

Dawson tipped his head.

"You see, Inspector – my first husband – George is my second husband – anyway, I married at a very early age, early and foolishly, and my parents were dead set against the marriage from the start, but I was pregnant. In those days – well, my parents were right about Vic – my first husband – he wasn't any good. Mostly he drank, never held a job for more than two months running, disappeared for days at a time. A cliché, I know, but even clichés have their roots in reality. My parents bought us a house, but they put it in my name." She laughed, a dry, humorless laugh. "They didn't want Vic to sell it out from under me – which he would have done. My father also took out a very large life insurance policy on Vic. Very large. I remember my father saying, 'At the rate he's going, you'll be a widow soon, and you'll need some money.' "

Eggleton doodled impatiently in the margins of his notebook, but Dawson leaned back in his chair and crossed his legs, as though prepared to spend the night listening to Mrs. Alexander if necessary.

"My father was wrong. Vic lived far longer than anyone expected. He didn't die of cirrhosis or lung cancer or a car accident as one might expect, but of a brain aneurysm. He collapsed one morning and died in the ambulance on the way to the hospital." She took a deep breath. "I was happy for the first time in years, Inspector. I was no longer, 'that poor woman, married to that bum, Michaelson,' no longer, 'poor Dolores, having to work just to keep food on the table.' I could finally hold my head up."

vic michaelson Eggleton wrote.

"I sold the house my parents had bought for me – it held too many unhappy memories – and I purchased an old Georgian house here in Castlemont. It took a lot of time and effort, but I refinished most of it by myself with weekend help from my son, Stephen. I met George when he came to design my garden area," she continued. She smiled, remembering those days.

"Color," he had said. "Masses of color. If not with flowers, then with foliage." Usually she had provided glasses of iced tea, which they sipped while strolling the grounds, planning as they went.

As he supervised the work, and his visits lengthened, they had moved inside in the late afternoon for cocktails. There they talked of literature, music, food, travel – and her garden.

"Would you like to go to the symphony with me?" he had asked one afternoon, setting his cocktail glass down with an unnecessary thump.

It's about time, she thought. "I'd love to," she said.

Their courtship was gentle and unhurried. Some evenings they went out, some evenings they fixed dinner together and then watched a movie on her TV. But most of the time they just talked. He spoke lovingly of the wife he had lost to multiple sclerosis, his eyes moist. She touched briefly on her husband's death, her eyes dry. When he asked her to marry him, she said, "Let me think about it for a while." He had not pressured.

"I was gun shy about marriage, Inspector, and I had a significant amount of money from the life insurance policy, so when George asked me to marry him, I had a private detective run a check on George's background." She smiled. "I know it doesn't sound very romantic, but at my age and with my experience, romance is only part of it. The essence of the report was that George had worked as an accountant for a bank in Kansas City for twenty-five years and was imprisoned for embezzlement of funds. He was apprehended in an attempt to replace the funds and was sentenced to two years in a white-collar detention facility. While he was in prison, he studied landscape architecture. He was paroled early."

"But you married him in spite of the report."

She stood and began to pace the floor. "I married him *because* of the report, Inspector. The report included a copy of the charges filed by the bank as well as the issues raised in his defense. His wife had MS and, according to the report, it was important to her to remain in her home. That worked for a while, but, finally, during the last two years of her life, it became necessary for skilled nursing around the clock. Naturally, insurance didn't cover what was needed to pay for that kind of care, so George siphoned funds from a dormant account under his responsibility at the bank. When his wife died, George sold the house and attempted to reimburse the account. Which was when he was caught. An audit."

She stopped her pacing and poured herself another glass of water, again drinking deeply. "In all honesty, from the sound of the report and because George had been an exemplary employee, I doubt the bank would have pressed charges, given the extenuating circumstances. However, the bank he worked for had just merged with a much larger bank, so top management did press charges. George pleaded 'no contest.'" Dolores put the empty glass down and returned to her chair. "These have been the happiest years of my life, Inspector. I *wanted* to marry a man who had cared so much for his first wife he would go to those lengths to insure her comfort."

"Your husband knows you hired a private detective?"

"I don't know. He might."

Eggleton glanced up from his notes, his face registering surprise.

"Does he know you know about his prison term?"

"Yes." She glanced at her watch. "Do you have any more questions for me, Inspector?"

"I do," Dawson replied. "Several more. Did you talk with Mrs. Cunningham this afternoon?"

"She came over and sat by us. It was getting on in

the party, and she'd been talking to just about everybody else. I think we had both hoped she would ignore us, but we weren't so lucky."

"What did she discuss with you?"

"Oh, she asked about how long we'd been married, and didn't we have an anniversary coming up soon, and were we going to take a trip to celebrate. That sort of thing."

"Any reference to your husband's past?"

"She alluded to his background as an accountant."

Dawson leaned forward. "What exactly did she say?"

"Exactly? I don't remember exactly. She mentioned she certainly hoped, if George did take a trip, he would not be gone too long, because he does such a fine job as treasurer of the church. Then she said something about 'shame on you, all that accounting skill and parading as a landscape gardener,' or words to the effect."

"What did your husband say?"

She laughed. "He's feisty. He said, 'shame and parading have nothing to do with it. I worked as an accountant for years and decided to change vocations."

"But this made you nervous?"

"Of course it did! Maybe she was just guessing, but if she did know something about his prison record, or if she even suspected, she'd blab it all over town."

"Isn't it possible, given your husband's skill as treasurer, she had just assumed an accounting background and it was nothing more sinister?"

"You're right, of course. Gwen always triggered my paranoia."

"But whatever the reason, it was important to you she

keep her mouth shut."

"I would rather she kept her mouth shut!" She flushed. "Are you suggesting I – or George? What utter nonsense!"

Dawson's voice was stern when he replied. "There is no *nonsense* – as you put it – in a murder investigation. And you have to admit you have a motive." Then he smiled, a small, tight smile. "Given your paranoia."

"Surely one doesn't commit murder for such a petty reason, Inspector."

"Murder has been committed for much less reason than you have, Mrs. Alexander. Besides, wanting a prison record kept quiet is hardly a 'petty reason.'"

Dolores sat tall in her chair and looked Dawson straight in the eye. "If the story of his prison record came out, people would understand why he borrowed the money. It might be awkward for a time, but we'd survive just fine." She pointed her finger at Dawson. "In fact, many people would respect him for the care he took of his wife. I know I do."

"So do I, Mrs. Alexander," Dawson said. "But it doesn't alter the fact you thought information of that nature in Mrs. Cunningham's hands could be detrimental to you both."

She smiled. "You're right, Inspector. Gwen could make a child's tea party suspect, but I assure you neither my husband nor I had anything to do with her death." She leaned back as though her denial of complicity settled the matter.

"What did Mrs. Cunningham do after she finished talking to you?"

"She excused herself. Said she needed to use '*the little*

girls' room.' Which, given the size of her, was ludicrous."

Dawson, who had to agree the picture conjured of the very large Mrs. Cunningham in 'the *little girls' room*' was indeed ludicrous, suppressed a smile.

"Did you go into the kitchen at all during the party, Mrs. Alexander?"

"Once. To get a glass of water."

"When?"

"Just before Gwen stopped to talk to George and me. By that time I'd had several glasses of sherry, and alcohol always makes me thirsty."

"Was anyone else in the kitchen while you were there?"

"No. Mavis had put out a pitcher of ice water and some glasses by the sink. I helped myself and put the glass in the sink and left."

"Did you notice the bottle of nicotine?"

"No. Not really. I couldn't tell you if it was on the sill or not. I'm sorry, Inspector."

Eggleton saw Dawson close his eyes briefly. So far nobody had seen anything. The answers they had received during their interviews seemed almost rote. He jotted *rote* in his notebook.

Dawson continued. "Did you go into the hall for any other reason? To use the bathroom, perhaps?"

"No."

"Did you see anyone in the hall on your way to or back from the kitchen?"

"No." She paused, frowning. "I take it back. I think I saw Linda going into the bathroom as I was going to the kitchen."

"Did she see you?"

"I doubt it. Her back was to me, and the bathroom is quite a ways down the hall."

Dawson stood. "I appreciate your candor, Mrs. Alexander."

She made a wry face. "It would appear my candor has landed me in the suspect pile."

Dawson smiled at her. "If I have more questions, I'll get in touch with you."

"Yes, I expect you will," she said standing and starting for the door. "Inspector, if this – this information about George doesn't have to come out, can it be kept quiet, do you think?"

"I can't make any promises, Mrs. Alexander."

"Still, if it's not necessary. . ."

"Well," said Eggleton as the door closed behind Dolores, "finally someone who was willing to talk."

Dawson, looking thoughtful, nodded. "Yeah. 'Consortium of guilt.' What do you think?"

"Looney tunes. Do you think the fact Mr. Alexander has been in prison is significant?"

"What I think is probably each person at this party has a secret he or she would like kept, and Mrs. Alexander is the only one who's owned up to their particular secret. The day planner: *acct?* by Alexander's name. Which may give validity to the other notations."

"Even the bishop?"

"Huh?"

"Secrets."

"Especially the bishop." Dawson paused. "I think."

"And Doctor Glasco?"

"Maybe." He shook his head as though to clear away the implications inherent in his friend's possible guilt. "You know," he continued, "she said much the same thing as . . ." He paused, frowning. "I think it was Mrs. Gentry – check your notes, Bill – said something about Cunningham not needing real information to find a cause for gossip."

He waited while Eggleton flipped through the pages of his notebook.

"Mrs. Liske."

"Mrs. Liske, then. What Mrs. Alexander said was almost identical to what Mrs. Liske said."

"Except the example she gave was different."

"I know. Mrs. Liske talked about suicide, broken marriages, lost jobs. Alarming, isn't it?"

"You know what I found alarming? Mrs. Alexander has a very loose version of the law. It's all right to steal funds if it's for a good cause. It's all right to commit murder if the victim is an evil person. Makes me glad I'm a Presbyterian. Rules are clearer there."

Dawson laughed. "I could hear your mind fidgeting back there, Bill. But you're right. Loose is a good word. Unfortunately, there's no law to get people like Cunningham put away. And, perhaps as we study this case in the community, we might find some people will paint Cunningham with a kinder brush. We'll see."

"Do you think anyone will mourn her death?"

"So far, it doesn't appear so."

"How sad."

"Yes. How sad. Let's see what the feisty landscape architect has to say."

97

GEORGE

George Alexander was a short, stocky man. His smile, broad and open, dominated his face. Dawson found himself instantly liking the man and wished for just one person in this parade of suspects he wouldn't mind finding guilty—well, maybe the bishop, but he was mature enough to realize that was about control. He gestured to the chair.

"You've been talking to my wife," Alexander said. "Quite a lady, isn't she?"

Dawson inclined his head. "It's been brought to my attention you went into the kitchen and took the bottle off the window sill—the bottle containing the nicotine."

"I did. It was a small bottle – I expect you're already seen it."

"Suppose you describe it for me."

"Well, it's like a medicine bottle." Alexander laughed. "You remember the dark brown medicine bottles your mother always had with the orange medicine? They had a little glass tube in them, and she would apply medicine to your scrapes."

avoiding? Eggleton wrote.

"And then, if your mother was anything like mine, she blew on it to make it stop stinging." Alexander smiled at the memory.

So did Eggleton.

Dawson had no such memory.

"Anyway, it was a bottle like that, with a little sticker – said *nicotine concentrate.* I put an eyedropper in it, so Andrew could count out drops to add to water for spraying the flowers."

"Which doesn't explain why you picked it up off the

sill," Dawson said.

Alexander smiled again. "Sorry. I picked it up, because, when Charles said it might be poison, the nicotine was the first thing I thought of."

"And?" Dawson persisted.

The cheerful expression left Alexander's face, aging him in a moment. "I brought it. I wanted to be sure my prints were on it."

"Pretty fast thinking, given the circumstances."

"Perhaps."

"Did you think your prints wouldn't be on it?"

Alexander bowed his head, a small smile returned to his face and he peered up at Dawson, not unlike a small boy caught at mischief. "I knew I didn't administer the poison, Inspector. Which meant, if the nicotine was in fact used, someone else handled the bottle. Therefore, if their prints were on it, mine would smudge them; if their prints were not on it, it meant they had wiped the bottle, and it was surely murder."

"But you're telling me now."

"I'm telling you now. It was a foolish thing for me to do."

"Or perhaps because you're aware your wife already told me."

George Alexander pulled himself straight in the chair. "We discussed it before you arrived, Inspector. We agreed we had both acted foolishly."

"You have obstructed the investigation, Mr. Alexander. Willfully obstructed. Which is a felony."

"Perhaps, 'unthinking' would be better than 'willfully.' And certainly, while I have no great love for the police, it was not with malice toward the police. Rather with compassion toward the guilty party. Whoever did this acted under great duress."

"Nonetheless. . . "

Alexander's voice turned hard. "Nonetheless be damned, Inspector! I have spent time in prison for acting outside the law. And I would do the same again tomorrow if I had to. The law is narrow! It doesn't . . ."

"Narrow?" Dawson interrupted – his voice sharp and loud. "Narrow?"

Startled, Eggleton looked at Dawson. Dawson rarely raised his voice, and certainly, in Eggleton's memory, never to an interviewee. "Narrow?" he said again. "In that it doesn't condone murder? Come now, Mr. Alexander."

Alexander continued. ". . . it doesn't understand about the suffering that drives a person over the brink of its circumscribed confines. It makes no allowances for the grey shadings between its black and white words. Yet grey is what colors our white deeds and dilutes our black. The law leaves grey to the skilled orator or the benevolent judge." He jerked his head toward the door. "That woman out there," he said, apparently forgetting Mrs. Cunningham's body would have long since left the premises, "has probably been responsible for more deaths in this community than a serial killer!"

"Surely that's an exaggeration, Mr. Alexander?" Dawson interrupted.

Alexander's eyes blazed at Dawson. "Not when I count at least two suicides I know of, one medical abortion that should have taken place and didn't because Gwen convinced the mother it was a sin – now the mother is dead, incidentally – died during the birth that should never have taken place, and two people who just gave up living because of the malicious gossip spread by Gwen. No. I don't consider myself exaggerating one bit! Yet she remained untouchable by the law you," his voice shook with emotion as he leaned forward, jabbing his finger at Dawson, "you so valiantly uphold. Now someone, someone who has probably never intentionally harmed anyone else in their life, may well go to prison for her death. I did my small part to protect that person, or, if not protect him or her, to join in the guilt, to show my support." He sat back, his voice resuming its normal tone. "I suspect you will find I am not alone in that gesture."

"So you're convinced she was murdered," Dawson said.

"We wouldn't be here if you didn't think she'd been murdered."

Point for Alexander Eggleton thought as he jotted *touché* in the margin of his notebook.

George Alexander put his elbows on the arms of the chair and made a steeple of his fingers, pressing them to his lips. "You know, Inspector, I find it interesting I confessed to you I had spent time in prison, and you didn't even raise an eyebrow."

"Perhaps it's because I already knew you had spent time in prison."

A slow smile crossed Alexander's face. "My wife."

Dawson shrugged. "And the fact we ran all the names as soon as I arrived."

"Ah, yes. Technology. A wonderful thing. It enabled Dolores to run a check on me when I proposed to her

– technology and a private eye. You see, Dolores is a very cautious woman. Given her first marriage and all . . ."

"She told us about her first marriage," Dawson broke in.

"Yes, well, then you can understand when I say she has had to be cautious. Anyway, when I asked her to marry me, and she asked for time to think it over, I knew she was probably doing a check on me. It was confirmed the evening she accepted me. She called the nursery that day and left a message with the secretary. It said, "Tell Mr. Alexander Mrs. Michaelson says 'Yes.' So that evening I went over to her house with a bottle of champagne and a bouquet." Alexander's face softened to a gentle smile. "Not roses, either, Inspector. Roses would have been cliché. It was a mixture of flowers: English Country they call it."

Eggleton made a note about *roses* and *clichés* and *English country bouquets*.

"Of course, with her garden, it was coals to Newcastle. Anyway, Dolores was in the kitchen getting a vase for the flowers, and asked me to get the champagne glasses out of the hutch. Dolores's desk was right next to the hutch, and on her desk was an envelope from Jerrard's Investigative Services. I assumed she had hired them to make inquiries." George pursed his lips. "In retrospect, I've wondered if she didn't leave the envelope there and send me for the glasses on purpose. So I would know she knew."

Eggleton cleared his throat.

George glanced at Eggleton and gave a small laugh. "Anyway, before I gave her the ring – which I had been carrying around in my pocket since before I asked her – I told her she needed to know something about me she might find troublesome. And then I told her about my time in prison, and why I had gone there. I didn't tell her I knew she'd had a PI investigate me. Anyway, my prison record didn't deter her from caring about me."

"Would you have told her if you hadn't seen the PI's report?"

"Absolutely! You can't enter a marriage with something like that hidden."

"I suspect the circumstances of your *crime* played in your favor."

"She told you?"

"About your first wife? Yes."

"You see what I mean then, Inspector, when I say the law does not allow for extenuating circumstances."

"I still feel we're talking apples and oranges here, Mr. Alexander. Siphoning off funds to pay for the care of an ailing wife, especially funds you attempt to repay, hardly falls into the same category as murder."

"I couldn't agree more, Inspector. In fact, you prove my point beautifully. Can the law differentiate? It said I committed a crime, and I must pay for it. It was unable to take into account the circumstances forcing me into the action I took. Now you, as an individual," and he stabbed his finger in Dawson's direction, "can make the distinction, but you, as the law, can you make the same distinction?"

"Well, I do have to ask – couldn't you have borrowed the money?"

"The insurance paid eighty percent of staggering bills: therapy, hospitalizations, medications, not to mention around-the-clock nursing care. The remaining twenty percent cost me all our savings. After those were gone, it was hundreds a month out of pocket. I couldn't sell the house because it meant so much to her to be in her home. If I could have afforded to repay a loan, I could have afforded the nurses' salaries. That was what I used the money for – the money I took – for the nurse's salaries." Alexander took a handkerchief from his pocket and wiped his forehead. "The law," he continued, "will prosecute the person who killed Gwen. It will be unable to take into account the circumstances that forced someone to kill her."

"Murder is a much more serious crime than embezzlement, Mr. Alexander."

"And I'm sure the sentence will be correspondingly more serious, Inspector. Probably the same as for a murder premeditated and carefully executed, for gain or lust."

"By the standards of premeditation, this crime falls into that classification. Premeditation does not necessarily mean someone plans the crime months ahead of time. The decision to commit this crime may have been almost momentary, but the planning of doctoring the sherry she was drinking falls into the category of premeditation."

"A person who was trying to save him or herself – or maybe someone else?"

"You're telling me you think this murder, if it was indeed murder, should be viewed as self-defense?" Dawson sounded incredulous.

"Oh, yes. That is exactly what I'm telling you."

"Against what?"

"Against the tongue of Gwen Cunningham. And there again, the law won't view the tongue of Gwen Cunningham as a weapon. Whereas, in reality, her tongue was a deadly weapon."

Dawson leaned back in his chair. "Well," he said, "I would love to argue the fine points of the law, Mr. Alexander, but the reality is we're not here to determine if a person deserved to be killed but rather who killed her. I have several more interviews, and I'm afraid I've allowed us to get sidetracked."

"Sorry. Just let me say one thing. Without qualification, I would rather face a knife than the tongue of Gwen Cunningham."

"If you had something to hide."

"Even if I didn't Inspector. Even if I didn't. Facts meant little to Gwen."

"Ah, but you did have something to hide."

"Not hide, Inspector." His voice was scathing. "Something I would have preferred not become public knowledge. There's a difference."

Another point for Alexander, Eggleton thought, who was likening the conversation to a tennis match.

"Aren't you splitting hairs, Mr. Alexander?"

"No. The person I care most about in this entire world is Dolores. Since Dolores already knows about my past, I had no reason to fear exposure."

"But you'd rather it not happen."

Alexander pursed his lips. "You're right, Inspector – but not to the point of killing Gwen Cunningham. Given the nature of my crime, exposure at Gwen's hands would be far easier to ride out than standing trial and subsequent sentencing for her murder. No, Inspector. Keeping my past a secret is a preference, but not one for which I'm prepared to commit murder." He leaned forward in his chair, his hands clasped in front of him.

"May I back up for a moment? You just said, 'if it was indeed murder' or words to that effect. Do you doubt it was murder?"

"For the moment, I am acting on the premise it was murder."

"But you have some reason, however small, to doubt it was murder."

point Alexander!

"Suicide has been mentioned, Mr. Alexander. Would you think it a possibility?"

"I think it would be very convenient for us all if it were suicide."

"That's not what I asked. I asked if you thought it a possibility."

Eggleton jotted *dawson scores.*

"I don't know. I didn't know Gwen all that well. I suspect very few people did. She wasn't a woman who anyone really wanted to make the effort to know." He paused, running his hand through his hair. "Let me hypothesize. Suppose Gwen could see us now. How thrilled she would be to view the pain and anxiety all those she left behind at the sherry party are experiencing. Let's take the hypothesis one step further. Suppose you never do find the guilty party." He held his hand up as though to forestall any comment by Dawson. "Purely speculative thinking, Inspector. But just suppose you never find 'who done it,' which is what would happen if it were an unconfirmed suicide. Think of the stigma following us the rest of our lives. Gwen would have loved that."

Dawson's tone was dry, like brittle leaves, fallen to a forest floor. He spoke slowly. "If you were worried about the stigma of being thought guilty, perhaps you should have thought twice about taking the nicotine bottle from the sill."

"Point – Dawson," Eggleton muttered.

"Yes Sergeant?"

"Nothing, Sir. Just clearing my throat."

"Fair enough, Inspector," Alexander said. "I acted first and thought later. I'm doing my best to undo the damage I might have done."

"Are you saying you hope the guilty party is apprehended?"

"Not at all. I'm simply saying by picking up the bottle I probably didn't further the cause of the guilty party either way, but have landed myself in a heap of trouble for obscuring evidence. I expect I will be severely reprimanded."

mocking d, Eggleton wrote.

"At the very least," Dawson said.

Alexander raised his eyebrows. "A threat, Inspector?"

"A fact, Mr. Alexander." Dawson stood, rubbing his fists into the small of his back. "You were talking about Mrs. Cunningham enjoying the spectacle of this interrogation."

"I can see Gwen committing suicide, provided she had some valid reason for doing so – such as a terminal illness – in this manner to throw suspicion on the rest of us. It would be perfectly in keeping with her personality. Sort of a last hurrah, don't you think?"

"I wouldn't know, Mr. Alexander. I didn't know Mrs. Cunningham."

"Ah, yes." George Alexander stood. "If you have no further questions . . . "

Dawson gestured Alexander back to his seat and took

his own. "A few, Mr. Alexander. Just a few more. Did you at any time leave the drawing room."

Laughing, George Alexander sat down. "Drawing room! I love it! Mavis has got you doing it. Everything here is so elegant one forgets most of us call it the living room." His face sobered. "No, Inspector. Not even to go to the *little boys' room.*"

Dawson's eyebrows shot up. "*Little boys' room*, Mr. Alexander?"

"Just mimicking Gwen. We were talking with her this afternoon, and she excused herself to go to the '*little girls' room.*' I apologize. Unless you were there, it couldn't be remotely humorous. No, I didn't leave the drawing room at any time."

"When did she go to the *little girls' room?* Early in the party? Late?"

"Oh, quite late. Not too long before she . . ." He paused. "Not long before she died."

little girls' room – late Eggleton wrote.

"I see. And you didn't go into the patio?"

"Well, yes. I did. I guess I consider it an extension of the drawing room."

"For what reason?"

"For what reason did I consider it an extension of the drawing room?"

Dawson sighed. "For what reason did you go into the patio?"

"Oh. Well, we all did – just sort of wandered in and out. It was warm outside, and Mavis's garden is a show-place. Naturally, I would want to see it. I spent a few minutes visiting with Andrew – told him about the nicotine

– said it was in the kitchen and after the party I'd show him how to use it."

"Did you go into the kitchen during the party?"

"No. I went in at the beginning of the party and put the bottle on the sill, but I didn't go back in."

"Did you notice anyone going out into the hall – in the direction of the kitchen or the bathroom?"

"I suppose lots of them did. I don't remember specifically."

"When Mrs. Cunningham excused herself to go to the *little girls' room,* did you notice if she went directly?"

Alexander frowned, as though picturing the scene in his mind. "I don't remember," he said finally. "I know she started in that direction, but I didn't see her actually go out of the door and into the hall."

"Did anyone know you were bringing the nicotine?" Dawson asked, changing directions.

"Oh, I think almost everybody did?"

Dawson looked surprised. Eggleton scribbled.

Alexander continued. "Last Thursday night we had a vestry meeting. Father Greg was late, so we just sat around talking."

"Where did this meeting take place?"

"In the conference room at the parish hall. There's a big table in there and plenty of room for all of us. Anyway, Mavis said something to me about aphids– said she thought her aphids had nine lives, because nothing Andrew used on them seemed to work. So I told her I'd bring her some nicotine concentrate – which incidentally is no longer on the market as an insecticide–and I'd show Andrew how to use it."

"Who else was there —at this meeting?"

"Mavis of course, Charles – although I think he got a call on his cell and stepped out to have privacy. I don't know if he was there when I said I'd bring the concentrate. Linda was there. And Sandy. Gwen of course. Father Greg came in late —after we discussed the aphids."

Eggleton scribbled names.

"So everybody here today could have heard you say you would bring the nicotine Saturday.?"

"Right."

"Was Mrs. Gifford there?"

"No."

"Mrs. Alexander?"

Alexander shook his head. "She's not on the vestry. She's just here today because spouses were invited."

"What were you talking about?"

"Huh?"

"This afternoon. You said you were talking to Mrs. Cunningham. What were you talking about?"

George Alexander took a deep breath and let it out noisily. Then he leaned back in his chair, and crossed his legs.

"Are we keeping you?" Dawson, sarcasm heavy in his voice.

"Sorry. I'm sure I'm going to repeat what you've already heard from the others and Dolores."

"We'll see," Dawson said and made a gesture for Alexander to proceed.

When he finished, Eggleton jotted *account agrees with wife's— seems credible.*

Dawson stood. "Thank you, Mr. Alexander," he said. "You can go on home now."

"Oh, I think we'll stick around for a while."

Dawson nodded. "If I have more questions, I'll be in touch."

Eggleton waited until the library door closed behind Alexander. "A worthy opponent, I would say."

"Feisty little bloke, isn't he? Like his wife said."

"But telling the truth, I think."

"Yeah. Me too."

"Almost an air of 'you can't touch me' about him. You know, my wife has a friend . . ."

Dawson rolled his eyes.

" . . . lost a husband and a baby in a car accident. She's like Alexander – there's this attitude: there's-nothing-you-can-do-to-me-that-hasn't-already-been-done sort of attitude."

"You're a bit like Miss Marple, Bill. Everybody reminds you of somebody."

"Speaking of Orient Express . . ."

"Were we?"

". . . what you were talking about with Mrs. Alexander. You know, in that book none of those people were charged with murder."

"You do keep me humble," Dawson said.

"Do you think you can get Mr. Alexander on handling the bottle?"

"I doubt it. Besides, it would be a small victory."

"Do you think he's covering anything?"

"No. But I've been rethinking his wife."

"Oh?"

"Think about it for a minute, Bill. She talked only about her husband and his past – a smoke screen, maybe, to keep us away from getting to her? And did we fall for it?"

"She didn't answer your question when you asked her if she had anything to hide. I made a note of it."

"You make me a better detective, Bill."

"You know what amazes me," Eggleton said, trying to look modest, "is all these people seem to think if this *was* a murder, it was justified. The Big M, Jake!"

"I think what we learned from Alexander that's important is all these people knew ahead of time about the nicotine."

"Except Mrs. Gifford and Mrs. Alexander."

"And the bishop," Dawson said.

"And the bishop. You know, Sir. I really am learning a lot from this investigation."

"Are you? Well, just remember, even if they are cliché, your wife may prefer roses."

"How'd you know what I was thinking?" Eggleton said, his voice jumping like an adolescent boy's.

"I'm a detective, Sergeant. It's what I do." He looked at his list of party guests. "I suppose I should talk to Charles," he said finally. "Get it over with." His voice was weary, and Eggleton could tell Dawson didn't want to interview his friend.

CHAPTER SIX

Interview: Charles Glasco

An evil disease, say they, cleaveth closely to him; and now that he
lieth down, he shall rise up no more.
Ps. 41:8

Doctor Charles Glasco sat in a bentwood rocker in a corner of Mavis's kitchen. With Dawson's permission, the little party had moved from the morning room and was gathered around a large oak table: Nancy, holding Father Greg's hand, Dolores Alexander, who was waiting for George to finish his interview with Dawson, and the bishop. An officer sat quietly by the door.

Andrew, with the proprietary air of one who is used to the house, was busying himself bringing condiments from the refrigerator door: mustard, ketchup, mayonnaise, and setting the bottles on the table. Finally, he opened a crisper and brought out a head of lettuce and two large tomatoes which he placed on a cutting board in the center of the table.

"Andrew!" Mavis exclaimed as she set out a stack of plates and silverware. "Let's get dishes for those things!!"

"Nonsense, Mavis. It feels more like home this way," George, who had just stepped into the kitchen, said. "And put those plates away. Don't you have paper plates in this house?"

"George! I wouldn't dream . . ."

"Get them!" George ordered, grinning at the uniformed policeman. "Or I'll jump our watchdog and go buy some."

Mavis shrugged and went to her pantry closet where she began rummaging on the shelves. After several minutes, she triumphantly held up an unopened package of Christmas paper plates. "Are you satisfied, George?" she asked.

"Perfectly," he said, looking at his watch. "It's going to be a very long night, my friends. Better get some nourishment." He ripped the plastic wrap from the plates and set them on the table: a merry, discordant addition to the scene. Mavis lifted a large salad bowl from the refrigerator and handed it to Andrew. "Just set it on the table," she said as she reached back into the refrigerator, removing packages of cold cuts and cheeses.

Nancy laughed, the sound high-pitched and strained, unlike her usual breathy laugh. "Mavis, do you keep food like this on hand in case a group of people arrive at your house to be questioned by the police?"

"Actually I was supposed to have the Garden Club here for a luncheon meeting tomorrow after church, so I had this food ready. But I called Sally Jo a while ago and canceled. Any other night I'm afraid the cupboard would have been bare."

The bishop stood and motioned for George to take his seat. "If you don't mind, I'll take Nancy's car and go back to the rectory to wait for you both," he said to Father Greg.

Father Greg reached in his pocket for his keys. "Take

mine. It's the Prius. I think there's a police car parked in back of Nancy's."

"Don't you want something to eat?" Mavis asked.

Looking at the bishop's drawn face, the normal light tan of his skin an ashen shade, Charles thought food was probably the last thing the bishop wanted, and he wondered what had been discussed in the library.

"I'm just tired. Maybe I'll eat something later, but not just now."

"Well," Nancy said, "there's plenty in the refrigerator. Help yourself. Oh, and tell Renee to stay until we get there. You don't need to baby sit after what you've been through."

"Thank you, Nancy," he said. Then leaning down, he kissed her lightly on the cheek and nodded in the direction of the library. "You'll do fine." Turning to George and Dolores, he squeezed their shoulders. "Goodbye, Andrew," he said, shaking the little man's hand. Then, crossing the room, he took Charles' hand in both of his, clasping it tightly before turning to Mavis and touching his cheek to hers. "Goodbye everybody. See you in church." His voice caught on the word 'church,' and he hurried from the room. Nancy folded her arms on the table and put her head down; her shoulders shook. Father Greg gently rubbed her shoulder.

Leaning his head against the back of the rocker, Charles closed his eyes. Death, he thought. So much death. It was a leitmotif playing its minor tune through his life, starting with the death of his father when he was ten years old, followed by the death of his mother when he was nineteen – and now patients – and Gwen Cunningham.

Thinking how his mother would have loved the

sherry party that afternoon, he smiled. "Sherry," she often said. "Stimulates the appetite." After she became ill, even sherry didn't help.

He had come home from college for Christmas vacation, his mind dizzy with thoughts of nubile freshman girls and preoccupied with excuses for the low grades he knew his mother would question. He had been so full of himself, he scarcely noticed the fatigue circling her eyes, nor did he question her long daily naps.

Over spring break, he visited with his roommate's family, and so, when summer came, and he returned home once more, he was not prepared for the sight of his mother in the high hospital bed that dominated the living room, her body a tiny mound beneath the white spread, her huge eyes a vivid blue, the only color against the white pillowcase. What hair she had left was white, her skin a pale gray. A formidable German housekeeper-cum practical nurse bustled through their home, shushing him, fixing him hearty meals, and setting small tables to rocking and dishes to vibrating in her wake.

After scolding his mother gently for not notifying him of her health, he settled into a routine of sitting by her bed each day, spinning improbable tales of Brunhilda – as he called the practical nurse – tales that brought a tiny smile of conspiracy to his mother's face. He read aloud to her and wiped her forehead with a cool cloth. He forgot the soft-breasted maidens of Hightower Dorm. One day, after Brunhilda had bathed and toileted her, his mother turned her head toward the I.V. stand by her bed. From it dangled a bag of colorless liquid. A tube led from the bag to her arm, where tape held a needle in place.

"I don't want any more," she said, her voice so soft he had to lean across her to hear her words. Her breath was hot and sour against his cheek.

"What?" he asked, sorry he had made her use her meagre store of strength to speak again.

"I don't want any more," she repeated. "They're coming today. Tell them . . . no more." She closed her eyes, exhausted by the effort.

When the doctor arrived, accompanied by his starched nurse, Charles cleared his throat and stood tall, his hands clenched, his nails biting into his palms. "She doesn't want any more," he said. He tried not to look at his mother, tried not to see her eyes watching him, praying for him to convey her message.

The doctor looked up from his watch where he had been counting the pulse of the dying woman. "What did you say?"

Again, Charles cleared his throat. "I said she doesn't want any more." His voice sounded high-pitched and unnatural. "She told me she doesn't want the intravenous feedings."

The nurse crackled in her uniform, her head and shoulders stiff with disapproval. She continued to remove the empty bag from the I.V. stand.

"That, young man, is not her decision, nor is it yours, to make," said the doctor. He stepped out of the way as the nurse reattached the tube to a new bag, bloated with the life-sustaining fluid.

Charles looked at his mother. Her eyes brimmed with tears, and he felt his own coursing down his cheeks. His face smarted with impotency and rage.

The doctor and nurse turned to leave, both rigid with indignation. "We will be back in two days," the doctor said at the door. "I will not expect any significant change in her condition in that time," he added, his eyes piercing in their scrutiny of Charles.

Charles sat in the chair next to the bed. "I'm sorry, Mom," he said, bending to lay his head on the white spread. Her fingers found his curly hair and gently ruffled it.

"You tried," she whispered.

His mother did not ask him to speak to the doctor again, nor did she ask him to unhook the bag, but Charles saw her feeble attempts to reach the needle with her free hand. Again and again she tried to lift her arm across her body, her fingers groping for the needle that eluded her by inches. Each time she lapsed into an exhausted sleep, only to wake and begin her attempts once more. Charles wept.

It was two weeks later Brunhilda woke Charles in the early morning hours. "She's gone," Brunhilda said. They stood together, their cheeks wet with tears, at the foot of the bed, and Charles realized he didn't know Brunhilda's real name; he was ashamed he had made fun of her. They watched as the bag dripped its fluids into the dead woman's body. Her eyes were open and staring, her arm reaching for the needle, her fingers frozen claw-like.

In answer to Charles' call, the doctor and his brisk nurse arrived within the hour. The doctor's eyes darted to the I.V. with its plastic bag, then to the needle, still taped to the dead woman's arm. His eyes flickered toward Charles, and then he turned to Brunhilda. "Elsa," he said, "did any.

. .?" Then he stopped. Quickly he went through the motions of determining death, a meaningless ritual by a doctor who played by the rules. His signature on the death certificate was hurried and illegible. While the doctor called the mortuary, the nurse unhooked the apparatus that had prolonged life and then pulled the sheet over the dead woman's face. Charles stood by, weeping. Elsa put her arm around him.

As he rocked in Mavis's comfortable chair, he smiled at the thought he had exchanged his preoccupation with bra size for a preoccupation with grade point – a grade point which earned him a scholarship to medical school. Then his attention returned to the gathering in the kitchen.

He watched as the group made their sandwiches; passing the jars of condiments, sharing knives, stabbing forks into meats and cheeses, layering on tomatoes and lettuce, vying for creativity. They smiled at one another, laughed occasionally – small laughs that stopped abruptly, as if inappropriate for the occasion.

"Aren't you going to have something, Charles?"

Charles jumped slightly, startled by Mavis' voice.

"Maybe in a little while, Mavis," he said, looking up at her face, beautiful in spite of fatigue. "You OK?"

Her smile was weak. "I'm fine. I think I'll make some fresh coffee," and she returned to the sink.

Charles watched as she went through the familiar routine of grinding beans and filling the pot. Knowing there was comfort in small, mundane tasks, he didn't offer to help her.

"Inspector Dawson would like to see you, Doctor

119

Glasco."

Eggleton's entrance into the kitchen had gone unnoticed, and Dolores, taken unawares, dropped the knife she was using to spread mayonnaise.

Mavis whirled around from the sink. "You startled us, Sergeant," she said. "Would you and the Inspector have time for a sandwich before you continue?"

Eggleton, whose stomach had been rumbling for the past hour, looked hopefully at the array of foods spread on the table and turned back to the library. "I'll ask him, Ma'am," he called over his shoulder.

But Sergeant Eggleton was destined to be disappointed. "I want to get this over with, Bill," said Dawson. "It's not a bloody social event."

Dolores, seeing Eggleton's dejection when he reported back to the kitchen, handed him the sandwich she had just finished making. "Just take your time getting back to the library, Sergeant," she said. "Tell the Inspector Charles was on the phone to the hospital or some such."

Eggleton raised his brows as he took the sandwich. "Lie to the police?" he asked, his tone mocking.

Nancy laughed again, the same unnatural laugh as before and twisted the pearls. Father Greg pulled her hand away. At the sink, Mavis made a choking sound, and Charles, unable to determine if he had heard a sob or a laugh, glanced at her with concern. George coughed discreetly into his napkin.

Eggleton reddened. "Sorry about that." He smiled at Dolores and took a large bite of the sandwich. "Thanks," he said, his mouth full of ham and cheese. "You're a life saver."

Lieberman had returned Gwen Cunningham's purse to the library, and Dawson was hunched over a small table spread with the contents when Eggleton entered with Charles Glasco. Noting Eggleton was chewing, Dawson raised one eyebrow and, with a tiny smile, pointed to the corner of his lip. "Mustard," he mouthed. Eggleton, to whom blushing came easily, blushed – and took his place at the desk.

Doctor Glasco made his way across the polished hardwood floor of the library in long, distance-consuming strides, and Eggleton wondered if Glasco might have done field and track at one time. Or perhaps basketball. "What do you have there?" Glasco asked.

"Contents of Mrs. Cunningham's purse," Dawson said. "It's all been printed. Take a look – especially at the prescriptions."

Glasco pulled his glasses from his breast pocket – a handkerchief from his pants pocket. He put the glasses, one lens at a time, into his mouth, clouding the lens with his breath and then carefully wiping it before holding it to the light to check for clarity.

stalling Eggleton jotted.

Finally, placing the glasses on his nose, Glasco folded the handkerchief and returned it to his pocket. Only then did take up the little bottle. "Ambien, Doctor Reinquist," he read, holding out his hand for the next bottle. "Ativan, Doctor Abernathy." He handed the bottles back to Dawson.

"So," Dawson said when Glasco had completed his inspection. "What can you tell me about them?"

"Ambien is a sleeping medication. It's used for

insomnia. But it does have some serious side effects.

"Such as?"

"Depression is one of them." Eggleton gave a quick glance in Dawson's direction, but Dawson's face revealed nothing. "Night walking. Paranoia if withdrawn suddenly," Charles continued. "You'll notice the Ambien is from Reinquist. The other prescription, the Ativan, is an anxiety medication. That's from Doctor Abernathy. Also, she's used two different pharmacies for her prescriptions. Evidently didn't want one doctor to know what the other was prescribing."

"Drug interaction?"

"Maybe. But I'll wager there was more to it than that. Knowing Reinquist, I suspect he was an easy mark for the Ambien. Abernathy wouldn't be so easy."

"I'm not sure I understand," Dawson said.

"Ambien should be used sparingly and under strict supervision. Also, it should be withdrawn gradually as soon as possible." Glasco paused, frowning. "I don't want to impugn a colleague, but quite frankly, I don't see Reinquist doing that kind of follow-up. I suspect if you check the pharmacy . . ." he picked up the bottle in question, "Payless – you'll find this prescription has been long-standing." He pointed to a notation on the label. "Right here it indicates three refills; probably renewed with periodic calls to the doctor. She was a regular user."

"And Doctor Abernathy would handle it differently?"

"I imagine." He took off his glasses, returning them carefully to his breast pocket.

"Any side effects from the . . . " Dawson paused, glancing at one of the bottles, "Ativan?"

"She shouldn't have been drinking alcohol with either. Either could have caused a problem."

"Such as a convulsion and subsequent death?" Dawson asked, moving to his chair and gesturing for Glasco to be seated.

Charles shook his head, frowning. "I doubt it," he said. "It's possible, I suppose. It'll be interesting to see what the post-mortem shows in the way of alcohol content." He slumped low in the chair facing Dawson's, crossing his long legs at the ankle. "Also, just what prescription drugs were in her system at the time? If she took the Ambien before bedtime last night, it probably passed through her system by this afternoon."

"So the depression side effect would be only for the duration of the drug in the system? How about alcohol interaction."

"With Ambien, the depression would last longer than the drug itself."

"Would suicide be a possibility, given the presence of the drug?"

"Yes. Suicide is frequently a result of depression. The literature shows suicidal thinking to be associated with Ambien. That's why monitoring of the drug is so essential. Although, insomnia is frequently a symptom of depression, so it's not known for certain if Ambien causes a type of chemical depression or whether the depression is there and the Ambien merely exacerbates a symptom." He chuckled. "The chicken-and-egg question."

"Could she have done it deliberately?"

"You mean suicide?"

"It's been suggested. What do you think?"

Recalling his afternoon conversation with Gwen Cunningham, Charles knew what he thought.

He had been sipping sherry– and wishing there was something besides sherry to drink– as he watched Mavis Dillon rearrange the already perfectly-aligned napkins and decanters while listening to Gwen Cunningham. Seeing Mavis's frozen expression, he wondered what Gwen was saying.

Mavis had closed the French doors, a slight wind having come up, and the little party was gathered inside. Glancing around the room, he noticed the other guests were involved in quiet conversation. Linda and Sandy were in the corner of the room by the fireplace visiting with the bishop; Linda stood close as though seeking warmth from a fire that was not burning. Her arms were folded tightly – her sherry glass stood empty on the mantle. The bishop had his hand on Sandy's shoulder, and he was smiling at her. As Charles watched, he saw the bishop squeeze Sandy's shoulder slightly. Then, setting his own glass on the mantle, the bishop took the glasses of the two women and walked to the sideboard, stopping to chat with the Alexanders and Nancy.

Nancy had pulled a chair close to where George and Dolores Alexander sat on the love-seat, her head bent close in conversation. Her golden hair was bright in the late afternoon sun shining through the windows; a contrast to the somber expression on her usually animated face. She smiled slightly when the bishop stopped beside her chair. The sunlight caught the faceted sherry glasses he was carrying and his gold pectoral cross. Charles turned his gaze back to

Mavis and Gwen Cunningham. Mavis was pouring sherry from a decanter, and her hands shook slightly. *Perhaps I'd better see if I can rescue Mavis,* he thought.

"Oh, Charles," Mrs. Cunningham said as he approached. "I was just telling Mavis I would prepare a family tree for Carol Anne's wedding gift." She smiled at him. "I think she's afraid of some skeletons in the closet," she said, giggling. "I've assured her I will be the soul of discretion." She turned to Mavis. "Haven't I? I'm going to get right on it tonight."

"Mavis," said Charles ,"perhaps you would show me the . . . " He had been going to say 'Victorian Blush rose,' but Mrs. Cunningham broke in.

"So sad about Danny Resnick, don't you think?" she said, her hand on Charles' arm.

"He was extremely ill, Gwen," he said.

"Still, one didn't expect him to be taken quite so quickly, did one? I realize he had Lou Gherig's Disease, but still, it doesn't usually move so rapidly."

"It's difficult to tell how a disease will progress."

"You will excuse me," Mavis said as she finished straightening a fan of cocktail napkins. "I really want to speak to Nancy." She gave him a tiny smile and walked off toward Nancy Gifford who had left the Alexanders and was standing by the bookcase scanning the titles. "Nancy," Charles heard Mavis say. "You're looking elegant today. I love your dress."

Mrs. Cunningham's eyes followed Mavis. "A dear girl, but one does wonder what she is hiding."

"Hiding?" Charles asked. "Mavis? I hardly think . . ."

"Oh, there's something about her she doesn't want

known," Mrs. Cunningham interrupted. "As I said, skeletons in the closet – secrets, you now." Smiling sweetly, she turned to the bishop who stood at the sideboard, decanter in hand. "Everyone has secrets, don't they Bishop." She held up her glass. "Just a splash since you're pouring." She lifted the filled glass in a mock toast before turning back to Charles. "Ah, yes," she continued, nodding her head slightly. "Secrets." The bishop gave her a sharp glance as he turned away and started back toward the fireplace. "By the way, Charles," she said. "I'm so interested in this new concept of physician-assisted death that's going to be on the ballot. I hear many physicians actually favor the bill."

Taken aback by her non-sequitur, Charles stared at her.

She clicked her tongue. "From what I hear, a number have already done it – assisted their patients, I mean. Talk about secrets!" She raised the sherry to her mouth, staring at Charles over the rim of her goblet. "What do you think about it?" she asked, tossing her head back and downing the sherry.

Charles shuddered; *sherry should be sipped* he thought – *Gwen Cunningham should be gagged.* "Physician-assisted death? I haven't given it much thought." A lie, since he had thought of little else during the last week. "I suppose there is a case to be made for both sides of the argument."

"Nonsense!" Gwen Cunningham snapped. "It's murder, pure and simple. I suppose you're going to say people who are dying anyway should be given something to ease them on their way. Well, I consider it a blatant disregard for God's rules." She fingered the heavy bracelet on her left wrist. "People die in God's own time, not some doctor's time."

"What about extreme pain?" Charles asked, mentally kicking himself for rising to her challenge, yet unable to stop himself. "Are you opposed to people who are terminally ill and in extreme pain receiving some relief?"

She raised her eyebrows. "I guess I know where you stand," she said. "However, I would hardly consider murder 'some relief' as you so casually put it."

"What would you want if it were you?" Charles said. "I think that's the question you have to answer."

"I certainly wouldn't want some doctor giving me pills or a shot to hasten me on my way," she said. "I have every confidence God will deal with me as is appropriate." Again she fingered her bracelet, this time the one on her right wrist."

I doubt He'll be so cruel, Charles thought, glad he could find some glimmer of humor in the conversation. "Well, it really isn't an issue yet, is it," he said, "since the bill hasn't come up for a vote? You will excuse me now," he continued. "I want Mavis to show me something in her garden."

"I suspect it's more of an issue than you might think," Mrs. Cunningham said to the doctor's back, but loud enough for him to hear. "And Margaret Billings was very ill, too," she added as she turned and made her way across the room to the brocade loveseat where the Alexanders sat.

"I asked what you thought about Mrs. Cunningham committing suicide."

With an effort, Charles pulled himself back to Dawson's question. He had no intention of saying anything about his conversation with Gwen Cunningham concerning physician-assisted death and people dying in God's own time, so he said, "What I think is hardly relevant. I don't know if she would have committed suicide or not. I didn't know her well enough to even make a guess. But I would wonder why, when she had a full bottle of sleeping pills – I'm sure you noticed the prescription was filled yesterday, so she probably picked it up sometime today before the party – she wouldn't just take a handful at home. Much less messy than the scene . .. ." He gestured in the direction of the drawing room.

Dawson, his forehead creased with concern, leaned forward. "Charles," he said, "you can help me – if you will. Nobody cares this woman is dead. Nobody. I can't get a handle on what happened here, because everybody is protecting everybody else." He pointed at Charles. "You, too, I suspect. And an entire room full of upstanding citizens has tampered with the only evidence I might have."

"You know I'd help you if I could, but I can't"

With a sigh of resignation, Dawson leaned back in his chair. "Can't or won't," he muttered.

"Can't Jake. I can tell you what I saw happen, which I expect you've already heard. My initial reaction was poison. Now I'm not so sure, given the Ambien and Ativan you showed me. It could have been a drug and alcohol interaction, nothing more sinister. Can you wait for the autopsy?"

"If I do, and it turns out to be poison – which you thought it might be and which Henchcombe is ninety-nine per cent sure it is – I've lost valuable time. I have to go on the assumption of poison in order to get as much information as close to the event as possible. If it turns out to have been accidental – or suicide – well . . ." He shrugged, leaving his thought unfinished. "Now, tell me what you and Mrs. Cunningham talked about this afternoon."

about time, Eggleton noted.

Charles pursed his lips and stroked his chin. "Well," he said. "She was talking to Mavis – something about a family tree for Carole Anne's wedding – I didn't pay much attention – then Mavis left, and Gwen started talking to me about two of my patients."

Dawson, remembering the notation beside Glasco's name in Gwen Cunningham's book, remained poker-faced.

Eggleton wrote *two patients.* In the margin, he jotted *dillon- family tree.*

Charles continued. "Danny Resnick had Lou Gehrig's Disease – very advanced – and Margaret Billings had battled pancreatic cancer for a number of years. Both died last week."

"What specifically did she have to say about them?"

"Nothing, really. Just that it was a shame, is all."

Eggleton jotted *not likely.*

"Did she imply anything unusual about their deaths?"

Charles felt his heart skip a beat at Dawson's question. He thought about his two patients, remembering their anguish-ridden faces as they begged him for something to end their suffering.

* * *

"Some pills, Doc," Danny had said, his speech barely intelligible. ". .. . take myself. You not invol . . ." He made a hollow, broken sound, someplace between a laugh and a sob. "Before . . . hardly swallow. . ." His condition had

129

deteriorated beyond what the home health care nurse could provide, and, having no one else to care for him, a nursing home was the alternative – and immediate.

Charles smiled at Danny. "I'll see you tomorrow," he said.

"Strong," Danny whispered.

"Strong," Charles said, squeezing Danny's shoulder. Danny's eyes filled with tears.

Margaret had said much the same thing as Danny. The room where she lay was hot and smelled of the decay permeating her ravaged body. "Please help me," she begged as her face twisted with pain. "I can't stand it anymore. Can't you give me something?"

"We've ordered morphine shots as necessary," he had said.

"I know. But they're . . . not very effective anymore." She gasped as another spasm hit her. "If there was something . . . I could take myself." Her eyes were luminous, like his mother's – as though they were the only living part of her body. "You understand. . ."

"Yes," he said. "I understand."

Margaret's daughter stood at the door as he left. "She wants to die," she said.

"I know," Charles had responded, once again remembering his mother's words. 'I don't want any more.' He would order additional morphine.

* * *

Charles knew he had to live with his conscience, which he had no problem doing, but he was not about to

130

share any of that with Dawson.

"Imply?"

"That's what I heard about her," Dawson said. "She implied things."

"No," Charles lied. "She just said it must be hard to lose a patient. I said, 'yes, it is,' and then I left her and went to talk with Mavis about her roses."

"Did you go out into the hall at all during the afternoon?"

"Once. To use the bathroom."

"Did you see anyone while you were in the hall?

"No."

"Did you go into the kitchen at any time?"

"Jake!"

"I have to ask, Charles. You know that."

"Yeah, I know. No, I didn't. Not until we all went into the kitchen. After – you know. You've heard about that."

Dawson stood. "Thanks Charles," he said. "You go on home now."

"I'll stick around awhile – keep an eye on Mavis."

"Tell me about Mrs Dillon. Widowed? Divorced? Married but the husband is absent, what?"

"She's widowed – has been for years. Has one daughter about twenty-five years old. Beautiful girl – plays violin with the San Francisco Symphony. The daughter's getting married in a couple of weeks, a young maestro from Russia. Of course, Mavis is thrilled; that girl is her life."

Eggleton scribbled *girl is her life.*

"No lack of funds," Dawson said.

Charles Glasco raised his eyebrows. "For sure. Dillon

left her well off – or his family did. I guess they're all dead now. Anyway, Mavis is not hurting."

all dead?? check. Eggleton wrote.

"Obviously," Dawson started toward the door. "Well, if you think of anything, let me know."

Looking at his friend, Charles saw the weariness in Dawson's face, and for a moment, felt a rush of tears to his eyes. He blinked them back. "Death stalks me, Jake," he said. "I've seen so much of it."

"I know."

"I guess you have, too," Charles said.

Dawson nodded, and together the two men walked out of the library. Over his shoulder, Dawson said, "Get Mrs. Gifford, Bill. I'm going to find the bathroom."

CHAPTER SEVEN

Interview: Nancy Gifford

...seeking goodly pearls...
Mt. 13:45

As she waited for Inspector Dawson to return to the library, Nancy Gifford wandered about the room, stopping for a moment to stare at the picture on the wall – wild game spread out on a table, a gun leaning carelessly against the table leg. Her finger twisted the pearl necklace. Then she remembered what Gwen Cunningham had said that afternoon, and she jerked her hand away.

"You know, you're going to break your beautiful necklace if you don't quit twisting it. It would be a shame to lose even one of those gorgeous pearls. They are lovely." Gwen had reached out a plump hand as if to touch the necklace. Nancy pulled away, flinching slightly.

"My, my," Gwen Cunningham said, raising her eyebrows. "I imagine they were a gift from Father Greg. I'm so glad you got them. I saw you in Meyerson's looking at pearls one day just before Christmas." She took a swallow of sherry and licked her lips. "I don't think you saw me; I was in the office visiting with Marjorie. Anyway, you were looking at them so longingly, and I thought to myself, I thought, I just know Father Greg can't afford something like that, but she does want them so."

Over Gwen's shoulder Nancy saw the bishop watching them, his face filled with concern. Seeing he had caught her eye, the bishop gave her a tiny wink. She dipped her head slightly. She could hear Dolores out on the patio, laughing.

"Well, we don't pay Father Greg half what he's worth," Mrs. Cunningham went on, "and I've said so many times, but I'm glad to see he managed. You can always tell quality," she added, leaning close to Nancy, peering at the necklace, and for one panicked moment Nancy wondered if Mrs. Cunningham might ask to rub them on her teeth.

Which was what the jeweler – a jeweler in the town where Greg had been Associate Priest before he took the position in Castlemont – had suggested when Nancy had taken her mother's pearls to be restrung. She had planned to wear them for the Diocesan convention dinner, when she noticed the string had deteriorated over the years.

"They're very nice," the jeweler had said, "but of no great value."

"Are you sure?" Her mother had been so certain of their worth.

"Here." He handed her another string of pearls. "These are real. Just run those both across your teeth, and you can tell the difference. The real ones will be rough."

She didn't bother to run them across her teeth; she took her mother's pearls home and restrung them with dental floss – and wore them rarely.

Gwen's attention to the pearls made Nancy remember her mother's simple faith.

When money was short, and it so often was, her mother would say, "We'll be OK, Honey. We have the pearls. Your daddy gave them to me when we got married, and he wouldn't want us to go hungry, so if I need to, I can always sell them."

Neither believed she would, but knowing the pearls were there, warm, gleaming on a bed of blue velvet, gave Nancy and her mother the security they needed, a hedge against poverty. The jeweler's few words had destroyed the memory and tarnished the image of the father who had died before she was born.

"Have a seat, Mrs. Gifford," Dawson said, as he came into the room. "I apologize for keeping you waiting."

Nancy sat, her hands tightly folded in her lap. "That's all right," she said. When she spoke, her voice was soft and breathy, giving Dawson the impression of someone fragile and naïve.

"I have just a few questions, Mrs. Gifford . . . "

Nancy broke in. "She really did a lot for the community. Gwen, I mean. And for the church. If you needed help with anything, you just had to ask and she . . ." She stopped, her voice dwindling to a whisper.

"I'm sure she did, and I will want to know all about that, but for now I need you to tell me what happened here this afternoon."

Nancy's hand went, almost reflexively, to the necklace and she began twisting it. "I don't know what I can tell you. Gwen collapsed, and Charles said he thought it might be poison." She shrugged. "I'm sure you've heard that already."

Dawson noticed she was twisting the strand of pearls to the point where they could break at any moment. "Would you like Sergeant Eggleton to pour you some coffee?" he asked, hoping to distract her from the pearls before the three of them were searching the carpet for stray beads. "Or tea?"

She shook her head, giving the pearls yet another twist.

Dawson leaned back in his chair and crossed his legs. "Tell me, Mrs. Gifford, how did you meet your husband?"

Eggleton stole a quick glance at his watch and put his pencil down.

Nancy looked puzzled, as though wondering what relevancy her meeting with Greg could possibly have. Then her hand dropped to her lap and she laughed; a sound as delicate and breathy as her speech.

"I met him in college," she said. "We were in philosophy class together – he was working on his masters at the time – I was still an undergrad."

"You laugh at the memory, Mrs. Gifford. It must be a pleasant one."

"It was the first day of class and Greg arrived late. He had this gorgeous, tall redhead with him, and the professor gave them both a look that could kill." She put her hand to her mouth. "Sorry," she said. "Maybe not the best choice of words."

"Clichés happen, Mrs. Gifford. Go on."

"Well, I thought he was extremely handsome, but every time I saw him, he was with the redhead, so I figured they were an item. Then one day when I was studying in the library he came up to me and said he'd forgotten what the philosophy assignment was. 'Chapter six in the text,' I told him, 'and the questions at the end.' It's funny how you remember the tiniest things." She laughed again. "Then he asked if he could buy me a cup of coffee."

"That was the start of it, Inspector. He confessed he hadn't forgotten the assignment at all; he just wanted to meet me, and I said, 'what about the redhead?' and he told me she was his cousin, so they hung out together. Then he said, 'But now I know you, so we could hang out together, too.'" She sat back and spread her hands in an open gesture. "And there you have the story," she said.

"It's a delightful story," Dawson said. "And you were married while you were in college?" Dawson asked.

"No. We were both on scholarship and marriage was out of the question. My mother died just after I graduated from high-school, and I lived with one of the counselors from the high-school while I went to college."

"You were fortunate." Dawson said. "To have that kind of help, I mean."

"Yes, I was. I had actually turned down a tuition scholarship, because after my mother died, I couldn't afford food and rent. I went to work for Woolworths, clerking at the cosmetic counter."

The same counter where, while in high school, she had shop-lifted small items such as lipsticks or nail polish – information she would not be sharing with Dawson.

"My high school counselor came in. She wanted to know what I was doing working at Woolworths because she knew I had gotten the scholarship. When I told her, she insisted I live with her – she has a huge house. She pulled a few strings to get the scholarship reinstated, and I lived there until Greg and I got married, which was right after we graduated – he had a Masters in Psychology and I had a Bachelor of Arts. Then he went on to seminary, and I worked – secretarial mostly. A B of A doesn't get you too far."

Nancy Gifford appeared to be more relaxed, and Eggleton picked up his pencil. He knew reminiscence time was over, and Dawson would start to hone in. He was right.

Dawson leaned forward. "Mrs. Gifford, I'd like to go back to this afternoon."

Nancy put her hand to her chest.

"I need to know just where people were during the party, so I have to ask questions of the people who were there. Now, did you leave the room? Or should I say rooms – drawing room, patio - at all this afternoon?"

Nancy frowned.

"The kitchen or the bathroom?" Dawson prodded.

"I went into the kitchen to get a glass of water."

"Did you see anyone while you were in the kitchen?"

Again Nancy frowned. Finally she said, "Not actually in the kitchen. Before I went in the kitchen, I saw Mavis and Gwen talking on the stairs. When I came out of the kitchen, Gwen was headed down the hall toward the downstairs bathroom, and Mavis was gone. I guess she was back in the drawing room."

"Did you hear anything they were saying?"

"I'm sorry, Inspector. I didn't. I nodded to them and went on into the kitchen."

"Did you notice the bottle with the nicotine on the window sill?"

"No. I just got a drink. Mavis had ice water in a decanter and some glasses on a tray by the sink. I got a glass of water and took it back into the drawing room."

"Did you see Mrs. Dillon when you got back?"

"No. But I wasn't looking for her either."

"Did you see anyone else go to the kitchen?"

"I wouldn't have known if someone was going to the kitchen – it's catty-corner across the hall from where we were," she said.

"Did you see anyone go out into the hall?"

"I suppose so. People were milling about between the patio and the drawing room. The bathroom is across and down the hall from the drawing room, so it would be natural some people would use that bathroom. If you're asking me specifically – no. I don't remember anyone going out to the hall." She closed her eyes. "I'm trying to picture in my mind," she said, "but I can't recall any one person. I'm sorry, Inspector."

"Was Mrs. Cunningham carrying her sherry glass when you saw her?"

Nancy opened her eyes wide and shook her head. "I don't remember. Sorry."

"Did you talk with Mrs. Cunningham this afternoon, Mrs. Gifford?"

"Briefly."

"And what did you talk about?"

Nancy shrugged. "She mentioned what a fine man Greg is.' She laughed softly. "I had to agree."

"And?"

"And what, Inspector?"

"And was that all that was said?" Dawson asked, an

edge to his voice.

"Oh, we talked a little about Greg's salary. I should say she talked about it. I didn't say anything. She said he wasn't paid enough for what he did. It seemed in poor taste to agree with her – or to even discuss it."

"Anything personal, Mrs. Gifford?"

"Surely my husband's salary is personal, Inspector."

touché! Eggleton wrote.

Dawson sighed. "I mean about you personally?"

Nancy's hand went to the pearls, and again she began the relentless twisting as she recalled Gwen Cunningham's words.

So much for putting her at ease, Eggleton thought, glancing at his watch. *Waste of time.*

"Those definitely are quality," Gwen had said, peering at the pearls. "Much nicer than the other set you had. Oh, those were lovely, don't get me wrong, but these are the real thing. I suppose you've read in the paper Meyerson's has been having some trouble with shoplifters."

Gwen Cunningham's sudden change of subject shook Nancy, and she had reached out to the back of the sofa to support herself.

Mrs. Cunningham went right on. "I think they should tighten security, and I told Marjorie so. Marjorie and I were in college together, you know, and we have lunch every so often, but she said too much security would offend their customers, make it look like they couldn't trust them. Well, I told her, I said, Marjorie, obviously if you're being shoplifted, you can't trust people, and even the most innocent have a dark side to them." She smiled. "I'm sure you'd agree with that, Nancy, even the most innocent-appearing have a dark side to them."

* * *

It had been rainy and cold that December day when she went into Meyerson's Jewelry to have the clasp on her mother's pearls tightened. Greg had suggested she wear them for a Christmas party they were attending. She had never told him what the jeweler said about the pearls, and, although they had lost any meaning for her, except to elicit anger at the father she had never known, she still wore them on occasion. Rushed because of the season, the clerks at Meyerson's, usually poised, looked harried. One clerk, his thin, brown hair disheveled, was showing a tray of pearl necklaces to an older, heavyset man and a young woman dressed in a leather jacket, mini-skirt and low-cut blouse.

"I don't know, Sweetie," the young woman was saying. "I think something a little . . .' she paused, searching for a word.

"Flashier maybe," the man said, a slight smile on his face.

"Well," she said, making a little pout. She turned her attention to the display behind the counter. "Ohhh, Sweetie," she squealed, leaning across and treating the clerk to a delightful cleavage as she pointed. "Just look at that one!"

As the clerk turned away, reaching for a crimson dais on which rested a ruby pendant, Nancy stepped up to the tray of pearls. With a quick, economical movement, she slipped her mother's pearls from her raincoat pocket, placed them on the velvet tray, and palmed the string adjacent. It was in the pocket of her raincoat almost before she realized what she had done.

Her heart thudding, she wandered away from the counter where the clerk was discussing the ruby pendant with the older man, stopping occasionally, pretending to admire some display or other, and finally made her way to a carousel of earrings: semi-precious gemstones, 14-karat gold, fresh-water pearls, none of them very expensive – certainly not like the jewelry in the glass cases or behind the counters. She selected a simple pair of gold loops and held them to her ears. Nodding apparent approval to the image in the mirror, she took the earrings to the counter where she waited for a clerk. No one stopped her as she left the store with earrings in a small silver bag and a pearl necklace in her pocket.

* * *

Since that day at Meyerson's, she had hated the pearls and herself. Now she could only assume Gwen had seen her in Meyerson's and was letting her know. In that moment, Nancy decided she would return the necklace to Meyerson's as soon as she could. Somehow.

Gwen Cunningham was still talking. "I'm sure you and Father Greg see the dark side of many people."

"Oh, hardly," Nancy said, wondering if her voice registered her fear. "Mostly we see the good side of people," she added, noticing the bishop had turned his attention to Mavis.

Mrs. Cunningham followed the direction of Nancy's gaze. "Speaking of the dark side," she said. "I can tell you Mavis Dillon is not all she's made up to be. You'll notice she just appeared in this town out of nowhere."

"Really, Gwen," Nancy said. "She came from someplace. Perhaps she has painful memories and prefers not to discuss it. Besides, it was years ago."

"I'm sure she has memories, but I suspect they're not all painful. Someplace along the line she picked up an awful lot of money."

"Having money hardly constitutes a dark side, as you put it," Nancy said. "Besides, you're not exactly poor yourself, Gwen."

Gwen Cunningham sniffed. "Mine is family money," she said.

"Perhaps Mavis's is too."

"Maybe. But you mark my words. Something will show up sooner or later about her."

Sooner if you have anything to do with it, Nancy thought, sorry for Mavis Dillon, but glad Mrs. Cunningham's attention was elsewhere. Her relief was momentary. Mrs. Cunningham talked on.

"I'm going to congratulate Father Greg on his excellent taste – next time I see him."

"Excuse me?"

"The pearls. They're beautiful, and I'm glad he was able to get them for you. I'll just tell him how splendid they are. I am quite an authority on jewelry, you know. I have many fine pieces myself – although mine are in the bank. Now, you just stop twisting them, or we'll all be on our hands and knees looking for them." She smiled coyly at Nancy and walked off.

A ridiculous picture, thought Nancy, viewing Gwen Cunningham's massive backside. But she felt heart sick. Even if she slipped the pearls through the mail slot at Meyerson's that evening – even if she told Greg the clasp had broken, and she had lost them – nothing would stop Gwen Cunningham from saying something to Greg about Meyerson's.

Of course, she thought, *I could tell Greg the truth; after all, confession is his business.* But even as she thought it, she shied away from the idea: confession is different when it comes from your wife.

Now the Inspector repeated his question, asking if Gwen had said anything personal to her.

Nancy had been looking at the picture on the wall – the picture of the dead bird. "No, Inspector," she said finally. "Nothing personal."

lying, Eggleton jotted.

Dawson's sighed. "That will be all, Mrs. Gifford," he said. "Perhaps we'll talk with you again."

She rose from the chair. "Yes," she said. "Of course." At the door she turned back to Dawson and Eggleton. She looked at them for a moment, but "Shall I close the door?" was all she said.

"Please," Dawson said, and the heavy door swung shut behind her.

"She almost said something else, didn't she?" Eggleton said. "Then she changed her mind."

"Yes. I think so."

"The sins of omission," Eggleton said. "Like everybody

else we've talked to."

"Yeah. I noticed. Maybe she'll be more forthcoming when I see her again."

"She'll be a wreck by then."

"I'm counting on it," Dawson said with a tiny laugh. "And I'm already a wreck," he said.

"She was sure giving those pearls a workout," Eggleton said.

"And the notation in Cunningham's book was Meyerson's. That's a jewelry store in town."

"I know. You think there's a connection?"

Dawson shrugged. "Don't know. Meyerson's the name of the one person who might have been a friend of Cunningham." He looked at his watch. "How many more do we have out there?"

"Just Mrs. Dillon. Say, have you noticed how they all call the living room the *drawing room?*"

"Uh, huh."

"I'll have to remember to tell Laura about that. Shall I get Mrs. Dillon?"

"Give me ten, Bill," he said and leaned back in his chair. "Ten," he said again and held up his fingers.

CHAPTER EIGHT

Interview: Mavis Dillon

Then shall the virgin rejoice in the dance...
Jer. 31:13

Mavis Dillon (neé Mavis Jennings, formerly Margo London, formerly Maggie Logan) busied herself at the kitchen sink, washing dishes that could easily have gone in the dishwasher. Although, because of George Alexander's insistence on paper plates, there weren't many. Mavis was troubled. Having spent years lying about her past, she now wondered if she could maintain the lie at the hands of a skilled interrogator. She found the warm suds soothing.

* * *

Maggie Logan was seventeen when she ran away from home. The night before she left, her father, who had fashioned himself after the prophets of the Old Testament, found her dancing in front of her mirror to the music in her mind. He pushed her to her knees.

"Whore!" he cried.

"Jezebel!" he screamed.

"Harlot!" he yelled.

Then, falling on his own knees, he prayed for his sinning child, accusing her of actions she had never considered. Her mother, ever ineffectual in the face of her brimstone husband, stood meekly by, twisting the belt of her bathrobe.

Nor was it the first such incident, although for Maggie it would be the last. For years Maggie's mother and younger sisters had cowered before the wrath of a vengeful God as personified by Mr. Logan who saw sin in the very breath they drew. Lifting his craggy face to the ceiling, his jutting beard quivering with emotion, his eyes gleaming with an inner fire, he begged God's blessing on each meagre meal, seeming inordinately grateful for what Maggie considered very little. He pleaded for mercy upon the worthless souls of his family, listing their sins as he perceived them. Elaborating with tedious detail, should God be slow to understand the enormity, he spoke of such iniquities as a slip showing beneath a skirt, curlers in the hair, and inappropriate gaiety on the Sabbath.

Sundays were days of silence, dreaded above all days by the three Logan daughters. In silence they dressed in the drab clothes Mr. Logan considered suitable for Church. In silence they drove to the tiny structure in town where the single most exciting event was the singing of a hymn. In rapture, Mr. Logan lifted his face as the preacher spoke, punctuating the poor man's prose with loud 'Amens.' Home again, he permitted the girls to sit in their church clothes and read from the scriptures. Silently. A cold meal, loudly praised for its very simplicity, completed the day, and the girls went early to their beds.

As did Mr. and Mrs. Logan, where Mr. Logan took his pleasure with a great display of grunts and groans, and made the young Maggie wonder at the hypocrisy of his insistence on silence. Later, after Mr. Logan had fallen into a sound and satiated sleep, Mrs. Logan would creep to the parlor in her nightgown and robe where Maggie could hear her crying softly.

Except the night before Maggie left home – the night Mr. Logan woke and found her dancing. Early the next morning, knowing it would be a terrible hardship on the family, she took thirty dollars from her mother's housekeeping money. Until then, Maggie's greatest sin had been to dance on a Sunday. Dancing – and hating her father.

The bus ticket to Las Vegas cost twenty-five dollars.

In Las Vegas, she divided her days and nights between waiting tables in the coffee shop of the Painted Desert Casino and watching the dancers rehearsing for the great floor shows. Alone in her tiny studio apartment, where her sole luxury was a full length mirror, she practiced the steps she saw the dancers execute. After a year of observing and practicing, she answered an audition call where she made it to the back row of the chorus.

The work, which had looked so glamorous to Maggie, was grueling. Long rehearsals, followed by two shows each evening, took their toll on all the dancers. Still, Maggie loved it. As the months – and then several years – passed, Maggie moved to the front of the chorus, and, on occasion, to dance a solo part. She felt lovely in the magnificent costumes with the heavy headdresses and voluminous skirts; that her breasts were bare did not bother her. She paraded proudly along the ramp leading out into the audience, enjoying the men ogling her. Occasionally she would see a craggy face with a jutting beard looking up at her, the eyes gleaming in the stage lights, and she would remember her father. Only the obsession is different, she thought.

One night after the late dinner show, as she was taking off her makeup, Jeannine, one of the dancers, said, "Mags, you look tired."

"I am," Maggie said. "I'm real tired."

"How long you been doing this?"

Maggie frowned. "Couple of years," she said after a while.

"Jesus! You know, there are easier ways to make a living than on your feet."

Suzanne, seated next to Jeannine, laughed. "I'll say! On your back!"

Maggie smiled at them in the mirror as she smeared a second coat of cold cream on her face.

"Yep," Jeannine said. "I'm out of here next month. I've got this contact for a job. First class all the way. One man a night. You interested?"

"You're talking about escort service?" Maggie said, thinking how her feet hurt and that she would have about four hours rest before she was back on them at rehearsal.

"If that's what you want to call it." Jeannine snorted slightly. "It pays well, they screen the men. It's a class operation. And you're beautiful. You'd be great."

Maggie said nothing, putting her makeup away and sweeping the used tissues into the waste basket.

Despite Maggie's attempts to forget it, Jeannine's offer stayed with her. The few men she had taken to her bed since her arrival in Las Vegas had given her little pleasure, and she often wondered if there was something wrong with her.

"Nonsense, honey," her friend, Denise, had said. "You just haven't been in love, is all. Wait'll you find somebody like my Frankie. Then you'll get all the pleasure you can stand."

But Maggie hadn't found any Frankie, and nightly she nursed her bleeding feet. With each bloodied cotton ball, Jeannine's words came back to her. One night, about two weeks after Jeannine's offer, her legs shaking with fatigue, she brought the subject up about the escort service.

"You'll have to change your name," Jeannine said. Again they sat in front of the makeup mirror; cold cream jars and crumpled tissues littered the counter. "Maggie Logan just isn't gonna cut it."

"Margo," Maggie said. "Margo London," and in that moment she knew she was committed. Perhaps, she thought, her father's accusation hadn't been so far off the mark. It was one of the last times she thought of her father – or any of the rest of her family.

* * *

Mavis drained the sink and refilled it, letting the warm water run over her hands. The kitchen had cleared over the course of the evening, leaving Charles in the rocker in the corner of the kitchen – Mavis knew he wouldn't leave until the police were through with her. Andrew, Nancy and Father Greg sat at the kitchen table, talking quietly about Greg and Nancy's upcoming trip to Scotland. The uniformed policeman, placed with them to keep them from discussing the matter uppermost in their minds, kept his nearly-invisible watch by the door.

151

"Let me do those," Charles said, appearing at her elbow.

"Oh. You startled me," She smiled. "It's not necessary. I need something to do."

Charles raised his eyebrows. "So do I."

"Sorry. I seem to have forgotten I'm not the only one upset by all this. I guess I'm next."

Charles put his hand on her shoulder and squeezed. "I think they talk for a while between interviews," he said.

They were speaking softly, and the policeman moved to a position near the refrigerator. Mavis smiled at him.

"Here," she said, slipping her apron off. "Since you're offering. . ." She put her arms around Charles' waist, tying the apron behind him and handing him a towel. Then she sat down in the rocking chair, composing herself for what was to come. It had been a long time since she had thought about Felipe.

* * *

She had been working as an escort for eight months when Felipe Contreras, a Las Vegas mob boss and wealthy client of the service, set her up in an apartment. "I want you out of the business," he said in his precise and heavily accented English. "My women do not go with other men. You will be mine exclusively."

She had considered herself lucky, but had known it was temporary at best; men like Felipe seldom stayed with one mistress long. Still, it was a relief to limit herself to the demands of one man, and she decided to enjoy her good fortune while it lasted. *Tomorrow will take care of itself,* she thought.

But less than a year had passed when, despite precautions, she found she was pregnant, and it was with trepidation she told Felipe she needed money for an abortion.

Felipe's reply was instantaneous and said with passion. "It is my child, and it will be born! I am Spanish – Spanish men have children!"

"And when you're finished with me?" she countered angrily. "What then? Do you expect me to return to the old life with a child?"

"You will not return to the old life. I will provide for you and the child."

She had known he was wealthy, but it was not until he established a trust fund for her and the child that she became aware of just how wealthy he was. That his gains were ill-gotten had not bothered her. In return, he asked she provide a home for the child and one picture a year, sent to the attorney who would administer the trust.

"And," he said, "you will never reveal your existence or the child's existence to my family. My lawyer will supply you with a new identity and will monitor your life. If you reveal anything about me to anyone, or should the picture of the child fail to arrive, the trust will immediately be revoked."

"This is a child you will never know."

Felipe's reply reflected the barrenness of his life. "I will know the child is mine. It is not enough, but it is better than what I have now."

Understanding Felipe's offer meant she would never have to work, never have to consider marriage, never again have to submit herself to the demands of any man, she agreed. Felipe's lawyer, with the help of a skilled forger, 'borrowed' the identity of a child named Mavis Jennings who died in 1969 at the age of two, and Margo London became Mavis Dillon, neé Mavis Jennings, widow of Stephen Dillon.

* * *

"You okay?"

It was Charles, still wearing her apron, his face drawn with concern.

She gave him a small smile. "I'm fine. Just enjoying being off my feet for a while. Thanks for taking over."

I expect they'll be calling you any minute."

She glanced at the clock on the kitchen wall. Had it only been ten minutes since she had handed the towel to Charles? "Yes. I expect they will."

* * *

The birth of her baby brought Mavis at last an understanding of the word *'love.'* She realized she wanted only the best for this beautiful child – a little girl she named Carole Anne – and to provide the very best, she needed to be the very best she could be.

When Carole Anne was just a few months old, they moved from Las Vegas to San Francisco. In her luggage, Mavis carried all the documents, real and counterfeit, she would need to start her new life: Social Security, Carole Anne's birth certificate, her own birth certificate (in the name Mavis Jennings), a marriage license for Mavis

Jennings and Stephen Dillon, a death certificate for Stephen Dillon, a diploma from Harvard Law School for Stephen Dillon, a diploma for a Bachelor of Arts degree from the University of Michigan for Mavis Jennings.

Once there, Mavis purchased a modest home in San Francisco and spent her days caring for her baby and procuring the antiques that would furnish her future house and furnish her with a family history and a San Francisco background. She was courteous to her neighbors, but did not encourage friendships. She hired a private tutor who taught her elocution, cancelling the Midwest twang of her youth. She read widely, studying art, politics, and literature, just as she had studied dancing. She bought used college textbooks – mostly Harvard Business Law – and, in what she thought was a more masculine handwriting, wrote the name of the fictitious Stephen Dillon.

Sometimes Carole Anne would say, "Tell me about my grandma," or "Do I look like Daddy?"

And Mavis would get out a family album – pictures she had collected from discarded scrapbooks at thrift stores and antique stores – anonymous people who might well have passed for Carole Anne's ancestors.

"This was your grandma on her wedding day."

"Gramma," Carole Anne would say.

"Just look at your daddy's dark eyes. They're like yours."

"Daddy," Carole Anne would say.

"This is the house your daddy lived in when he was growing up."

"Daddy's house," Carole Anne would say.

By the time several years had passed, the girl who had

been Maggie Logan had become the woman who was Mavis Dillon: beautiful, poised, articulate, and well-educated.

When she felt she was ready, Mavis bought another home north of San Francisco, this time a Victorian in the wine country town of Castlemont. Every day, with Carole Anne either in her car seat or at nursery school, Mavis drove to Castlemont to supervise the restoration process with contractors and decorators. In the evenings, while Carole Anne played on the carpet with her doll house or plunked tunes on her tiny keyboard, Mavis carefully wrapped the precious antiques and packed them for moving. Carole Anne was four years old when Mavis sold their San Francisco house, and they moved to their new home.

The residents of Castlemont had been curious about the restoration of the lovely old house - and curious about Mavis as well - and called on her. She took them through, and as they exclaimed over the beautiful vases and silver pieces, the gracious French provincial furniture, and faded tapestries and carpets, she gave the history of each piece.

"This was the bedroom set used by my husband's grandparents."

"The silver service was a wedding gift to my husband's parents."

"This vase has been in my family for several generations."

Because she had studied the provenance of each piece she had purchased, asking questions about its age and authenticity, her stories were consistent and almost accurate. Thus she built legitimacy for Carole Anne and for herself.

Carole Anne had grown into a beautiful and gracious young woman. Her talent and love of music was apparent at an early age, and lessons with the finest violinists in San Francisco and abroad earned her, at the age of twenty-four, first desk, second violin with the San Francisco Symphony.

It was at a rehearsal of the Symphony she met Sergio Sokolov, the brilliant young maestro from Russia, and the toast of the international community, when he visited as the Symphony's guest artist. Since then, Carole Anne and Sergio had been as inseparable as their schedules allowed.

Now, in just two weeks, Bishop Kindermann would preside over the wedding of Carole Anne at St. Francis Church. Although San Francisco society had urged them to be married at Grace Cathedral, Sergio had said he preferred the simplicity of St. Francis in Castlemont with the reception to follow in the garden of Carole Anne's home.

After years of cementing the fiction of the wealthy and prestigious Dillon family, Mavis would see Carole Anne well married – as long as she could maintain the fiction with Inspector Dawson.

* * *

"Inspector Dawson would like to see you, Mrs. Dillon," Eggleton said.

Mavis stood. "You don't need to do any more, Charles."

"I'll just finish the coffee pot," he said. "I'm rather enjoying it."

"Whatever works," she said with a small laugh.

"Will the Inspector want to talk with me tonight, Sergeant, or may I take Nancy and go on home?" Father Greg asked.

"I'll check."

"Just let me pour myself a cup of tea, Sergeant," Mavis said, taking a fragile bone china cup and saucer from the counter and pouring from a pot on the table. "Do you and the Inspector need anything?"

"No. Thank you anyway. We're fine," Eggleton said, eyeing the remains of pound cake on a plate.

"Come along, then," and, balancing her cup, Mavis led the way out of the kitchen and down the hallway to the library. Eggleton watched her walk, appreciating her magnificent carriage and firm calf muscles. She triggered some elusive thought, but when he tried to grasp it, it was gone. *Ah, well,* he thought. *Better not to try too hard. It'll come.*

"Father Gifford wants to know if you'll be talking with him this evening, or should he take Mrs. Gifford and go home?" Eggleton asked as they entered the library.

Dawson looked at his watch. "It's late," he said. "See what time tomorrow he could squeeze us in. Perhaps after the confirmation service."

"I'll check," Eggleton said, heading back to the kitchen where he delivered his message and helped himself to a slice of pound cake.

It was on his return to the library, after dismissing Father Greg and Nancy, Eggleton remembered what it was Mrs. Dillon had reminded him of. Hurrying to the desk, Eggleton wrote quickly.

"He said 1:00, Sir. I've made a note so you'll remember." He handed Dawson a small piece of paper.

ask her if she's ever been a dancer, the note said.

"Thank you, Sergeant," Dawson said, running his

finger along one side of his lips before he slipped the note into his pocket.

Red faced at being caught again, Eggleton brushed crumbs from the corner of his mouth.

Dawson turned to Mavis. "You're exhausted, Mrs. Dillon," he said. "I'll be as brief as I can."

"Thank you, Inspector," she said, her voice low and without inflection, as though the fatigue she felt permeated even her vocal chords.

"Is there a Mr. Dillon?" Dawson asked.

"My husband is deceased," she replied. "He died shortly after our daughter was born."

"I see. A Harvard graduate?"

"I'm sorry?"

"Your husband. He was a Harvard graduate?"

She frowned. "How did you . . . ?"

Dawson turned his head in the direction of the book-shelves. "I was thumbing through some of your books, Mrs. Dillon. I saw his name in several textbooks on business law." What Dawson did not mention was the names were written in a rather feminine handwriting. He would explore that avenue later.

"Yes," she said. "Business Law."

Dawson continued. "Now, about this afternoon, did you have any occasion to speak with Mrs. Cunningham?"

"Briefly. We talked for a while about my daughter's wedding. She's being married in two weeks – June twenti-eth." Her face brightened slightly. "To Sergio Sokolov," she added. "The conductor."

wedding – june 20 Eggleton wrote.

Dawson nodded. "Quite a match! You must be

pleased."

Those had been Gwen's exact words that afternoon.

"You must be pleased, Mavis. Such a delightful event. A marriage made in heaven, surely."

For once, Mavis found herself agreeing with Gwen. If anything as corny as a marriage made in heaven is possible, she thought, this is it.

"You're probably terribly busy with the wedding preparations. I expect the Dillons will turn out in force for the big event," Gwen continued.

"I'm afraid Carole Anne is the last of the Dillons," Mavis said, wishing the words back immediately she had said them.

"Oh, surely not! Such a fine family and so wealthy? I can't imagine there are no relatives *someplace.* Unless there are a few skeletons even in your fine closet." Gwen Cunningham's eyes held Mavis's.

"Don't be silly," Mavis retorted, laughing slightly. She heard her laugh; it sounded strained, and she turned to the sideboard, rearranging a bowl of roses. "Unfortunately, they have all died out . . . Carole Anne is the last"

"Oh, how tragic!" Mrs. Cunningham said, pointing at Mavis with a shortbread cookie. "I'll tell you what I'm going to do. It isn't right this fine family should die out. Although it won't really, because I'm sure Carole Anne and Sergio will have children, but they won't be Dillons now will they, so I am going to turn my attention to doing a family tree for Carole Anne."

Mavis gasped and turned away from the flower arrangement.

"Now don't you say a word. It will be my pleasure. I'm a registered genealogist; it's a hobby of mine you know, and I have resources most people don't have."

"Oh, please don't . . ."

"Nonsense! It's not a bit of trouble. I'm always glad of an excuse to do it. Just think, won't it be a treat for Carole Anne?"

"Carole Anne knows a great deal about her family origins," Mavis said, hoping the tone of her voice would put a stop to Gwen Cunningham's plans. "I've been very careful to see she was fully educated in her family history."

"I'm sure you have, dear. But, naturally, you are limited. That's not criticism, of course, but with the publications I receive and my contacts, to say nothing of my computer programs, I have much greater access than you could possibly have. Of course, I won't have it done in time for the wedding, since I will have to put out feelers on-line and in the periodicals – do some research, but, better late, as they say – I'll get started this evening. In the meantime, I'll just send a congratulations card with a little note about what I'm doing."

"I would really rather . . ." Mavis stopped. What could she say?

Gwen topped off her sherry glass and reached for another cookie. "I know I'm going to find out all sorts of interesting things." She leaned toward Mavis conspiratorially. "Here comes Charles. Have you noticed – he can hardly keep his eyes off you? Well, this is a lovely party! And I'll just get right on our little project. I know you'll be pleased," she said and turned her attention to Charles Glasco.

"I am pleased about the marriage," Mavis said, pulling her thoughts back to the Inspector. "Anyway, Gwen and I talked about the wedding for a bit, and then Charles joined us, and after a few moments, I wandered off." She leaned over to place her cup and saucer on the table beside the chair. "I left Charles with Gwen."

"So you didn't discuss anything with Mrs. Cunningham other than what you've told us about your daughter's wedding?"

"No, I don't think . . ." She fixed her gaze on the crown molding. "Not that I remember."

does remember – not saying Eggleton wrote in his notebook. *won't look at d.*

"I've heard she could be . . . " Dawson paused . . . "very direct, Mrs. Dillon. Perhaps even tactless. Did you find that to be the case?"

Mavis' pale face flushed, and the knuckles of her clasped hands showed white. "I don't know, really. Certainly, any conversation with Gwen was a challenge."

"In what way?"

"Oh, sometimes she asked embarrassing questions, or said something – as you said 'tactless.' "

"I see," Dawson said. "And what embarrassing questions did she ask you?"

"I wasn't talking about me. I – I just meant sometimes – well, you never knew . . ." She stopped speaking and stared at her hands as though she had just discovered them.

"But she has asked you embarrassing questions in the past," Dawson persisted.

Mavis looked at Dawson. "She asked embarrassing

questions of everyone, Inspector. I'm sure I received neither more nor less than my share, but I believe I am sufficiently capable of deflecting any queries from Gwen Cunningham should I choose not to answer them. Or was capable," she amended, her eyes lowered again to her lap.

"So you're saying there are things about your life you didn't want her to know," Dawson said.

"Oh, come now, Inspector," Mavis said, her voice scornful. "She was an acquaintance, not a bosom friend."

Eggleton jotted *bosom friend.*

Looking at the cool, poised Mavis Dillon, Dawson wondered if she even had a *bosom friend.* Whatever her secrets, it was unlikely she would share them with anyone, least of all the police.

"Besides," she continued, "you're making more out of a brief discussion about my daughter's wedding than needs be made."

"Perhaps," Dawson said, leaning forward, his forearms on his thighs, his hands clasped in front of him. "Did Mrs. Cunningham go into the kitchen during the party?"

"I don't know," she said. "It's across the hall from where we were, so she might have, but I wouldn't necessarily have known."

"Did she leave the living room and patio area at all?" Dawson asked.

"I do know she left to go to the bathroom," Mavis said, fingering the porcelain bird on the table beside her armchair.

"And how is it you were aware of that?"

Mavis smiled. "I went upstairs to change into some low-heeled shoes." She looked down at her feet, encased in ballet slippers. "Not these," she said with a little laugh. "About the time you arrived, I dropped all pretense of being a hostess and just got comfortable. But earlier in the day I was wearing high heels, and my feet began to hurt, so I went upstairs to change into a lower pair, and when I came down, Gwen was climbing the stairs."

"She was going upstairs to the bathroom?"

"She was going upstairs to snoop, Inspector," Mavis said, her voice hard. "I asked her where she was going, and she said she was looking for the bathroom. I turned her around and directed her to the one downstairs."

"Perhaps she didn't think there was one downstairs," Dawson said, apparently forgetting for a moment the grandeur of the house."

Eggleton glanced up sharply from his notebook; Mavis picked up her cup and saucer. She said nothing.

"Or perhaps, as you say, she wanted to snoop," Dawson said, leaning back in his chair.

Eggleton lowered his head to hide a smile.

"When did this take place, Mrs. Dillon?"

"Just shortly before . . ." Mavis's voice grew husky. She began again. "Just shortly before . . . she died."

"Was she carrying her sherry glass when you met her on the stairs?"

"I don't . . ." She stopped. "I think I would have noticed."

"If she wasn't carrying it, do you have any idea what she might have done with it?"

"None whatsoever, Inspector."

too emphatic,' Eggleton jotted beside her response.

"Could she have put it on one of the hall tables?"

"Perhaps."

"But you didn't see her do that?"

Mavis shook her head.

"Do you know for a fact she went into the bathroom?"

"If you mean, did I stand and watch until she walked in the bathroom door, no. I pointed out the door to her and returned to my guests."

"What would she have seen if she had gone upstairs, Mrs. Dillon?"

"Just the bedrooms."

"And why didn't you want her to see the bedrooms?"

"Perversity, Inspector," Mavis said with a tiny smile. "Bloody-minded perversity. Had it been any one of my other guests, I would have turned right around and given them a tour. Although, most of them have been here many times, and have been through the house. However, Gwen had not been here often, and then only in the receiving rooms downstairs. I had no desire to have her in my more private rooms."

Eggleton wrote *receiving rooms* on his note pad and drew a smiley face.

"Mrs. Dillon, did you see anyone go into the kitchen during the party?"

She pursed her lips. "Nancy – that's Nancy Gifford – went in while I was coming downstairs with Gwen," she said. "I saw her later in the drawing room with a glass of water, so I assume that's what she went in to get. Otherwise, I wouldn't know who might have gone in. As I said, the kitchen is across the hall from the rooms where we were, so anyone could have gone into the kitchen, and I wouldn't have known. I assume some people did, since there were several glasses in the sink."

"Did any of your guests inquire as to the location of the bathroom?"

"No. Most of them have been here before. And you were back and forth between the drawing room and the kitchen?"

"Many times."

"Do you dance, Mrs. Dillon?"

Her face went pale, and the cup and saucer clattered in her hands. She turned to the table and carefully placed them beside the bird. When she turned back, Dawson could see her composure had returned. "Surely you're not asking me for a date, Inspector," she said with a tiny laugh.

It was Dawson's turn to flush, and he shot Eggleton a glance which clearly said, *I'll get you for this.*

"I phrased that the wrong way, Mrs. Dillon. Have you ever been a dancer?"

"I danced in my youth. The usual lessons girls take. Nothing more. Why do you ask?"

Out of the corner of his eye, Dawson saw Eggleton straighten himself into a very erect position, and he took a stab at Eggleton's meaning.

"Your carriage, Mrs. Dillon."

"Ah," she said, sounding relieved. "Deportment lessons, Inspector. Part of my growing up, along with ballet, tap, piano, and French."

"A privileged childhood," Dawson said as he stood. "Your parents?"

"Deceased," Mavis said and stood as well.

"Doctor Glasco mentioned Mrs. Cunningham told

him she was planning to research a family tree for your daughter as a wedding gift."

Again the color drained from Mavis Dillon's face, but she recovered quickly. "Yes," she said. "Yes. A generous thought."

Dawson had seen her moment of alarm – the remark or fatigue? He would do some research of his own before he pressed the issue. "I may have more questions for you later. For now, I suggest you get some rest."

"Thank you," she said. "Andrew will see you out."

Dawson raised his eyebrows. "The gardener? He's still here?"

Mavis smiled. "Don't be misled, Inspector. Andrew has had a few drinks, but I assure you, he's quite sober. And, he's not about to leave me alone in this house after what's happened."

"Your daughter doesn't live with you, then?"

"No. She has an apartment in the city. Her symphony hours make a long commute difficult." She started out the door, then turned back. "Andrew and his wife Fiona are the dearest people I know in Castlemont, Inspector. They treat me like a daughter," she said, closing the library door behind her.

"Well," Dawson said, running his hand through his hair. "Since you were writing notes to me, you might have mentioned your reason for suspecting she had been a dancer."

"You did fine. Her posture was what I was thinking of. And her way of moving her body."

"Let me guess. She reminds you of someone."

"My sister."

"Your sister? She's a dancer?"

"Remember the night the prostitute was murdered? We went back to your apartment. I told you about my sister."

The crime scene had been especially grisly, and, after they left the scene, they retired to Dawson's condo where they shared a significant amount of Wild Turkey. Sometime, around two in the morning, Eggleton began to talk about his sister who danced, bare breasted, at a Las Vegas casino. "My father says she's little more than a proshtitush," Eggleton had told Dawson.

Dawson nodded. "I remember," he said.

"It's the way Mrs. Dillon walks. Like she was balancing one of those enormous headdresses the Vegas dancers wear. Vicky walks the same way. Second nature. Hours of practice and two shows a night." Eggleton laughed, a small, bitter laugh. "The family wonders what Vicky will do when she gets too old to dance."

Dawson looked down at his hands. "That's what made you think of Vicky? Her posture?"

"Initially. But when you were talking to her, her slipper slipped off her heel. She has a real high arch. Lot of dancers have high arches."

Dawson shook his head. "You're a man of unplumbed depths, Bill." He began to stack glasses, empty cups and crumpled napkins on a tray. "So you think she was a dancer in her youth, maybe even a showgirl, and that might have been what Mrs. Cunningham was referring to when she wrote 'Mavis-background.'"

Eggleton made a face. "Put that way, it seems rather

a leap, doesn't it?"

"All the same, it may be an accurate leap. It rattled her a bit when I mentioned it."

"Rattled the cup and saucer is more like it. You have to admit she came out of it quite well. 'Surely you're not asking me for a date, Inspector,' Eggleton said, mimicking Mavis's precise way of speaking.

Dawson threw a crumpled napkin at him. It fell to the floor. "She is a beautiful woman," he said.

Eggleton leaned out of his chair to pick up the napkin. "Man," he said, his voice muffled from beneath the desk. "I hope she doesn't turn out to be the guilty party. I think you're smitten."

"A quaint turn of phrase, Sergeant."

Eggleton emerged, smiling.

"And I'm not," Dawson added, stroking his chin. "I wonder if the glass was tampered with when Mrs. Cunningham set it down to go into the bathroom."

"If she set it down. Mrs. Dillon didn't know – at least she said she didn't know."

"You think she might have been lying?"

"Oh come on! They're all lying – except Alexander."

"Huh!" Dawson said. "But if she did set it down . . ."

"Who else would have seen her set it down and seized the opportunity?"

"Mrs. Gifford."

"Ummmmm. . . I'm going to have to question Mrs. Gifford again about what she saw in the hall." Dawson said.

"Whoever took it had to work fast to get it to the kitchen, put the drops in, return it to the hall table – if that's where Mrs. Cunningham left it – all the time running the risk someone would see him or her. After all, it probably didn't take Mrs. Cunningham too long to go to the bathroom."

"I don't know," Dawson said. "From what we know of her, she probably spent some time going through the cupboards while she was in there."

"Yes. But could whoever took the glass count on that?" Eggleton asked, sounding skeptical

"Unless," Dawson continued, oblivious to Eggleton's tone, "there was a substitute ready, just waiting for Cunningham to put hers down so they could make a switch. Which would mean the murderer was carrying around a sherry glass all through the party – just waiting for an opportunity."

"Not necessarily all through the party. It could be somebody prepared the doctored glass after they talked to Mrs. Cunningham and then carried it around, waiting for the opportunity."

"You're right, Bill. I'm just thinking out loud. I don't think any one of these people came to the party planning to kill Mrs. Cunningham. It has to have been something she said that triggered their action."

"Did you notice Mrs. Dillon's reaction when you mentioned the family tree?"

"I did. Of course, she could just have been very tired, but I want to do a little research myself before I broach the subject with her again."

"I wonder what else they talked about that she didn't mention. Actually, I wonder that about all of them," Eggleton said, slipping his pencil into his pocket. "They're all so damned polite. Like it was some sort of gracious party instead of somebody dying."

"I know," Dawson said, running his hand through his hair again, combing it into gray spikes. "I'm bushed," he said. "I'll look up the sainted Andrew and tell him we're leaving. Oops! One thing. Is there any sample of Mrs. Dillon's handwriting on the desk?"

"Just an address book," he said, handing it to Dawson.

Dawson opened the book and carried it to one of the library shelves where he pulled out a large volume. Opening it to the front cover, he scanned the address book – holding it next to the larger book.

"Interesting, Bill."

"What?"

"I'm no handwriting expert, but the writing in the two books looks similar – not identical, but there are similarities. Seems strange she would write her husband's name in his text books. Students usually write their own name in their texts."

"And this means. . .?"

"It means work for another day."

"Uh huh," Eggleton said as he gathered the tray and tucked his notebook under his arm. "When are we going to talk to Andrew?"

"Tomorrow. I'll arrange a time with him," Dawson said, taking the tray from Eggleton. "I'll take this. You get Mrs. Cunningham's purse." He started for the doorway, then turned back. "By the way, Sergeant. We're going to church tomorrow."

"That'll make 'em nervous."

Dawson smiled.

PART TWO:

THE INVESTIGATION

CHAPTER NINE

The Small Hours

But while he thought on these things...
Matt. 1:20

Sunday, June 7

Jake Dawson leaned back in his swivel chair and put his feet on the desk. It had been nearly eleven o'clock when they left the crime scene. Now, at one in the morning, the noisy daytime activities of the police station had softened to a gentle hum of low voices and the occasional telephone call, muffled through Dawson's closed door. He rubbed his face with his hands.

They had left Mavis Dillon's house, seen out by Andrew. "Aye, and it's a harrd night ferr us all," Andrew, his burr thick with whiskey and the hour, had said as they left. "Ye'll be talkin' wi' me tomorrow, will ye?"

Dawson assured him they would.

"I'll nip on home, while Mavis is at cherrch," he said, " but me wee wifey and me, we'll be back here errly in the afternoon," He shook his head. "The poor gerrl. An' that lovely Carole Anne aboot t' be married." He shook his head again and closed the door behind them.

In the car, Eggleton spoke. "You don't really think I'm going to be able to take notes when you interview him, do you?"

"I expect the whiskey lubricated his brogue. I doubt he'll be so Scottish by tomorrow.

"Huh!" Eggleton grunted. "God! I'm tired."

"You go on home when we get back to the station," Dawson said. "I'll go over your notes."

"Let me at least get them typed so you can read them," he said.

"And miss your comments in the margins?" Dawson replied. "I don't think so."

So Eggleton handed his notebook to Dawson. "You ought to get some sleep. You're probably just as tired as I am."

Dawson shrugged. "Later maybe – I'm not tired right now."

Eggleton knew from experience 'later' meant what sleeping Dawson did would be on the cot in the locker room. "Want me to stay for a while?" he asked.

"No. You get some rest. Tomorrow's going to be a long day. Remember, we're going to church."

Although Eggleton regularly attended St. Paul's Presbyterian Church, he had never known Dawson to attend church except for weddings and funerals. "I won't know how to act in an Episcopal Church," he said. "All that kneeling and up and down stuff."

"Neither will I."

"I thought you were a recovering Catholic."

Dawson ignored him. "We'll sit in the back and do what the people in front of us do – shouldn't be too hard."

Eggleton looked doubtful.

Remembering Eggleton's skepticism, Dawson smiled.

He thought briefly about quitting for the night, and then took another sheet of blank paper and made four columns:

Name/Access/PK for Previous Knowledge/**Motive (1-10)**

NAME	ACCESS	P/K	MOTIVE (1-10)
Liske	yes	yes	?lesbian relationship
Gentry	yes	yes	?lesbian relationship
Bishop	yes	no	?(son)
D. Alex.	yes	no (?)	Geo's record Ck. previous husband's death
G. Alex	yes	yes	prison record
Glifford	yes	no	?(ck. Meyerson Jewelry)
Glasco	yes	yes	?(ck death of Resnik /Billings
Dillon	yes	yes	?(ck. background

He made his notations in pencil. Numbers would come later.

He swung his feet to the floor and drew his chair close to the desk where Eggleton's notebook lay open.

Pulling a sheet of blank paper from a drawer, he wrote TRAFFIC PATTERN at the top, and sketched Mavis' floor plan. He made a copy on the copy machine – a ploy he would use when they visited Mrs. Liske and Mrs. Gentry – and then, meticulously combing Eggleton's notes and chuckling over the margin notes as he read, he drew traffic paths to and from the drawing room, the kitchen, and the bathroom. He used colored pencils, a different color for each guest.

At the bottom of the page, he made a neat legend, labeling each person by their color: red for Gwen Cunningham. To some, he could attach an approximate time, but without a clearer definition of all the times involved, the sketch was incomplete. By the back kitchen door, he placed a question mark; he would ask Andrew if anyone had used that door - or if Andrew himself had used the door. He would have to get information about Andrew's comings and goings that afternoon. He made a note to call Andrew in the morning and make a time to meet with him after the church service.

He set his sketch aside when an officer knocked on his door. "Can I get you a coffee or anything, Sir? I'm about to go off duty, but if you need anything, I'll be glad to get it for you. I think there's some coffee left in the pot in the break room."

Dawson made a face at the thought of the hours-old coffee. "Thank you, officer. I'm good. Almost ready to close down myself."

Yes, Sir," the officer said. And the door clicked shut.

On a new piece of paper Dawson wrote: <u>SUICIDE</u>.
Then below he listed a series of questions and answers.

Q. *Why?*
A. *Depression, disease, blame on party participants*
Q *If C. committed suicide, why such a painful method?*
A. *May not have been aware of painful aspects of the drug*
Q. *Was list in daily planner meant to cast suspicion on party participants?*
A. *If suicide, yes*
Q. *Does daily planner contain similar references to persons attending social gatherings on other dates?*

Dawson pulled Gwen Cunningham's daily planner from the evidence bag and, beginning with January 1, thumbed through, stopping to read the cryptic notations for some of the social events she had attended. He recognized two – thought them of interest.

Chamber of Commerce/Dinner: Mayor/sec.

"Holy shit! The mayor," he muttered and returned to his list.

School Board/Potluck: Rudy & Meg/rlnsp
Q. *If suicide, was C counting on nicotine?*
A. *Probably (Vestry meeting)*
Q. *If Alexander hadn't brought nicotine, would she have used Ambien instead?*
A. *Probably not, if motive was to*

cast suspicion on party participants

Q. Was C sufficiently depressed to commit suicide?

A. ? Check with Fr. Gifford

Q. If C depressed enough to commit suicide, could she have carried through a social afternoon with no one recognizing her depression?

A. ? Check with Fr. Gifford re: previous experiences.

Q. Would a depressed person consider suicide when not experiencing a depressive episode?

A. Check w/shrink

Q. Could C. have displayed normal behavior so close to suicide?

A. Check w/shrink

Q. Who would know more about GC?

A. Marjorie Myerson (Meyerson's Jewelry)

He would transfer his sketch of the house and his ACCESS/KNOWLEDGE/MOTIVE matrix to the white board on Monday after he'd talked to Eggleton and filled in some of the blanks. Dawson looked at his watch: two-thirty. Then, taking Gwen Cunningham's Daily Planner to the copy machine, and beginning with January first, he copied each page, ending with Saturday, June sixth. Finally, removing his jacket from the back of his chair, Dawson turned off the lights and headed for the men's locker room. He wondered if he would be able to sleep and thought maybe he should go home. But the thought of home gave him no pleasure; he needed the gentle buzz of the station at night. It was 3:00 A.M.

Across town Eggleton slept. He had come home to find the house dark except for the light over the stove. A note on the kitchen table read: *Sandwiches and fruit in the frig. We love you. L&B*

Sitting in the soft light of the kitchen, Eggleton wolfed down the sandwiches and munched an apple. Then more slowly, he sipped a brandy. Gradually, he felt the day's tension slip away. He put his dishes in the sink and tiptoed to his daughter's room.

Two year old Elizabeth Marie lay flat on her back, her legs sprawled in her little Snoopy pajama bottoms. The pajama top was hiked up over her round belly, and Eggleton pulled it down, careful not to disturb her sleep. Her tattered blanket binding was clutched in her fist; her thumb was in her mouth. Eggleton knew thousands of fathers around the world had seen the same scene, but he thought what he saw must be the most beautiful. Leaning over, he kissed Beth's cheek.

After brushing his teeth in the guest bathroom where he kept a spare toothbrush for such nights, he tiptoed to the walk-in closet he shared with Laura, closed the door, turned on the light and stripped off his clothes. In his pajamas he tiptoed again, this time to bed. A street lamp cast a small light in the room and he paused to look at Laura. She was a pretty woman, not beautiful, but pleasantly pretty with glowing skin and sweet features. She would blur gently into middle age as her mother had done, the already-soft lines and angles of her face and body becoming less defined as the years passed.

Laura would be disappointed he couldn't attend church with her and Beth in the morning. They sat together as a family, Beth between them with her picture book of Bible stories. Laura worked as a paralegal, and she said she felt guilty enough about having Beth in daycare all week without sending her off to the nursery at church, too. "When she was old enough for Sunday School, it will be different," Laura said, but while she was so little, Laura wanted her with them as much as possible.

Beth loved her Bible book and sat quietly, turning the pages with exquisite care, murmuring softly as she retold herself each story, while the minister gave his sermon. Occasionally she would climb into Eggleton's lap – knees, elbows and the corners of the book jabbing him – to whisper in his ear about one of the pictures. It was a precious time to Eggleton; he, too, would be disappointed to miss church with them, but it wouldn't be the first time.

He slipped between the covers, sliding his back against Laura's. If she had been awake, she would have called it 'bumping bottoms,' but she wasn't awake.

Eggleton slept.

When Eggleton arrived at the police station the next morning, he found Dawson seated at his desk, rumpled and unshaven. "You look like hell," Eggleton said.

"Good morning to you, too, Sergeant."

"Go clean up. I'll buy breakfast," Eggleton said.

"Didn't you already have breakfast?"

"Has that ever stopped me? Go take a shower. You

got a change of clothes here?"

"Of course, Mother," Dawson said. He stood and stretched. "Be right back."

It was a transformed Dawson, sharp in a fresh shirt, tie, lightweight jacket and sharply creased slacks, his hair still damp from his shower, who sat across from Eggleton in the back booth of the Omelet House Café. He watched as Eggleton poured syrup on pancakes and sausage. "I don't know where you put it," he said, shaking his head.

Frowning, Eggleton looked at Dawson, then back at his plate. "It's just a short stack," he said.

Dawson sipped his orange juice before setting the glass aside to spread marmalade on his English muffin.

"More coffee?" the waitress asked, slipping the check under the syrup saucer.

"Not for me," Dawson said.

Eggleton, his mouth full of pancakes, nodded, pointing to his cup with his fork. The waitress splashed coffee into the cup, then swished away, the large bow on the back of her apron bobbing in time to her walk.

"So," Eggleton said when his mouth was empty, "what time is church?" He used his napkin to sop up the coffee in his saucer.

"Eleven," Dawson answered, glancing at his watch. "It's nine now, but I want to get there early." He lowered his voice. "For one thing, I want to be sure we get a seat in the back, and for another, I want to hear what they're saying." Looking around the café, he added, "It's pretty empty. I guess we can work here for a while." He pulled his sketch of Mavis Dillon's home from his pocket and laid it on the table.

"Do you think everybody will know we're cops? At church, I mean," Eggleton asked, holding up a sausage on his fork and eating off one end of it.

Dawson had never thought of himself as looking like a policeman, but, seeing Eggleton, his navy suit jacket tight across his shoulders, his shirt buttons straining beneath his tie, his large face simultaneously tough and anxious, Dawson figured Eggleton to be the profile of the quintessential cop. He chose to ignore Eggleton's question.

Pointing to the sketch, Dawson asked, "Can you fill in any more times?"

Eggleton studied the sketch while he ate. "Not off hand," he said through a mouthful of pancakes. "Did you check my notes?"

Dawson nodded.

"Then that's probably all we've got." He looked questioningly at Dawson. "We going calling?"

Dawson nodded again. "We'll start with Mrs. Gentry and Mrs. Liske," he said. "Tomorrow morning, very early, while they're hurrying to get ready for school, we'll pay a quick visit."

Eggleton pursed his lips and raised an eyebrow at Dawson. "Why not at church today?" he asked, pouring syrup on a last small piece of sausage.

"I want to see how they live," Dawson said. "When they're caught off guard."

"And what are we hoping to find?"

"Evidence of their quote *relationship* unquote."

"You're still convinced, huh?"

"No, Sergeant. I'm not convinced. If I were, we

wouldn't be going. I'm open, but I want to be convinced, one way or the other."

"So, how will we determine if they're having a *relationship* by dropping in early in the morning?"

"You will have had a lot of coffee before we arrive, and you will need to use their bathroom. On the way to the bathroom, you will probably pass bedrooms, see who's sleeping where, are two beds mussed or one?"

"Maybe one makes her bed as soon as she gets up," Eggleton countered. "Or maybe both do."

"We can but try, Sergeant."

Eggleton frowned. "Besides," he said, "even if the bed is unmade, what would it tell us?"

"Surely you can tell if one person got out of a bed or two, Bill. You just don't want to think those two ladies . . . , " he paused, leaving his sentence incomplete.

"Are having a relationship," Eggleton finished for him. "I guess you're right. I don't."

"Because they remind you of your Aunt Alice or some such."

"Aunt Sarah," Eggleton said. "*And* Aunt Sarah is *devoted* to Uncle Trigger!"

There was a long silence while Dawson looked closely at Eggleton.

"What?" Eggleton ask.

"Do I even want to know?"

"Know what?"

"Trigger.'"

"Oh, that. He shot himself in the hand when he was a kid. Lost his trigger finger."

"Makes perfect sense," Dawson muttered and folded

his hands on the table. "Well, you're going to have to put your preconceived ideas aside, Bill. Cunningham said 'relationship,' and I want to know what she meant."

"Seems awfully underhanded, if you ask me," Eggleton muttered.

"Well, I didn't ask you, but I'm willing to listen to another suggestion."

"Why not just lean on them? Call them in one at a time? Mrs. Liske'll crack, for sure."

"I don't know," Dawson said, frowning. For a few moments he was silent, poking holes in his napkin with his fork. At last he said, "We may have to. Actually, none of them seem likely, you know what I mean? Not one in the entire bunch."

"You'd be the first to tell me a murderer doesn't necessarily look like a murderer."

"You're right," Dawson admitted. "Besides, we don't know for sure it is murder, do we?" He returned the sketch to his pocket and pulled out his sheet of questions and answers concerning suicide. "Actually, I'm sure – you're not."

The waitress appeared at his elbow, her hands on her hips. "You want anything else?"

Dawson looked up, startled. "No. No thanks," he said, turning the sheet of paper over.

"Cops, aren't you?" she asked.

"Uh," Dawson said noncommittally. He stood. "Time to get going, Bill." He shoved the paper into his pocket and handed the check to Eggleton. "I think you said you were buying."

While Dawson and Eggleton ate breakfast and

186

studied Dawson's charts, Nancy Gifford was getting her children ready for church. Her hands shook as she buttoned Becca's dress and Sammy's white shirt. The bishop and Greg had left early in the bishop's car. The bishop, usually talkative, especially in the morning, was strangely silent. Across town, Sandy and Linda lay curled around each other, gently soothing, each reluctant to get out of bed. Doctor Charles Glasco put on his suit and put his phone in his pocket, praying it would vibrate with a call from the hospital, and he would have an excuse to skip church. Mavis Dillon dropped one of her earrings down the drain while trying to put it on. Andrew drank a cup of very strong coffee. The Alexanders dressed for church and then drank coffee on the porch and read the Sunday paper.

Dawson and Eggleton were seated in Dawson's car in the church parking lot when Dawson again pulled the paper from his pocket.

"Thought we were going to church."

"We are – this'll just take a minute. Something for you to think about if the sermon gets boring. *Suicide,*" he read to Eggleton. "*Why? Depression . . .?*"

"According to the bishop, she'd been depressed for years," Eggleton interrupted.

"Maybe it'll be easier on the bishop if it's suicide."

"Ya think?" Eggleton said, a faint smirk on his face. "Come on! It'll be easier on all of them if it's suicide."

Dawson ignored Eggleton. "Maybe it was getting worse – the depression. We'll ask Father Gifford. Called him this morning. We've got a one o'clock with him."

"You suppose he'll know?"

"He might. Besides, I plan to see this Marjorie Meyerson tomorrow. She appears to be Mrs. Cunningham's only friend, at least the only one anybody's mentioned. She might have more information than Gifford." He continued with his list. *"Disease. We'll know more after the autopsy,"* he said.

"When do we get those results?"

"I talked with Hench this morning. He hopes to have preliminaries by late afternoon." Dawson turned back to his list. *"Blame on party participants."*

"Rebecca," Eggleton said.

"Huh?"

"The story. Rebecca was terminally ill, but no one knew it. She staged her own death to look like murder, and her husband spent his life with that cloud over him."

"I remember," Dawson said. "DuMaurier. It's been known to happen in real life, too. Somebody takes their own life, even if they aren't ill, just to make life miserable for someone else."

The two men stared at the list for a while. Finally Dawson said, "I can't come up with anything else: depression, a terminal illness, and sheer meanness."

"I think some people kill themselves to free up other people, allow other people to go on with their lives."

"Awfully noble, Bill, and hardly in keeping with what we know of Mrs. Cunningham."

Eggleton shrugged. "I thought it was a general list," he said.

Dawson gave Eggleton a sideways glance, shaking his head as he wrote: *Nobility.* "I have more lists to go over with you," he said.

"The result of your sleepless night?"

Dawson nodded. "They can wait," he said glancing at his watch. "I think it's time we went in." Folding the sheets of paper, he stuck them in the inside pocket of his jacket.

CHAPTER TEN

A Service of Confirmation and Holy Communion

But where shall wisdom be found?
Job 28:12

June 7

A canopy of grape vines covered the breezeway leading from the parking lot to the church; bunches of green grapes, heavy with delicious potential, hung low. Sunlight filtered through the leaves, dappling the faces of parishioners as they made their way – talking together in low voices – to the tall, double doors that opened into the sanctuary. A few held out welcoming hands to Dawson and Eggleton.

Doctor Charles Glasco broke away from his position by the door and came toward them. "I thought I might see you here today," he said, clapping Dawson on the shoulder and handing each of them a thick pamphlet. "The whole service: hymns, lessons, everything all in order," he said. "So you don't have to fumble with the prayer book and the hymnal.

"Thanks,"

"I'd sit with you, except I'm ushering."

"That's OK," Dawson said. "Just as soon be fairly inconspicuous."

"Right," Glasco said with a tiny smile.

"Inconspicuous," and hurried back to his position by the doors.

"Do you sometimes get the impression we have 'cop' written all over our faces?" Eggleton whispered.

"I think you've asked that question before."

Inside, stained glass captured the sunlight, painting it with shades of rose, amber, purple, green, and cobalt blue, before sending it on to play across the burgundy carpet and polished oak pews. The scent of flowers, candle wax, and just the faintest hint of incense from some past high mass filled the sanctuary. Looking around, Dawson was struck with the memories of his own childhood when he was an altar boy, making his way slowly down the aisle of Mary Magdalene Catholic Church, swinging the censer and trying to avoid his mother's eyes which shone with pride and tears. He blinked some tears of his own and slid into a back pew next to the aisle, pulling his knees aside to let Eggleton ease past. All around them people were taking seats, lowering kneelers and slipping to their knees in prayer. Eggleton raised his eyebrows in a question, a look close to panic on his face, but Dawson shook his head.

Although he had hoped to overhear some talk about Gwen Cunningham, he'd heard none. He assumed the quiet conversations of the parishioners in the breezeway dealt with Mrs. Cunningham's death, but he could not make out what they were saying. Inside, all was quiet save for the occasional whispered, 'good morning,' and the squeak of lowered kneelers.

Suddenly the tower bell rang, a single voice sending the call to worship to the town, the vineyards, the surrounding hills, and as the last toll faded away, the organist began a Bach Prelude and Fugue: *The Great G minor.* One of Dawson's favorites: he closed his eyes and gave himself over to the music.

A faint scent of perfume, followed by a tap on his shoulder, brought him alert, and he turned to see Mavis Dillon standing beside the pew. "If you slide over a bit, I can sit with you and help you through the service," she whispered.

Caught between the desire to maintain a low profile and the desire to sit next to this lovely woman, Dawson quickly sorted his priorities and, nudging Eggleton, slid over to make room for Mavis. She smiled at him, and, lowering the kneeler, sank to her knees. A streak of sunlight fell across her honey-colored hair.

Eggleton wondered what she was praying for.

Charles Glasco, holding the hand of a beautiful young girl dressed in white lace and wearing a white veil, walked down the aisle, followed by a straggle of young people. The girls were similarly dressed in white, while the boys wore neatly creased flannel slacks, starched shirts, and clip-on ties. The boys' sleeked-down hair bore damp comb tracks. Charles released a ribbon cordoning the front pew and herded his charges into their seats.

Seeing the youngsters struggle between dignity and the desire for space, Dawson suppressed a laugh as they wriggled, jabbed, and settled themselves. Charles returned to his position by the entrance.

Glancing around, Dawson saw Nancy Gifford and two small children seated near the front of the church. As he watched, Dolores Alexander walked down a side aisle and slipped in by Nancy. Out of the corner of his eye, he saw Sandy Liske and Linda Gentry slide hurriedly into a back pew. He wondered where George Alexander was.

The fugue ended, and the sanctuary darkened as Charles closed the doors. Except for the rustle of clothes as people shifted expectantly in their seats, all was quiet. The silence lasted for several moments, but even the young people in the front pew sat motionless, their mouths slightly open, looking toward the back of the church to the two great doors.

Suddenly three sharp knocks sounded, and beside him Dawson felt Eggleton start – saw his hand move reflexively to his inside pocket. "Put your hand down," Dawson whispered, his teeth clenched.

Through the doors they could hear the voice of the bishop. *"Open unto me the gates of righteousness that I may enter."* All around them people stood as the doors opened, and the organ began to roar with the opening hymn. Dawson felt his insides vibrate, an almost primal sensation. Mavis opened her pamphlet and gestured to Dawson and Eggleton to do the same.

The bishop stood framed in the doorway, magnificent in his cope and miter. He stepped in and then moved to one side as the procession began. The white-gloved crucifer – a girl of about fifteen – carrying a large gold cross and flanked on either side by a torch bearer, was first down the aisle. Following the three, was an acolyte carrying the banner of St. Francis. The choir, wearing dark red robes, entered next, singing as they walked: *Lift high the cross, the love of Christ proclaim.* George Alexander's deep baritone boomed as he passed, answering Dawson's question as to his whereabouts. Beside Dawson, Eggleton joined in with a lusty tenor. Dawson stood silently. They're all here, he thought. All except Andrew.

Following the choir was Father Gifford in a green chasuble, the color of Pentecost. He was a handsome man Dawson recognized from various functions around town. The bishop followed Father Gifford, his cope of ivory brocade billowing with each step he took, the multi-colored sunlight glistening on the braid and jewels of his miter. In his right hand, he carried a simple wooden staff, the symbol of his role as shepherd of his flock. Dawson felt goose bumps start on his arms; beside him Eggleton blew his nose. Some tough policemen we are, Dawson thought.

Mavis held her thick pamphlet toward Dawson, pointing to the hymn. Dawson shook his head slightly. "I don't sing," he whispered.

"Sad," she whispered back.

When the hymn was over, Father Gifford stepped in front of the altar, and, raising his arms, gave the Invitatory. The service began, and both men relaxed into their seats.

Linda Gentry came forward to read the Epistle. "*See then that ye walk circumspect, not as fools, but as wise, redeeming the time . . .*" She paused, looking up at the congregation before continuing. Her eye caught Dawson's, and her voice faltered. "*. . . be . . . because the days are evil.*"

At announcement time, Father Gifford spoke of Gwen Cunningham. "As most of you know by now, Mrs. Gwen Cunningham died suddenly yesterday." There was a rustling among the people in the pews, but Dawson heard no great gasp or intake of breath, and he knew the word had spread long before the service began. "She has been a great asset to this parish in many ways, and her talents will be missed. We have not yet set the time of her memorial service, but you can call the church office Monday to see if we have more information. Our prayers today will include prayers for the peace of her soul."

"Diplomatic," Eggleton muttered.

"Uh, huh."

Mavis shifted in her seat and Dawson was acutely aware of the woman next to him – beautiful, carefully dressed and groomed, her perfume a delicate hint of flowers – aware, as one might be of a fine painting or a porcelain vase, but he felt nothing. She prompted no quickening of his heart, no flush of warmth to his loins – a situation he realized was rare for him; he usually found proximity to a beautiful woman mildly arousing. If given the invitation to lie with her, he realized he would refuse – not that he thought for a moment he would be given the invitation.

He pulled his thoughts back to the service and found it moving – the young Candidates for Confirmation so serious as they took their confirmation vows, the poetic liturgy of the Eucharistic service, the pageantry of the richly garbed clergy and assistants. The sermon, delivered without notes, by the bishop, was brief and eloquently presented. Dawson smiled as he remembered the bishop's confession he often gave the same sermon several times since he was always in a different parish. At the communion, Dawson and Eggleton remained seated as most of the people around them rose to go forward to the rail.

"Trappings," Eggleton muttered.

"Presbyterian," Dawson whispered.

Following the bishop's Benediction, the organist began the final hymn: *God of the prophets, bless the prophets' heirs.* While finding it difficult to picture the delightful children who had been confirmed that day as future prophets, Dawson was captivated by the words of the hymn:

Anoint them prophets, teach them thine intent:
To human need their quickened hearts awake;
Fill them with power, their lips make eloquent,
For righteousness that shall all evil break.

A high charge for such young people he thought – for all of us. He noticed the word *evil* had surfaced twice in this service. Knowing well staff had chosen the readings and hymns far in advance, he wondered at the coincidence. Or was there some greater power foretelling the evil act which had taken the life of the apparently-evil woman who died while drinking sherry at the bishop's party. Dawson shook his head at his own foolish thinking – Eggleton shot him a glance.

The procession leaving the sanctuary was every bit as majestic as the procession entering had been. The crucifer and torch bearers led, followed now by the Candidates, their faces serious, as if a cloak of responsibility had matured them in this brief time. Next came the choir, Father Gifford and the Deacons, and at the end, the bishop. As he passed the pew where Dawson stood reading verses and Eggleton sang full throat the beautiful words, the bishop gave a tiny inclination of his head, acknowledging their presence.

When the hymn ended, the procession moved out the double doors and again the bells rang, a full chorus now, each bell singing its own song, unmindful of the others, this time signaling to the town, the vineyards, and the hills something very important had taken place. The organist began an improvisation on the final hymn.

The two officers joined the crowd queued to exit the sanctuary. From the corner of his eye, Dawson could see Charles Glasco walking among the pews, picking up leaflets and returning kneelers to their position. As he stepped out of the church, he watched in amusement as doves flew from the belfry, their squawks of indignation grace notes in the cacophony.

"Tintinnabulation," he muttered.

"Poe," Eggleton said.

They stopped to shake hands with the bishop and Father Gifford. The bishop whispered, "Any word?" to which Dawson shook his head. Father Gifford said, "One o'clock, my office," and nodded toward a cluster of buildings adjacent to the church.

The breezeway and adjoining patio buzzed with word of Gwen Cunningham's death, as though Father Gifford's announcement had released a flood of pent-up conversation.

" . . . if her money will go to St. Francis . . ."

". . .said it was suicide."

"Always knew somebody'd do her in."

". . . gave so much . . ."

"Old bitch!"

"Michael!"

"No great loss, if you ask . . ."

"Couldn't have happened to . . ."

". . . Literacy Program at the .. .

" . . . suppose those two sitting with Mavis . . ."

"I heard the police think . . ."

A few people stopped to talk to Dawson and Eggleton.

"Haven't I seen you . . .?"

"Are you new in town?"

"You cops?"

"Will you be coming to St. Francis?"

"I know you from . . ."

"Could sure use a tenor like you in the . . ."

"Dawson. There used to be a Dawson, owned a vineyard."

"Will you join me for coffee in the parish hall?" Mavis asked as she caught up with them.

"We're meeting with Father Gifford at 1:00," Dawson said, looking at his watch. "I need to jot some notes first. Thank you anyway."

She smiled. "I'm hostess," she said. "I'll bring a piece of cake out to your car for you," and she turned and went into the parish hall.

"Yessss!" Eggleton said.

They were reviewing Dawson's notes when Mavis appeared at the car window, carrying a tray with Styrofoam coffee cups and paper plates of cake. Dawson opened the door.

"I feel like a car-hop," Mavis said, smiling.

"No danger," Dawson replied, taking a cup from the tray and passing it to Eggleton. "Thank you for your help during the service."

"It takes getting used to," she said, as she handed him a plate and plastic fork.

Finally, having distributed the coffee and cake, she stood, the empty tray dangling by her side. Dawson could see the tiny lines of stress around her eyes and mouth. He waited for her to speak. "I hope you get this sorted soon, Inspector," she said at last. "It's a terrible thing to have hanging over us."

"I hope so, too, Mrs. Dillon. We may need to talk to you again, you know."

"I know," she said and turned to walk back to the parish hall.

Dawson sipped his coffee. "They were all there, just going about their regular business," he mused, more to himself than to Eggleton. "But one of them's a murderer."

"Maybe," Eggleton said.

"You don't for a moment think this was anything but murder, do you?"

"Jury's out," Eggleton said.

"Huh!"

"Do we just wait here until time to talk to Father Gifford?" Eggleton asked, brushing crumbs off his suit jacket and on to the papers in his lap.

Dawson pointed to the clock on the dashboard. "It's only ten minutes, Bill."

"Time flies," Eggleton muttered. "Did you pick up anything interesting this morning?"

"Other than that you have a fine tenor voice? How come I never knew that?"

"Depths to plumb, Inspector. Depths to plumb. I mean from watching. And listening. Out there in the walkway."

"Not much. You?"

Eggleton shook his head. "Lot of talk, was all, but nothing specific. Just that there seems to be a feeling it wasn't such a bad thing."

Dawson sighed. "I've never known of anybody so universally disliked," he added.

"You noticed Father Gifford didn't try to give the impression it was a great sadness or loss."

"We certainly can't accuse anybody of hypocrisy, can we?"

Eggleton leaned back and closed his eyes. Dawson took his diagram of Mavis's house from the papers on Eggleton's lap, shook the cake crumbs out the window, and studied it. With his pencil, he drew a tiny goblet on the hall table. And a question mark beside the goblet.

Father Gifford's study was that of a scholar. A large desk stood in the middle of the room. Behind the desk and on two other walls were floor-to-ceiling bookshelves, jammed with books. The moment he entered, Dawson prowled the shelves; he always learned a great deal about a person from the books they read. More books stood in piles on a small table by the desk. Large windows, looking out on the courtyard, took up one wall.

"Shall I close the drapes?" Father Gifford asked.

"Up to you. I think everyone knows who we are and why we're here."

"Then I'll leave them open. It's a beautiful day; it would be a shame to close it out. Please, take a chair."

From their seats in front of the desk, Eggleton and Dawson could see parishioners wandering about the grounds; parents and grandparents posing with the candidates. The bishop, his cope encased in a large garment bag, stopped for a picture with some of the groups, before continuing on toward the parking lot. Father Gifford sat behind a desk cluttered with paper, books, and pictures of his family. He was frowning at a pipe rack.

"Nancy hates it when I smoke," he said, selecting one of the pipes. "Would you mind terribly?"

"Not at all," Dawson said. "I enjoy the smell of a pipe."

Eggleton said nothing as he pulled his notebook from his pocket.

Father Gifford scooped the pipe into a canister of tobacco, pressing the tobacco into the bowl with his thumb. Tobacco flakes scattered across his papers, and he tipped the papers into his wastebasket. "She says it's a messy habit." His eyes twinkled as he said it. "Wonder why she thinks that." He lit the pipe, drawing deeply. When he exhaled, the scent of the smoke filled the small office. Eggleton held his breath.

At last Gifford said, "Now, how can I be of help?"

Dawson got straight to the point. "Of the guests at the party, do you have any idea who might have wanted Mrs. Cunningham dead?"

"Oh, Inspector. I was afraid you would ask that."

"You asked how you could help."

"I was hoping you just needed information about Gwen."

Dawson inclined his head. "Very well," he said. "Let's start with information about Gwen. We've been told Mrs. Cunningham suffered from some form of depression. Was it your experience with her?"

"Yes. And I suspect the episodes were getting closer together and of greater severity," Father Gifford replied.

Dawson gestured toward the bookcases. "Textbooks on psychology, sociology, personality disorder, psychopathology. I see a diploma for a Master of Science in Psychology and Counseling in addition to the Doctor of Divinity."

"A tool in my work as a priest," Gifford said. "I don't practice in a clinical sense."

"Did she ever come to you for counseling?"

"No. Gwen wouldn't have admitted, at least to me, there was a problem. Her attitude was: tough it out – there's nothing wrong. There's frequently a lot of denial associated with depression."

"Did you ever suggest professional help?" Dawson asked, remembering what the bishop had told him.

"Just once. She left the church when I did."

"What did you do to get her back?"

"Nothing. In all honesty, I wasn't real sorry to see her go. She'd caused much heartache for some of my parishioners. However, it's a moot point, since she came back."

moot? Eggleton wrote

"Did she ever say why?"

"Why she left or why she came back?"

"Either."

"No."

"Given your experience as a clinical psychologist . . ." Dawson started.

Father Gifford held up his hand, the one holding the pipe. "Just a minute," he said. "My actual experience has been limited to internships and what work I do with parishioners. I have never worked as a clinician."

Dawson dipped his head in concession. "Given your

knowledge," he amended, "could a person suffering from depression function at a social gathering such as the sherry party yesterday afternoon?"

"You mean, during a depressive episode?"

Dawson nodded.

Father Gifford frowned and drew on his pipe.

Eggleton frowned as well.

"I wasn't there to observe her," he said finally. "But according to Nancy, she seemed perfectly normal . . . normal for Gwen."

"Can you be more specific about this . . ." Dawson paused. ". . . this hypothetical diagnosis of depression?"

"Inspector, I am very uncomfortable with the word *diagnosis*." Father Gifford rose from his chair and went to stand in front of the windows, studying the parishioners who were still roaming about the courtyard, giving a small lift of his pipe to those who saw him watching. He spoke, his back to the officers. "You need to develop a profile with someone in your department – a psychiatrist or psychologist – who can bring clinical experience to the profile – who can interview people who knew her. For that I would suggest her gardener be interviewed. He works two days a week in Gwen's gardens. He's one of the staff at the nursery where George works." Father Gifford laughed. "When Gwen shut herself away, the gardener would say to George, 'She's gone to ground.' I picture a small animal burrowing underground. Or rather a large animal." He turned and faced them. "I would also suggest your clinical professional interview Marjorie Meyerson. If Gwen had a friend in town, it would be Marjorie. They were in college together. And of course, I will be happy to sit down with any professional you suggest," he added and returned to his place behind the desk.

"Any evidence of manic behavior?"

"More just hyperactive – a bundle of energy, ideas pouring out of her – good ideas, creative ideas. She'd be restless, unable to sit still. But certainly nothing like a major manic episode that I ever witnessed."

"But major depressive episodes?"

"I repeat. I'm uncomfortable making these judgments, Inspector. Please consult with your experts"

"I will. Now, go back with me to my question: could she function if she were in the throes of a depressive episode?"

Father Gifford shrugged. "Some people are fine, making plans, talking about the future and an hour later takes his or her own life. However, since Gwen tended to hibernate during her episodes, I doubt it," he said. "Not without people being aware something was wrong. I can hypothesize, though, and say perhaps she was aware one of those episodes was coming on. For some people there is a warning. It's possible she pulled herself together for the party yesterday, knowing a major episode was just around the corner. I don't know, and there is no way of finding out."

"Several people have mentioned suicide."

convenient for him if it is Eggleton jotted.

"I've heard."

"What is your opinion?"

"How fortunate if it were so."

Eggleton drew a smiley face.

"Nothing more?"

"It's possible, Inspector. Especially if she knew a

major depressive episode was eminent. And, to compound that, if the episodes had been increasing in frequency and intensity, as I suspect they had been, yes. But I think it's more likely she'd commit suicide during the episode– when the thoughts of suicide can overwhelm the victim."

"So, possible, but not likely."

Father Gifford smiled and pointed his pipe at Dawson. "I feel like I'm repeating myself. I'm not the person to ask."

"The alternative is she was murdered," Dawson said scooting himself forward in his chair and leaning his forearms on the edge of Father Gifford's desk. "By someone at the party yesterday. So, getting back to my original question of the group at the party, who might have wanted Mrs. Cunningham dead?"

about time, Eggleton jotted, having been lost in the finer points of manic-depressive behavior and its variations.

Father Gifford studied his pipe for a moment, and then he said. "Which is why I said it would be fortunate if it were suicide – for all of us."

Neither man mentioned Nancy Gifford's presence at the party. They didn't need to; it hung heavily in the small office like the scent of tobacco.

"Do you have any information, any insight at all, that could point me to a motive?"

Father Gifford leaned forward in his chair, his forearms resting on the desktop. The two men were almost eye to eye.

faceoff? Eggleton wrote.

When Father Gifford spoke, his voice was sorrowful. "In this town, Inspector, Gwen Cunningham and motive for murder are almost synonymous."

"So I'm learning," Dawson said. "Give me some examples. Of motives, I mean."

Father Gifford hesitated, his lips pursed, the pipe at rest on the ash tray. At last he said, "One person I could tell you about without betraying a confidence would be Buddy Neuman. He married his childhood sweetheart, Debbie Madison. She was a diabetic, had been all her life, and both knew what that meant – no children. But something went wrong with their birth control method, and Debbie became pregnant. Well, her parents, Buddy, her doctors, even me – and while I am a proponent of choice, I always hope the choice will be to have the child – we all recommended abortion. But Gwen heard about it. She told Debbie it would be a mortal sin, and poor Debbie listened to her. She vacillated so long an abortion would have been unsafe, and no doctor would have performed it even if she'd agreed to one. A moot point because she died in childbirth, and Buddy was left with a baby to raise."

moot – twice. Eggleton thought he would try it on Laura.

Father Gifford shook his head. "The prognosis for the child isn't good – he's severely diabetic himself."

"I thought diabetes skipped a generation."

Father Gifford shrugged. "I've heard that, but I think it's a myth. It certainly didn't in Debbie's case. Charles Glasco cares for the baby free of charge, and what bills there are, I pay from my discretionary fund. Gwen knew nothing about it. If any of Gwen's money comes to St. Francis, I'll ask the congregation to vote a chunk toward the baby's medical care. There will come a time when Charles can't absorb it all. I think there would be a certain irony in that, don't you?"

"She seems to have been a very powerful influence," Dawson said, "if this young woman took her advice over the advice of you and her doctor."

"Debbie was vulnerable, and Gwen was a force. Some could stand against her, some couldn't."

Dawson leaned back in his chair. "Do you have anything else?"

"You mean like the story of Buddy and Debbie. Yes, but some of them would break a confidence, and, since they don't apply to the people present at yesterday's party, I don't think they'd be of interest to you."

"On the contrary, you're giving me a feel for the woman. For now I'll respect your wish to hold your confidences, but if I need information about one of the people at the party, I'll expect you to be forthcoming."

"Only if it doesn't violate my role as their priest," Father Gifford said.

Dawson frowned. "You'd let a murderer go free, even if you had the information to help me charge him or her?"

Father Gifford did not hesitate. "Yes," he said, tapping the bowl of his pipe into the ashtray before returning the pipe to the rack. Then he stood. "Gwen was like two different people, Inspector. She gave so much to the community –and she did so much damage to the community. It's the damage that sticks in my mind." He pointed to his watch. "Nancy and the kids are waiting for me."

The interview was clearly over.

CHAPTER ELEVEN

A Wee Chat With Andrew MacBride

Why do ye not understand my speech?
Jn. 8:43

June 7

"Let's leave the cars here and walk over to Mrs. Dillon's," Dawson suggested as he and Eggleton left Father Gifford's office. "It's just a few blocks, and we've been sitting a long time."

Eggleton, who was sweating and feeling constricted in the dark suit, would have preferred to drive, maybe even taking off his coat and tie and leaving them in the car. But Dawson, immaculate and cool-looking, strode off in the direction of Mavis Dillon's house without waiting for Eggleton to voice an opinion.

Eggleton jogged a few steps to catch up. "By the way," he said, "I don't like pipe smoke."

"Neither do I."

"Then why did you tell Father Gifford you liked the smell of a pipe?"

"Because pipe smokers frequently need something in their hands, especially in a stressful situation. And having his wife as a suspect in a murder investigation is probably pretty stressful for him. I thought it was interesting to see how much he actually smoked and how much he just played with the pipe."

"Hummm. He didn't smoke much, did he?"

"Nope."

"Nervous with us there – a lot of pipe English."

"Pipe English. I like that."

"Office smelled."

"Uh huh."

Summer was all around them. The bright green vineyards stretched up and across the hills in neat rows. In the gardens they passed, roses bloomed in a profusion of color. Men in tank tops mowed lawns while women hunkered in flower beds, surrounded by their tools and sacks of fertilizer. Defying disaster, two boys on skateboards skimmed past Dawson and Eggleton.

Eggleton mopped his forehead. "Duded up like this, we might be mistaken for Jehovah Witnesses," he said.

"Who has the most to lose, Bill?" Dawson asked, ignoring Eggleton's observation.

"You've mentioned that before; figure it out – we'll have our murderer – if this was really murder."

Dawson rolled his eyes. "The only one we know for sure about is George Alexander, and he doesn't seem to give a rat's ass if people know he spent time in prison." He paused to kick a rock off the sidewalk. "You have the name of Mrs. Alexander's first husband, supposedly died of an aneurysm?"

Eggleton patted the pocket that held his notebook.

"Check it out tomorrow. Make sure there was no question about his death. Anyway, she wasn't even listed in Cunningham's diary, so I don't think we'll find much on her."

"You know . . ." Eggleton said as they began the walk up the brick path leading to Mavis Dillon's front door.

Dawson had been admiring the garden. Masses of color bordered the lawns; trees provided shaded areas for the occasional small statue: a rabbit, a deer, a duck. He turned to Eggleton.

" . . .I did notice something today," Eggleton continued. "You mentioning the diary made me think of it."

By this time they were at Mavis Dillon's front door, and Eggleton said, "It can wait. I'll tell you after we've seen Andrew. Doesn't have anything to do with him."

"Fine," Dawson said.

Andrew answered their knock. "I'd like ye to meet my wee wifey, Fiona," Andrew said, introducing the Inspector and Sergeant to a tiny woman in her early seventies. Why Andrew referred to her as 'wee' was evident.

Andrew's thick brogue of the evening before had slipped away, nursed, Dawson figured, by a night's sleep and coffee. All that was left was a slight lilt, a few rolled r's and words that were part of his vocabulary, with or without whiskey. Looking at Fiona, with her cloud of white hair, her lightly powdered parchment skin, and the frilly blouse with ruffles up to her chin, Dawson had a fleeting impression of the fairies of folklore. Her warm smile welcomed them instantly. "Have ye had your lunch? We're a bit late with it today. Mavis just got home from church. She's upstairs having a rest, and I'm fixing us all a wee bite. You're welcome to join us."

"No thank you, Fiona," Dawson said. "We just want a quick word with Andrew, and then we'll be on our way."

Eggleton, who looked as though he would not have

been at all opposed to a 'wee bite,' gave Dawson a sideways look.

"Come with me, Sergeant," Fiona said, taking Eggleton's arm. "I need you to open something for me. Jars these days . . ." Over her shoulder she said, "He'll be right back, Inspector. You and Andrew start your chat." Then she pulled Eggleton into the kitchen and closed the door behind them.

Eggleton made sure he was finished chewing before he walked into the library. Slipping into his place at the desk, he wiped the corners of his mouth and then took out his notebook.

"OK," Dawson was saying. "You're saying you didn't speak to Mrs. Cunningham yesterday."

"No. She thought herself a bit above the common gardener, Inspector, so she didn't bother talking to me."

"Did you go into the house during the course of the party?"

"No need."

Dawson looked puzzled.

"I've a fine bathroom all fitted up in the shed, and a refrigerator. Nothing in the house I was needing."

"Are you telling me you didn't go into the house or that you had no need to go into the house?"

"Same thing, I'd say."

"Not quite."

"I didn't go in the house, Inspector, because I had no need to go in the house."

angels dancing Eggleton jotted in his notebook.

"Yesterday you said you were glad to be getting the

nicotine. Is that right?"

"Aye. It's been a bad year for the aphids. Mavis wants the garden perfect for the wedding. That's why I was working yesterday. Got a load of sod on Friday to patch the lawn."

"How long have you worked for Mrs. Dillon?"

Andrew pursed his lips as he thought. "Twelve years," he said finally. "Twelve years come October."

"You seem very fond of Mrs. Dillon."

"Aye. That I am. And my wee wifey, too. Like a daughter she thinks of Mavis."

"She's been good to you?"

"Aye. Always. When my sainted mother, God rest her soul, passed over, it was Mavis said I was to go to Scotland right away, went out and bought the tickets for Fiona and me. Wouldn't hear otherwise."

Eggleton made a note. *passed over.*

"She was ninety-eight. My mother."

Dawson, who didn't know whether to be sympathetic or amazed, said nothing, allowing an ambiguous silence.

At last he continued. "You were saying earlier, before my Sergeant came in," and here Dawson glanced at Eggleton with a tight-lipped smile, "that yesterday you were working mainly on the far side of the house, the side away from the patio."

Andrew nodded in agreement. "I had spots to re-sod. Also, I was giving everything over there a good trim and watering. Watered the lawn on that side, too."

"Did you see anyone go into the kitchen from that side of the house?"

Andrew considered for a moment. "No," he said

finally. "Not while I was around there. No one. Been foolish for them to come around there, what with me watering and mucking about."

"Could you see into the kitchen from where you were?"

"Not clearly."

Dawson persisted. "Could you have seen someone if they came to the sink, say?"

"Aye. Shadow-like. Wouldn't be able to see who it was though."

"So you did see people at the sink?"

"Aye. Couple times, I guess. Wasn't really looking."

"Do you know who it was?"

Andrew shook his head.

"Could you see if anybody took anything off the sill?"

Again Andrew shook his head. "Too dark in there."

"Did you see people talking to Mrs. Cunningham?"

"When I was over that way. They were all in and out of the house and on the patio, everybody talking. I remember she was talking to the Alexanders. Kept on at them the longest time. I wanted to ask him about one of my plants, but I wasn't going to get involved with her, so I let it be."

"So you didn't talk to her at all?"

Andrew shook his head.

"Did the others talk to you?"

"Aye. I'd say they all did one time or the other, even the bishop fellow, the one with the purple shirt and the big cross 'round his neck." Andrew shook his head as though unable to conceive of a man wearing a purple shirt and a necklace. "Commented on the rose bushes. Said he'd never seen any like 'em."

"Did you see Mrs. Cunningham put down her sherry glass at any time."

Andrew shook his head. "Wasn't paying attention. I wasn't really in with the party."

Dawson leaned forward, his elbows on his knees, his face close to Andrew's. "Do you know of any reason why Mrs. Cunningham might have been murdered, Andrew?"

There was the hint of a chuckle in Andrew's voice. "Aye. Just about anybody knew her had a reason. Doesn't mean they did, mind you."

"Well, it certainly looks as if *somebody* did."

"Did you ever think she might'a done it herself?"

"Do you think she might have?"

"Be just like her. Make it look like somebody else did it, her enjoying knowing they'd all be suspected." Andrew shook his head. "Just like her. Just like her."

"You didn't think much of her, did you?"

"Like I said, she had no time for the gardener. And I thanked my stars."

Dawson stood and held out his hand. "Thank you, Andrew. We'll let you get to your lunch now. If we have more questions, we'll be in touch."

"Aye," Andrew said, nodding. "Aye." In silence he followed them down the hall to the door.

As they walked back to the church parking lot, Eggleton shrugged off his suit jacket and pulled off his tie. He hooked the jacket on one finger and carried it over his shoulder. The tie dangled from the pocket.

"So what was it you wanted to tell me?" Dawson asked.

"Actually two things. First of all, I noticed how much the two ladies – Mrs. Liske and Mrs. Gentry – how much they went out of their way this morning to avoid us. We shook hands or spoke to everyone else that was at the party, but those two made themselves scarce. Guilty conscience maybe?"

"About something. What else did you see?"

"Mrs. Gifford. When you mentioned Cunningham's diary, I thought of the notation by Mrs. Gifford's name: Meyersons. That's the jewelry store in town, and yesterday Mrs. Gifford was twisting her pearl necklace – I figured it would break."

"Me, too."

"Well, nervous habit, or something about the necklace. So I'm putting jewelry store and necklace together, and I'm remembering yesterday she had on that really simple – I think it's called a sheath – bright blue dress, had her hair up on top of her head, pearl earrings and the pearl necklace."

"You're a regular fashion maven," Dawson said.

"Huh?"

"Go on."

"Today, she had on another dress sort of like it, navy blue this time, hair on top of her head, pearl earrings, but no necklace. And if ever a dress called for a simple pearl necklace, it was the one she wore today."

"You are amazing, Bill."

"Right."

"No, I mean it. Although where you got this expertise in fashion is definitely something I don't want to know, you're absolutely right. Great question: where was the pearl necklace?"

"Could be she broke it after all."

"Could be."

"If she'd worn gold earrings and a gold necklace, I wouldn't have thought anything of it. But the pearl earrings . . . got me to thinking. Like at the last minute she decided not to wear the pearls." He shrugged. "Whatever. She probably broke the pearls this morning, and I'm making too much of it."

"Or could be she didn't want to wear it for some reason having to do with the note in the diary and Meyerson's. I'm going to call on Mrs. Myerson at the store tomorrow. I'll see if anything pops up."

They walked in silence for a while, Dawson rehashing his conversation with Andrew, Eggleton wondering how to spell *maven*.

Dawson broke the silence. "You know, I've been thinking Andrew could have slipped into the kitchen by way of the outside door."

Eggleton, reflecting on the little lady who had fixed him a quick ham sandwich, said, "Nah!"

Dawson snorted. "You were just smitten with his wee wifey, Sergeant."

"A quaint turn of phrase, Inspector."

"But he might have."

"Huh?"

"Slipped into the kitchen."

"Or any of them," Eggleton said. "Walked around on the pretense of looking at the flowers, nipped in the side door, did the deed with the nicotine, back out the side door, carried the glass back to the patio, waited until

Cunningham put her glass down for a minute, made the switch, and no one the wiser."

"Andrew said he didn't see anybody. Besides, it would have been easiest for Andrew. The rest of them would have to leave the patio, go down that side of the house, around the end of the house, and down the kitchen side," Dawson said, ticking the progression off on his fingers. "Which would take some time and might raise questions from the other guests. Also, if Andrew was watering and tending the lawn on that side, their shoes could get muddy or at least wet. Forensics didn't report any sign of footprints in the kitchen."

"The same would hold true for Andrew."

"Unless he slipped his shoes off."

"Any of them could have done that."

Dawson persisted. "I still think Andrew is the logical one if we consider someone slipping in the kitchen door."

"What motive, Inspector? And when would he have gotten this theoretical poisoned sherry glass to Mrs. Cunningham? And how?"

They had reached the parking lot, empty now except for their two cars. They stopped by Dawson's door; Dawson clicked his key.

"Yeah. That's the problem," Dawson said, somewhat reluctantly. "When did anybody slip her a glass with nicotine in it? As to motive, I'd swear they all have one, but so far we've only got one for the Alexanders, and I suspect we have one for Mrs. Liske and Mrs. Gentry." He grinned at Eggleton. "Regardless of your Uncle Trigger. But Andrew and his wife seem awfully protective of Mavis. Suppose he knew Mrs. Cunningham was threatening Mavis about something in her past – or background as I interpret *b-k-g-d* to mean. That would give him a motive."

Eggleton looked doubtful. "Still when and how?"

"You're just in love with Fiona."

"Aye. That I am."

Laughing, Dawson punched Eggleton on the arm. "Go on home, Bill. We've done enough for one day. I'll call Hench – then I'm going to knock off, too. Tomorrow I want you to check on Mrs. Alexander's first husband. Also, six o'clock tomorrow morning – meet me at the station. No later."

"You still planning for us to visit Mrs. Liske and Mrs. Gentry?"

"Aye. That I am."

CHAPTER TWELVE

Dawson Makes No Friends

...now it is high time to awake out of sleep...
Rom. 13:11

June 8

Doctor Henchcombe was in Dawson's office when Eggleton arrived the next morning. Impeccably dressed at 6:00 A.M., Henchcombe sat perched on the edge of his chair, as though to sit back might compromise his immaculate appearance – or might emphasize the fact his feet didn't quite touch the floor. Three Styrofoam coffee cups sat on Dawson's desk; Eggleton selected one, opened it, and tossed the lid into the wastebasket.

"So it is poison," Dawson said.

"What?" Eggleton said. "The coffee?"

"Funny," Dawson replied, gesturing for Eggleton to pull up a chair beside him. He held the autopsy report so they both could read.

"Eighty-five milligrams of nicotine found in the stomach," Henchcombe said.

"What would be a fatal dose?"

"About sixty milligrams, although she was a large woman. For her, it might have been a bit more than sixty, but certainly not eighty-five. There was also a quantity of alcohol found in the stomach, an amount consistent with at least three glasses of sherry."

"With a fatal dosage of nicotine, it seems we can rule out death by interaction between drugs and alcohol," Dawson said.

"Is that a question or a statement?" Henchcombe asked.

"Yes."

Eggleton stifled a tiny laugh; he and Dawson continued to read.

"One hundred thirty-one kilograms? What does that mean in pounds, Doc?"

Henchcombe winced at Eggleton's choice of address and then glanced at his own copy of the report. "Two hundred forty pounds, one hundred seventy-eight centimeters in length - which would be five foot, ten inches in layman's terms."

"One coffee left, Hench," Dawson said taking the lid off his.

"Never touch the stuff," Henchcombe replied. "But thanks anyway."

Might stunt his growth, Eggleton thought.

"Five-ten, nearly two hundred and fifty pounds. She was a big woman," Eggleton said, making a face as he sipped his coffee. He set it aside.

Henchcombe nodded.

"Some erosion of the mucus membrane of the mouth, throat, esophagus and stomach," Dawson continued.

"Consistent with nicotine poisoning," Henchcombe said, his answers as crisp and concise as his mode of dress.

"Has nicotine in alcohol been used before in a murder, do you know?"

"Well, in fiction – Scotch and a martini. Actual case

histories– one woman killed her sister by dissolving cigarettes in water, and another woman killed her husband by mixing it in with his after-shave lotion. Both highly effective, I might add."

Realizing there was little to be said, Dawson and Eggleton were silent for a moment and then continued reading.

"This the suicide attempt you showed me Saturday?" Dawson said at last, pointing at a paragraph on the report.

Eggleton read aloud. "Small scar on palmer surface of right wrist measuring two point nine centimeters in length. Small scar on palmer surface of left wrist measuring three point two centimeters in length. Scar on left wrist of greater length than on the right, indicating it was made by the stronger right hand. Both scars are old, probably occurring during the early years of subject's life."

Dawson turned to Henchcombe. "One of the people we interviewed mentioned she always wore large bracelets, which they figured probably covered some scars," he said. "But I still reject the suicide theory. Chugging nicotine? Too painful a method." He picked up a coffee cup.

"Well, obviously slashing her wrists didn't do the job. Maybe she wanted a surer method," Eggleton said.

"You don't want this to be murder do you Sergeant?"

"You're right. I don't"

The two men read on.

"Would you look at that!" Eggleton exclaimed after a few moments. "No obvious disruption of the hymen." He looked at Henchcombe.

"I noticed this when examining the genitalia and reproductive organs for any pathology. It would appear the woman was a virgin. All indications are that, if she ever did have sexual relations, there was no actual penetration."

"So what about Mr. Cunningham?"

"Maybe why he's not around," Dawson said with a small smile.

"Maybe he never existed."

"I've been thinking about that, too. We might find out more about him when we go through her house this afternoon."

"But still a virgin . . ." Eggleton shook his head.

"I would imagine after a certain age it ceases to be a burden, Bill." Dawson said. "Also, I have an appointment with Marjorie Meyerson later this morning." He turned to Henchcombe. "She has the jewelry store downtown . Apparently Mrs. Meyerson knew Gwen Cunningham in college. Maybe she can tell us something about Mr. Cunningham."

Doctor Henchcombe cleared his throat. "If you're through with me . . ."

"Sorry Hench. I'm getting ahead of myself. Let me just finish the report in case I have more questions."

"Tissue samples from major organs showed no abnormalities except for thickening of arteries indicating arteriosclerotic changes. . . "

"High blood pressure," Henchcombe interrupted.

". . . and early stages of diabetes."

"Uh huh."

"Hmmm . . . no other evidence of disease – in summary, death by nicotine poisoning, old scars indicates a previous suicide attempt at an early age.'"

"That's about it, gentlemen," Henchcombe said,

standing and giving his trousers a slight tweak so the creases fell straight, breaking just slightly at the top of his highly polished shoes. He placed his copy of the autopsy report in a soft leather folder and turned to leave the room.

"Oh, Hench," Dawson called after him, "see what you can get me on ALS."

Startled, Eggleton looked at Dawson.

Henchcombe turned back, his face puzzled.

"Symptoms, progression of the disease, that sort of thing."

"Are you in a hurry?"

"Whenever," Dawson said. Then amended, "Tomorrow."

Henchcombe nodded and pulled the door closed behind him.

"Relax, Sergeant. It's not me."

"Resnik?"

"Uh huh."

"You know," Eggleton said, "these slacks just came out of the cleaners, this shirt . . ." and he pinched the fabric between his thumb and forefinger, ". . . this shirt is brand new, and I polished my shoes last night."

"Apropos of what, Bill?" Dawson asked, gathering the autopsy report and shoving it into his briefcase, along with his charts and diagrams and Mrs. Cunningham's daily planner.

"Apropos of Henchcombe. He always makes me feel scruffy."

"I just figure he's overcompensating for his work. Probably comes from mucking about in dead bodies all day."

"Gross!"

"You ready to make a call on the ladies?"

"I just hate the thought of this," Eggleton said, making a face at the Styrofoam cup in his hand.

"So do I."

"I meant calling on the ladies – not the coffee."

"You have a better suggestion?" Dawson asked.

"I do," Eggleton said. "We know what Cunningham put in her notebook was right on target about Alexander. What if we tell Liske and Gentry about the notations. We can say we've found the ones we've checked – we don't need to tell them we've only been able to verify one – have proven accurate, and we would like to get their take on *r-l-n-s-p*. You could press them– bring up the young man they told us about who was fired because he was gay."

"Forgot to tell you. I looked into that yesterday afternoon – it was just like they told us. Seems Gwen Cunningham was behind the firing."

Eggleton shook his head. "Geez!" he said. "What a bitch!"

Dawson's eyebrows shot up. "Speaking ill of the dead, Sergeant?"

"This one. Anyway, we could try – before I have to pull the potty performance."

"You do have a way with words, Bill. But yes. Out of respect for your sensibilities, I will do as you suggest. I will tell them her notations are checking out, and we would like to know just what she meant by *r-l-n-s-p*. And, if I don't get anyplace with that, you are needing the bathroom. Got it?"

Eggleton made a face.

"It's 6:20. Let's get moving."

They rode in silence, Dawson at the wheel, picturing his diagram of Mavis's house; Eggleton remembering Sunday afternoon with his family.

Eggleton had played hide-and-seek with Elizabeth for what seemed like hours, his throat almost sore from his cries of 'Oh, no! You found me again!" (a cry which sent Elizabeth in paroxysms of giggles), helped her with her little piece of broiled salmon, mashed potatoes and carrots, and sang her a song as he tucked her into bed. That was followed by two glasses of wine with Laura, a long hot shower, and when he crawled into bed, Laura pulled him to her. Their loving was long and slow, delicious with their wisdom of each other. Eggleton slept well.

Dawson's Sunday evening had not been as delightful. His condo was rather dark, and smelled musty when he arrived there in the late afternoon after his visit with Andrew. He raised the blinds, opened windows, and sat down at the piano to play a Bach fugue. He loved fugues; the subject, the counter subject, the tonal conversation and development, the point where all the pieces came together in logical fashion – if only a murder investigation was so well constructed. He called Henchcombe and learned Henchcombe was on his way to his parents' home for Sunday dinner, but yes, he would be happy to meet with Dawson and Eggleton at 6:00 Monday morning. Dawson hung up, feeling slightly depressed a man of Henchcombe's age, which he estimated to be near his own, was still having Sunday dinner with his parents. Or was he slightly envious? That evening Dawson dined alone: cheese, crackers, an apple, some grapes and Wild Turkey - neat.

The home of Linda Gentry and Sandra Liske was a well-maintained, standard, ranch-style house, about fifteen years old. Tree roses bordered the walkway leading to the front porch.

Sandy Liske answered the door. She was wearing an emerald green cotton dress. Her hair was styled and, as far as Dawson could determine, her makeup was complete.

"Inspector!"

"Good morning. May we come in? I have a couple of quick items to sort out with you and Mrs. Gentry."

"We're due at school shortly. Can't this wait?"

"I'm afraid not. We'll be brief. I promise."

She stepped aside to let them in, the expression on her face one of exasperation – and unease.

"Who is it, Sandy?" a voice called from the back of the house.

"The police."

"Police. At this hour?" Linda Gentry came into the room, carrying a mascara wand. She was dressed in camel colored slacks and a creamy cotton shirt. Her hair stood in tufts, and she ran her fingers through it nervously.

"They have some questions," Sandy answered, dropping onto the sofa, sighing deeply.

"Oh, Inspector," Linda said, sounding as irritated as Sandy. She glanced at her watch. "Surely this can wait. It's terribly inconvenient."

"Murder is inconvenient, Mrs. Gentry."

"Murder!" Sandy put her hand to her mouth. "But I

thought . . . I hoped . . ." Her voice trailed off.

"In this case, inconvenient for Mrs. Cunningham. We can talk now, or I can have you pulled from your classes later today. For questioning. Downtown. Your choice."

"Sounds like more of a threat than a choice, Inspector," Linda Gentry said, her eyes narrowed and angry. "Should I call the school and tell them we'll be late?"

"I'll try not to keep you long," Dawson said, placing his briefcase next to Sandy and opening it. "I just need you both to show me exactly where you went during the afternoon: bathroom, kitchen, patio, drawing room, hallway." He pulled the diagram he had drawn from his briefcase. "And a question about a notation we found in Mrs. Cunningham's daily planner," he added in an off-handed way as he placed the diagram on the coffee table in front of Sandy.

Sandy gasped. "Daily planner?" Her face was flushed, her eyes brimming with tears; she brushed at them, smearing her makeup.

She cries more than Elizabeth, Eggleton thought.

"Let's do the diagram first." Dawson handed each of them a colored marker; pink for Sandy, yellow for Linda.

Sandy bit the cap off the marker, but when she tried to mark her path through the house, her hand shook, and the pink jittered across the paper. Eggleton squatted beside her. "Let me help you," he said, gently taking the marker from her hand. "You show me where you were, and I'll mark it."

Sandy nodded, a look of resignation in her eyes. She pointed to the drawing room and the patio.

When Eggleton and Sandy were finished, Eggleton

pushed the diagram across the coffee table to Linda who quickly made yellow dashes between the drawing room, the patio and the bathroom.

"I hope this is what you wanted, Inspector. Perhaps we could finish getting dressed so we're not late for school."

Dawson opened his notebook. "Just one small thing, Mrs. Gentry. And then we'll get out of your way. Mrs. Cunningham made notations in her daily planner next to the names of the people who would be attending the party. By your names, she wrote *r-l-n-s-p*. Does that mean anything to you?"

Sandy and Linda looked at each other; Sandy's face flushed, Linda's taut.

"You see," Dawson continued, "there were notations by each guest's name as well as Mrs. Dillon's name. And, from what we've been able to check out so far, the notations have proved accurate."

Eggleton suppressed a smile.

"So I'm looking at *r-l-n-s-p*," Dawson said, apparently studying his notes carefully, "and I'm getting *relationship*. Would I be wrong?"

Linda Gentry sighed. "I'll call the school," she said, nodding to Sandy.

bingo! Eggleton jotted in his notebook.

It was Sandy who began the story. Her voice, tentative at first, grew strong, much to the surprise of both Dawson and Eggleton.

"Yes," she said. "Linda and I are in a relationship, a lesbian relationship – which is what you want to know, isn't it Inspector? This is the result of a long-standing friendship

228

which became something more a short time ago. Both of us had been married and very much enjoyed the marriage bond, and we quite honestly surprised ourselves. Recently, as I explained to you when you interviewed me at Mavis's house, we moved in together, ostensibly to save money toward our retirement. But also to celebrate the love we share on a regular and more intimate level."

Dawson found himself in awe of the woman who was speaking with such eloquence – so unlike the quivering Sandy of their previous encounters; Eggleton found himself blushing.

Sandy turned to Linda, who had stepped quietly into the room, as though passing her a torch. "When Gwen talked with us on Saturday," Linda said, "she mentioned our living together and reminded us, implying of course, school boards do not take kindly to homosexuals among staff. I said *implying*, but it was crystal clear what she meant. When she left us to talk to some other poor soul, Sandy and I, almost simultaneously, decided we would put this living arrangement aside, at least until we retired. We are both eligible for retirement at fifty-five, and it's just a few years off for both of us."

"I decided right then to buy a small condo in a new development not too far from the school. So, those plans were made before Gwen died," Sandy said.

"Just before," Dawson said.

"But before," Sandy said with emphasis. "Before. Which is important."

WOW! Eggleton noted.

Dawson stood. "Thank you Mrs. Gentry, Mrs. Liske. I appreciate your honesty. The sergeant and I will be on our way. I hope you're not too late for school."

"The principal and vice principal are covering for us until we get there," Linda said as she closed the door firmly behind the two police officers.

"Well, you were right, Bill," Dawson said as they got into Dawson's car. "Bringing up the daily planner was all we needed."

"Thank you, God!"

"Whoever."

"We sure saw a different side of Mrs. Liske."

"We did, Bill. What do you think prompted the change?"

Eggleton shrugged. "I guess she gathered strength to talk about the relationship." He fastened his seatbelt. "So this morning I'm supposed to track down Mrs. Alexander's first husband's death – I'll get on it as soon as I get to the station. Anything else?"

"Yes. Transfer the diagrams to a white board. Also, put a motive chart on the board and all the cryptic notations from her notebook. Like I told Hench, I'm going to meet with Marjorie Meyerson . . ." he said, glancing at his watch . . . "hopefully this morning. In the meantime, I'm going to call someone I know in Social Security – tell him you'll be coming in with questions. I'll give him the name, so he can get a head start. I want to know a lot more about Mavis Dillon."

"How do you know he'll be willing to do this?"

"We go back a ways."

"Ah," Eggleton said. He nodded his head in the direction of the house they had just left. "Where do you put these two on your motive scale?"

"Hard to tell. If they were afraid of losing their jobs this close to retirement, that would be a strong motive. They would probably still draw their retirement pensions at fifty-five, but the money would be less. So money could be a factor. As far as reputation goes? Who knows?"

"You said something to Doctor Henchombe about going through Cunningham's house," Eggleton reminded Dawson.

"Later this afternoon. You're going with me, and I'll ask Mrs. Meyerson to go with us."

"Think she'll be willing?"

"I'm the police, Sergeant."

"Aye. That you are."

"Thank you, Andrew. Want to get some breakfast?"

"Aye."

CHAPTER THIRTEEN

Coffee With Cream and Sugar

*Deliver my soul, O Lord, from lying lips and
from a deceitful tongue.*
Psalm 120:2

"Mrs. Meyerson– Inspector Dawson is here," the young woman announced as they entered the office at the rear of the jewelry store. Glancing around the room, Dawson saw it was simply and elegantly furnished.

Marjorie, who was standing, her back to the door, turned, placing the manila envelope she had been holding, on her desk. "Thank you, Victoria," she said. "And we'll have some coffee when you have a moment."

"Inspector Jake Dawson," he said, extending his hand.

"Marjorie Meyerson," she responded, taking his hand in hers. Then she turned back to the desk. "The strangest thing," she said, picking up the envelope and shaking her head. Dawson could see MEYERSON JEWELRY printed in large irregular block letters on the front of the envelope. He raised his eyebrows. "I'm sorry. I know you're here about Gwen. How can I help you?"

"Don't apologize," Dawson said, pointing to the envelope. "The lettering makes me curious. Tell me why it's strange."

Marjorie laughed. "Probably nothing. Just a small crime that has apparently righted itself."

"Oh, now I am curious."

"Are you sure?"

"I'm the police. We're inquisitive by nature."

Marjorie smiled and handed Dawson the envelope.

He tipped it, and a strand of pearls slid into his hand "Whoa!" he said. "Are these the real thing?"

"They are. They were stolen from us one day last Christmas season – right off the tray. And a strand of imitation pearls – very fine imitation pearls with a broken clasp – was left in their place. I think someone brought them in to be fixed, saw an opportunity to take the real pearls, and . . ." She made a small dismissive gesture. "We were so busy – always are near the holidays – and we didn't notice the substitution until things quieted down just before closing."

"Did you notify the police?"

"No. No one saw them taken, so we had no evidence to give the police, and we are very judicious in making a claim to our insurance company – our premiums are high as you can imagine. Some things we have to write off. Now, six months later, this envelope was slipped through the mail slot sometime last night. Victoria said it was on the floor with the mail this morning when she unlocked. Somebody had second thoughts."

Although not an expert in jewelry, Dawson thought the pearls he held in his hand looked remarkably like a string of pearls he had seen just two days earlier – being mercilessly twisted. He placed them around his neck. Yes. Very similar in length. He turned and faced Marjorie who looked at him with raised eyebrows. "You know what they say, 'Pearls go with everything,'" he said.

She shook her head but allowed herself a small smile.

"Sorry. I couldn't resist. So you think someone had pangs of conscience and returned them?" He slipped the pearls into the envelope and returned it to Marjorie.

"I do." She placed the envelope on her desk.

"Hummm," Dawson said, remembering the notation of 'Meyerson's' by Nancy Gifford's name in Gwen Cunningham's daily planner. "Did you happen to keep the strand of imitation pearls?"

"I might have. I keep some odd pieces of jewelry in my bottom drawer – for what purpose I don't know. If I have them, that's where they would be."

"If they are, would you be able to have the clasp fixed and let me take them?"

She looked at him quizzically. "Does this have anything to do with Gwen's death? Because that's why you're here."

"I'm sorry. About the pearls, I can't say. But yes. Mrs. Cunningham's death is why I'm here."

Marjorie looked as though she was about to say more, but instead opened her desk drawer. She removed a small cardboard box, and, setting it on the desk, rummaged through a jumble of broken brooches and bracelets, single ear-rings, and rings with missing stones. "Ah!" she said, holding up a string of pearls Dawson found very similar to the ones in the manila envelope on Marjorie's desk. He took them from Marjorie and again slid the stolen strand from the envelope. Placing them side by side, he could see the luminescence of the real pearls, but, to his untrained eye, he would not have been able to tell the difference if he hadn't had them to compare.

Just then the young woman who had brought Dawson to Marjorie's office entered with a large silver tray which held a silver coffee service, two china cups and saucers, silver spoons and a small china plate with scones. Dawson took the tray from her and placed it on the coffee table that stood between the two small sofas at the far end of the room.

"Aaron's here today, Victoria," Marjorie said, handing her the strand of imitation pearls. "Please have him repair the clasp on these. The Inspector will be taking them with him when he leaves, so tell him soon as possible."

"Of course," Victoria said, as though her employer's request was an everyday event.

"Now, Inspector," Marjorie said as she sat on one of the sofas and gestured Dawson to the other. "How can I help you with Gwen's death?" She leaned over to pour coffee into the china cups, passing one to Dawson, who, used to the thick ceramic mugs at the station or the cardboard containers from Starbucks, found the fragile cup and saucer a challenge.

"Cream and sugar?" she asked with a nod to the tray.

"Yes," Dawson said and lavishly added both to his cup. "It makes a dessert out of coffee."

Marjorie smiled. "That looks good," she said, promptly adding two sugar lumps and a generous splash of cream to her own cup. Then she sat back and, when Dawson asked about her relationship with Gwen Cunningham, proceeded to tell Dawson of Gwen's parents' visit to the college and the suicide attempt. She said she felt guilty about her role in helping Gwen decorate her dorm room with the posters and the Chianti bottle and how she had urged Gwen to try some makeup.

"I can understand you would feel that way," Dawson said when she finished her story.

She quickly blinked back what threatened to be tears. "So you think I did the wrong thing?"

"I didn't say that. I said I can understand how you might *think* you did the wrong thing. Which is different. What I think is you did the right thing. You helped her when she asked for help. You had no way of knowing what her parents were like or how they would respond. Gwen knew, but she went ahead with her plan anyway. Where would you say the responsibility lies?"

"She was only eighteen – and she wanted so much to belong."

"Yes. And you were eighteen – and wanted to help her."

Marjorie sipped her coffee. Finally she said, "Do you realize you're the first person I've told this to that has said you understand my feelings. Of guilt. Thank you."

Dawson inclined his head, never taking his eyes off the lovely woman in front of him. She was slender without being thin. A simple gray dress, lightly draped across the hips, emphasized a well-maintained figure that probably was not accustomed to cream and sugar in coffee. Her hair, dark and shot with silver, picked up the tone of the dress. She wore black hose, low-heeled black shoes, and accented her ensemble with a large silver pendant and silver loop earrings. She echoed the understated elegance of the jewelry store. Were her eyes gray? Or green?

"Let's go back to her parent's visit," he said. "You

mentioned Mrs. Cunningham's father looked as though he might be experiencing some degree of sexual satisfaction from his wife's display of anger. Did you have reason to believe Gwen might have been sexually molested by her father?"

"Oh, Inspector," Marjorie said, shaking her head, "isn't sexual abuse of children the thing we hear most about these days? It's as though, if you want to write a book or get on television, you have to have been sexually abused as a child. No. I had no reason to believe Gwen was the victim of sexual abuse, but I was naïve in those days and really wasn't even aware such things happened. It was a gentler time – perhaps it didn't happen as often." She paused. "Or perhaps I'm still being naïve."

"It's the first thing that came to my mind, given your description of her father." He paused, remembering Henchcombe's autopsy report. "There are many levels of sexual molestation – not all of which involve intercourse."

"Yes," Marjorie said. "There are. I will tell you Gwen suffered great emotional abuse at the hands of those parents. As you said, she was just a girl, trying to be like other girls, at least for that little bit of time. I saw those monster parents several times over the next few years while we were in college, although I made it a point never to be in their presence for long. They were sanctimonious, Bible thumping hypocrites, putting Gwen's acquaintances down at every possible opportunity, spouting scripture, and decrying the fall of the college."

"I wonder why they permitted her to continue there."

"It was a religious college so, first of all, I figured they thought a more liberal college would be even worse, and secondly – and it's hateful for me to say this – but I think they fed off finding fault."

"You obviously felt strongly about these people, Mrs. Meyerson," Dawson said.

"I did. And please call me Marjorie."

"Thank you. I will." He paused. "I imagine no one calls you Marge."

She smiled. "A few have tried."

Dawson laughed. "OK. Back to what I said. You obviously felt strongly about those people."

"I think the only way Gwen could survive in that household and hang on to their love was to bring them the stories of the transgressions of her classmates. I believe they got a secret pleasure out of hearing her tales, and the relationship fed on Gwen's college experiences– once they brainwashed her of her small try for freedom. Lord knows what went on in that family the summer after Gwen's suicide attempt." She shuddered.

"Were you there when her parents came to get her?" Dawson asked.

"No. Gwen was in the hospital, and I wasn't allowed to see her. Her parents came and picked her up at the hospital, and the dorm mother packed Gwen's things. I didn't see Gwen again until the next fall."

"How was she then?"

"Well, she was wearing heavy bracelets to cover the scars, but she never mentioned the suicide incident and neither did I. Still, I felt responsible for Gwen . . . guilt you know. Logic tells me if it hadn't been the makeup, it would have been something else, but logic and the heart don't always sleep well together." She stopped. "I haven't answered your question, have I? I'd say she was different. Harder. Colder. And very critical of everyone – always looking for some infraction of the rules."

"An emissary of a vengeful God."

"Or perhaps an emissary of her parents who believed themselves emissaries of a vengeful God. Some of the girls started getting anonymous letters and phone calls. Mrs. Starkley got some anonymous calls, too. I know Gwen was behind it." She paused, picking up a small napkin from the tray and folding it into accordion pleats. "A huge indicator was that the phone calls and letters stopped when she got sick, and they started again when she was well. After the suicide attempt, Gwen had times when she'd lock herself in her dorm room and refuse to come out. I guess she came out to use the bathroom when we were all in class or asleep, but I can honestly say, we never saw her during those times. I would bang on the door." Marjorie laughed, a small laugh, falling just short of humor. "But she would say, 'Go away.' I'd sneak food up to her and tell her it was by the door. Sometimes she ate it, but usually she didn't. I think that was probably the beginning of her periods of depression."

Marjorie took a deep breath and put the napkin back on the tray. "Also, the way I knew she was behind the phone calls and letters was she actually told me once – it was just shortly after she came back to school – she had called a girl named Rachael and told her she had seen her boyfriend kissing some other girl. Rachael broke up with him immediately. Gwen seemed proud of herself. I said I wouldn't speak to her if I ever found out she did something like that again – so she was real careful around me."

"But you suspected."

"More than suspected – but except for the incident with Rachael, I had no proof. Some of the girls would ask me how I could be friends with her, but I was very honest with them. I told them I felt some degree of responsibility for what happened." She picked up the napkin again and then put it down. "They were a lovely bunch of young women, Inspector. Tolerant and forgiving most of the time. I think they all recognized an unhappy person. A lot of Gwen's vindictiveness died on the vine – mostly people just ignored her. Not all, of course. Several romances collapsed because of Gwen, and I do know two girls were expelled for what was termed an 'improper relationship.' I don't think Gwen did anything directly; I think she told her parents about the relationship, and her parents notified the college."

Dawson, who didn't limit his practice of jumping from topic to topic to when he was interviewing suspects, changed the subject. "Let me tell you the names of the people who were at the party Saturday and see if you remember Mrs. Cunningham saying anything about any of them," Dawson said, flipping the pages of his notebook and reading aloud.

When he finished, Marjorie laughed. "She had a lot to say about most of them, but I don't remember anything specific. Usually I tuned her out when she got to gossiping, but, honestly I don't remember. . ." She stopped, frowning. "There was – let's see, last time I had lunch with her I think it was . . . she said something about Sandy Liske . . . something to the effect it was a good thing Sandy didn't teach sex ed." Marjorie shook her head. "I suppose she was talking about Linda and Sandy, but I wasn't going to give her the satisfaction, so I didn't say anything. And Mavis." Marjorie pursed her lips. "Poor Mavis. Gwen really disliked her. I was always afraid if Gwen ever got the slightest thing on Mavis, she'd never let go. Fortunately, Mavis keeps herself to herself. Otherwise. . ." She shook her head again.

"Any of the other people?"

"Nothing I can remember."

"If she disliked the people at the church so much, why do you think she continued in the church?"

"I've often wondered," Marjorie said, "and the only conclusion I can draw is, given her early, very fundamentalist upbringing, she couldn't turn her back on the church." She paused for a moment. "I'd hate to think she saw it as a fertile ground for her little hobby. And I don't want you to think I have anything against fundamentalist Christians, Inspector. Not at all. Gwen's parents used their extreme viewpoint to feed their own sick minds. They were an aberration. We hear about it all the time in the news – the extremist mentality."

Dawson nodded. "Why wouldn't she continue in a fundamentalist congregation?"

Marjorie shrugged. "I don't know. Maybe it was a small step of independence – from her parents. Who are, incidentally, dead."

"Besides St. Francis, what organizations did she belong to?"

Marjorie laughed. "What ones didn't she belong to would be a better question. Just about everything in town at one time or another. There was the Historical Society, Castlemont Docents, Friends of the Library . . ." She paused. "Garden Club I think, School Board, Genealogical Society,

City Council this past year." She shrugged her shoulders. "There may have been more; she always had some meeting or other to go to."

"Did you hear of her other . . . how should I put it . . . hobbies? People who were damaged by her rumors or gossip?

"Oh, Inspector. That could take a long time."

"I have lots of time," Dawson said, and poured a fresh cup of coffee for them both. The cream and sugar passed between them.

"This is delicious."

"Glad I could lead you astray," Dawson said – and immediately wished he hadn't.

She didn't seem to notice.

"Well, there was Debbie who died because she refused to have an abortion. Everybody in town knows about that."

"Father Greg told me yesterday. Do you know of other instances?"

She looked at Dawson as though deciding whether to answer him or not. Finally she said, "I'm not really comfortable with this, Inspector."

"I understand. But you must understand – if she was killed – I have an obligation to find the person responsible. Secondly, anything you tell me is in strict confidence unless it pertains directly to her death."

Marjorie sighed. "There was a man here in town, definitely not one of the guests at Saturday's party. Gwen told me she had found out he was involved with another woman. He and his wife had been having marital troubles, money and his work hours, teenage children, communication – at least that's what his wife thought were the problems – and they were getting counseling when his wife heard about the affair. Inspector – this has nothing to do with the people at the bishop's party."

"How did the wife hear?"

"She received an anonymous letter. When Gwen told me about the affair in the first place, I said, 'Don't you dare say a word to anyone, do you hear?' But Gwen got a funny little smile on her face, and I knew it was too late. Ironically, the husband had broken off the affair when the counseling started. It was all over when Gwen sent the letter, but the wife couldn't deal with the additional information, and she left him. Took the children with her and went home to her folks. In Southern California." She paused. "Inspector, I feel like I'm just spreading tales. I wish I thought it was doing some good."

"You're right, Marjorie. None of what you've told me is relevant to Saturday's party. However, you've given me a feel for just what her meddling was and how it affected others, and I'm very grateful. Tell me, how did she come to move here in the first place?"

Marjorie set her cup down and leaned forward, clasping her hands. "She came to Castlemont about twenty years ago. One day, out of the blue, I got a call. 'This is Gwen,' a voice said. I was preoccupied with my five-year old at the time. She was crying about a bad day at kindergarten or some such crisis, and it took time for the name to register. 'Gwen,' she said again. 'Gwen Kittleson. I'm in town and thought I'd look you up.' "

"I invited her over for dinner, and that was when I found out she was more than just in town; she'd actually moved here." Marjorie reached for her coffee cup and took a sip. "I wasn't anxious to renew a painful relationship, but of course I didn't say anything. She was full of her plans for renovating the Fischer estate, so I knew she had plenty of money. Any questions I had about her husband, since she said her name was Cunningham now, were hastily disposed of, which led me to believe he might be fictitious." She held her hand up. "I don't know that for a fact. But if I'm right, then don't you think it a bit ironic for her to choose a name containing the word *cunning*?"

"I hadn't thought of that," Dawson said, sipping his coffee.

"Sometimes I think she moved here because of me, sensing my feelings of guilt, perhaps, knowing she could manipulate me to some extent." Marjorie shrugged. "Of course, maybe it's just me being paranoid. Maybe she thought of me as her only friend. Anyway, we lunched together about once a month. I heard from other sources about her various activities of poking and prying into people's affairs, but she rarely mentioned anything. She would have known I didn't approve."

She sighed. "I didn't disabuse her notion we were friends until just recently, Inspector. When this happened – this business with the anonymous letter to the man's wife – I told her I didn't want to see her anymore."

"How did she take it?"

"She cried, phoned a couple of times, begging me to have lunch with her, but I told her I was busy. So actually, it's been several months since I've seen Gwen."

"Were you concerned she might spread some gossip about you?"

Marjorie laughed. "I would wish her luck, Inspector. I lead a righteous and boring existence, and I think the whole town knows that. No, I wasn't concerned. Anyway, there was often a kernel of truth in Gwen's viciousness – and I had no kernel for her to latch on to. My reason for befriending her at all was the guilt I carried, but she just pushed me to the limit – you can only play on guilt so long." She set her coffee cup in the saucer; it made a tiny bell of sound. "You know, Inspector, I think the real tragedy about Gwen is her potential was so great and so misdirected."

"Her potential?"

Marjorie sat back. "It was as though Gwen could read your mind or even your soul. She had an uncanny ability to see directly into a person. Just one small incident or clue, and she would build an entire scenario about that person. And very often with great accuracy. With those skills, she would have gone far as a therapist, or a doctor, or a clergywoman – someone in one of the helping professions. Or a detective, like you, Inspector."

Obviously not a helping profession, Dawson thought and smiled slightly.

"Instead she chose to misuse her gifts," Marjorie continued.

"Tell me more about this insight of Mrs. Cunningham's."

"More gossip," Marjorie said with a sigh. "Well, I remember once we were having lunch, and this elegantly dressed woman passed us. I commented on her exquisite clothes, and Gwen said, 'She shoplifts most of them.'"

"Oh, come now, Gwen," I said. "Have you ever seen her shoplift anything?"

"Gwen said she hadn't, but she had been in a store, the hosiery department to be exact, when this woman had been there, and she could tell from the way the woman kept watching the clerk the woman was planning to shoplift. I asked Gwen why she didn't stick around to watch and turn the woman in, and Gwen said, 'Well, Marjorie, I didn't want to get involved, you know.' Which was a laugh, but I let it pass. The funny thing was – several weeks after that lunch with Gwen – I read in the paper where this woman had been arrested on charges of shoplifting."

"Let me ask you this," Dawson said, again changing the subject. "Do you think Mrs. Cunningham's earlier attempt at suicide was simply a ploy to get attention?"

"No. I got a glimpse of the bloody water after the ambulance came. Mrs. Starkley forgot to lock the bathroom door. Ghoulish, but what can I say? We were teenagers. But if you had seen that, you would know it was a serious attempt. I have no doubt in my mind she meant to die – none whatsoever."

"Knowing her as you did, do you think she might have taken her own life this time?"

"Yes, I do," Marjorie said.

"In such a way as to place guilt on others?"

Marjorie's answer was emphatic. "In just such a way, Inspector – especially the vestry from the church."

"You're saying she would sacrifice her own life to get back at a group of people."

"Especially if she was in one of her depressed episodes, yes. Or sensed one coming on. Or was just coming out of one. Suicide is never far from the thoughts of a depressed person, so yes, I think it possible."

"You have some experience in the field of psychology?"

"I took a lot of psychology in college. For a while I thought I might like to pursue psychology as a profession. But during my last year of college I met and fell in love with a wonderful Jewish boy, David Meyerson. His family owned a jewelry store in Seattle, and I had gone in to buy earrings for my mother. We had coffee that afternoon – which led to other dates. So I finished my degree, and we were married the summer after I graduated." She smiled at the memory. "My parents weren't thrilled – they were casual Methodists and were fearful I would convert. That wouldn't have been the case. David was ethnically Jewish, not religiously Jewish. His parents were devout Jews, but it wasn't for him."

"And you were a Methodist girl."

"I went to a Methodist college and did all the requisite religion courses which I found of great historical interest, but, no, I was never enamored of organized religion either."

"I know your husband passed away some time ago. I read about it in the paper."

"Yes. David's been gone five years. A massive heart attack at the age of 50." She turned her head away for a moment, fingering the silver pendant.

"I'm sorry," Dawson said.

Marjorie turned back, looking hard at Dawson. "But you're not here about my history. And I also think you wouldn't be here if you thought Gwen's death was suicide. Would I be right in that assumption, Inspector?"

Dawson nodded, picking up one of the scones from

the plate and biting into it. Crumbs fell down the front of his sport coat.

"Just brush them off, Inspector. Scones that don't crumble aren't any good. Besides, we have a little hand vac for just this sort of thing." She bit into a scone. "Yum!" she said, and brushed at the crumbs that fell on her dress.

"Did you ever suggest professional help to Mrs. Cunningham?"

"Many times. Gwen would just laugh at me and tell me I was all the professional help she needed. One day I came right out and said it was too great a burden for me to carry, but Gwen became angry and said she was handling it."

"Yes," Dawson said. "That's often the way." He stood, slipping his notebook into his pocket, and brushing one last crumb from his jacket. "Can I help with the hand vac?"

She shook her head. "No, but thanks."

"By the way. Do you know who her executor is?"

"Her lawyer is Regina Stinson. Regina's a personal friend of mine, so, when I heard about Gwen's death, I took the liberty of calling her."

Dawson knew the name well. "I'll give her a call later," he said. "And thank you. You've given me some valuable insight. I want to go through her house," he added. "Would you go with me?"

"Me?" she said, standing as well.

"I don't know what I'm looking for, Marjorie, but I think you might be a help."

She looked doubtful. "I was only there a few times, Inspector."

"Please."

She sighed. "Of course," she said. "When did you have in mind."

"This afternoon."

"My goodness!" she said, walking to her desk and opening a large date book. She frowned, pursing her lips. "Ummmm. . ." she muttered, making pencil checks by several items. "I could go at three o'clock, Inspector."

"Perfect. Thank you! Shall I pick you up here?"

"Yes," she said and followed him out, pulling her office door closed behind her. "I'll walk with you to Aaron's workroom," she said. "We can pick up the necklace before you leave." Then she turned and faced Dawson. "Am I to understand you know who it belongs to?"

"Perhaps. Would you press charges?"

"No. I suspect this person has suffered enough angst. I don't want to add to that," she said, gesturing Dawson ahead of her into a small room where an elderly man, wearing a jeweler's magnifying lens, sat at a workbench. He looked up as she entered and handed her the pearl necklace. "Thank you, Aaron," she said.

This is a remarkable woman, Dawson thought, watching as she placed the necklace on a bed of cotton in a narrow silver colored box and tied the box with a silver ribbon. "I'm glad Gwen Cunningham had someone like you to mourn her."

"Oh," Marjorie said, her eyes bright with unshed tears. "I mourned Gwen over thirty years ago, when she slipped away in a tub of bloody water." She handed Dawson the box. "That's when she really died, Inspector."

"It's Jake."

" Jake."

CHAPTER FOURTEEN

Nancy Gifford Redux

As the thief is ashamed when he is found...
Je. 2:26

Nancy Gifford opened the door to Dawson. She was wearing a baggy black tee shirt that said I HATE HOUSEWORK in bright green letters, jeans, and a red scarf around her hair. In her hand was a dust rag.

"Inspector!"

"May I come in?"

"Of course." Looking down at her clothes, she added unnecessarily, "You caught me cleaning house." A vacuum cleaner stood in the entry hall. To the left, Dawson could see into a small room, which, except for being scrupulously tidy, was nearly a replica of Father Greg's office at the church: a desk, crowded bookcases, two visitor chairs. A staircase led to the upstairs rooms, while the entry hall jogged to the side of the stairs before leading to the rooms at the back of the house. It was an old house, with high ceilings, wainscoting, and highly polished, dark wood floors. Dawson noticed, while Nancy might sport a tee shirt proclaiming she hated housework, she was very good at it.

"Not your favorite chore, I take it."

She patted the front of her shirt. "Greg got tired of me borrowing his old shirts for cleaning, so he had this made for me." She gave Dawson a small smile. "He's not in," she said. "He's at the hospital making calls."

"I know. I called his office, and they told me he would be at the hospital this afternoon. It's you I came to see," Dawson said. "Without him here – or my sergeant."

"Oh!" The weak smile faded.

"I believe I have something that belongs to you," he said, pulling the small jewelry box from his pocket. He held it out to her.

Nancy studied his face as she reluctantly put out her hand to take the box. "What's this?" she asked, setting the dust rag on a small hall table.

"Why don't you open it and see."

Slowly, Nancy untied the silver ribbon and removed the lid. At the sight of the necklace, her eyes welled with tears, and she turned from Dawson. Her shoulders began to shake.

"You know, Mrs. Gifford, I think you should tell me about these pearls. Let's go to the kitchen. You can show me where the tea is, and I'll make us a cup while you get yourself sorted. Then we'll talk." He put his hand on her elbow and led her down the hall.

Nancy's sobs had subsided to an occasional sniffle, and the tea had gone cold when she finished telling Dawson the story of the pearls: how her mother thought they were real, how she and her mother had called them their insurance, and the trip to the jeweler when she found out they were fake. She told him about her anger at her father, and how she had taken the real pearls from Meyerson's. "I don't want Greg to know," she said. Dawson had lost count of the number of times she said it.

"Unless they're directly connected to Mrs. Cunningham's death, there's no reason he should know," Dawson assured her, "but I need you to tell me everything that happened Saturday."

"What could my taking the pearls from Meyerson's possibly have to do with what happened Saturday?"

"You'll have to let me be the judge of that," Dawson said.

"Besides, I still don't understand how you knew they were mine."

Dawson sighed. He could tell she was going to avoid discussing Saturday as long as she possibly could. That was all right; he had time. Stretching his legs out under the pine table, he looked around the kitchen. It was a busy, pleasant room. Childish drawings held in place with vegetable and fruit magnets covered the refrigerator. Bright canisters, a large cookie jar, a vase of flowers and jars of home-canned fruits decorated the counters. A blue checkered cloth, which matched the cushions on the chairs and the tall counter stools, covered the table where they sat. A bright yellow kitchen cabinet with glass doors held a display of yellow, blue and white pottery dishes. Rag rugs in shades of yellow and blue lay scattered on the floor.

"I had some clues, Mrs. Gifford."

"Ah, yes. The detective." Her voice was bitter, and Dawson wondered where her anger was directed.

He continued. "In her daily planner, Mrs. Cunningham made a notation under Saturday's date. It said, *Nancy – Meyerson's*. In addition, you were preoccupied with your necklace Saturday when we talked to you.

You twisted the beads until the sergeant and I thought you would break the strand. Then, this morning, when I went to talk to Mrs. Meyerson about Mrs. Cunningham, I happened to arrive just as she was sorting her mail. An envelope, addressed in block letters and containing the real pearls, was among the mail. I put it all together and came up with Nancy Gifford. It would appear I was right."

"It was a coincidence," Nancy said. "You being at Meyerson's at just the right time."

Dawson shrugged. "Being a coincidence doesn't negate its value as information."

"Did she have notes in her daily planner about the other people at the party?"

"Maybe we should just stick with the notation about you."

Nancy pulled a tissue from her pocket. It was soggy and useless, and she threw it at the wastebasket with an impatient gesture. Dawson stood and pulled a paper towel from the roll under the cabinet. "About Saturday," he said as he handed it to her.

Nancy blew her nose and put the towel in her pocket. "I was twisting the pearls at the party, and Gwen said something to me about if I didn't stop twisting them, they'd break and we'd all be on our hands and knees looking for them." Nancy stopped for a moment, tracing a line of check on the table cloth with her forefinger. Then she glanced up at Dawson. "I was nervous. I hadn't wanted to wear them, and I was feeling terribly guilty about taking them from Meyerson's, but Greg asked me to wear them for the bishop's sherry party, and I didn't know how to tell him I didn't want to, so I did." She swiped at her eyes with the back of her hand. "Well, Gwen went on and on about how beautiful the pearls were and how she was going to congratulate Greg on his good taste and about seeing me at Meyerson's looking at the pearls and how Meyerson's needed greater security." Nancy paused and took a deep breath. "Anyway, I had decided that day, before Gwen ever came up to me, I would return them to Meyerson's, and then I would just have to tell Greg I lost them."

Dawson nodded, thinking Nancy Gifford had some very childlike qualities: the tears, the breathy little voice, her long, convoluted sentences, and he wondered how she fared in her role as Rector's wife. *I don't like her very much* he thought and slapped his mental hand.

"What else did Mrs. Cunningham say to you about the pearls?"

Nancy took a tremulous breath before going on to relate her Saturday afternoon conversation with Gwen Cunningham, how Gwen had said they were so much nicer than the string Nancy usually wore.

"She didn't say something like, 'I know you took those pearls from Meyerson's, and I'm going to tell Father Greg,' or words to that effect?"

"Oh, no. Gwen was much too subtle. She said she was going to *congratulate*, and that was the word she used, *congratulate*, Greg on getting real pearls for me – just letting me know she knew. That's the way she was. She just let you sweat it out, imagine the worst." Nancy smiled wryly. "Since she was capable of the worst, it didn't take much imagination."

"And you thought if she did congratulate him on getting you real pearls, he would find out they weren't your mother's after all."

"Yes."

"You said he never knew your mother's pearls weren't real."

"Right. But if Gwen said something about this strand being so much nicer than the other strand, he'd figure it out."

"As a rule, would he know real pearls from fake?"

Nancy shook her head. "No. If it were a first-edition book, he would, but pearls and pop-it beads, or rhinestones and diamonds, it would be all the same to him unless he was told otherwise. He just likes the way they look." She smiled, a sad little smile, her face still damp from tears.

"Tell me about returning the pearls," Dawson said.

"It was about eight-thirty Saturday evening. Greg was upstairs reading to the children from one of the Frog and Toad books, so I called up, said I was going to run to Rite-Aid for something – did he want anything? I bought a package of padded mailing envelopes – I'm sure you saw it at Mrs. Meyerson's – and a black felt-tip marker. I printed the name on the envelope and stuck the necklace inside." She took a deep breath and continued. "I drove to the mall. There weren't many people around that end of the mall, so I parked a distance from Meyerson's and walked up to the store and slipped it through the mail slot. I'm positive nobody saw me. And then I came on home." She shrugged. "Actually, it was very easy, and I kick myself for not doing it sooner."

Dawson nodded as though agreeing.

"Does Mrs. Meyerson know it was me?"

"No."

"Are you going to tell her?"

"Probably not."

"Just probably?"

"Have you told me everything that happened Saturday – your conversation with Mrs. Cunningham and where you were during the party?"

"This sounds a bit like blackmail, Inspector."

"Perhaps. But if the pearls should prove to have a direct bearing on the death of Mrs. Cunningham, this information will come out."

"Which is a nice way of saying, 'If you murdered Mrs. Cunningham, Mrs. Gifford.'" There was bitterness in her voice again. "Am I right? Do I need a lawyer?"

"No. At this point, I have no reason to think you're any more responsible for her death than anyone else who attended the party."

"But now you think I had a motive for wanting her dead."

"The question would be, is it a strong enough motive to kill her?"

Nancy shook her head. "I didn't kill her. I'm not capable of such an action, not even to protect this secret. And I have told you everything."

"You asked if I would tell Mrs. Meyerson. You should know she said she wouldn't press charges. She felt whoever took the pearls in the first place had obviously suffered enough, or person would never have returned them. She would just like to forget the whole thing. So, as I said before, unless you have not told me everything, and I find out the pearls are significant to the death of Mrs. Cunningham, I will consider it to be a closed issue."

Nancy leaned her head back, her eyes closed. "Thank you, Inspector. Thank you from the bottom of my heart. I did a foolish thing and jeopardized the dearest thing I have – my family. I've learned a lot. I suppose I was so angry at my father . . ." She blew her nose again.

Dawson folded his arms and leaned toward her across the table. "He gave you a sense of security you wouldn't otherwise have had, Mrs. Gifford."

"But it was based on false information," she protested. "My mother thought the pearls were real. She might have tried to sell them."

"Perhaps your father knew she never would. Besides, I'm sure he thought he would live to take care of you both." He resisted saying *Get over it!*

"Still," Nancy persisted, "it was false security. And my mother and I believed in it."

"Some might say the same of religion," Dawson, who had had enough of Nancy Gifford, said softly.

She looked at him, startled. "They would be wrong, Inspector." There was no trace of the little girl about her now.

Maybe she's more mature than she acts, Dawson thought. He stood and picked up the cups and saucers from the table. As he carried them to the sink, he said, "Just one more question, and I'll let you get back to your housecleaning, Mrs. Gifford. Did you happen to remember any more about when you saw Mrs. Cunningham in the hallway? Perhaps you remember if she was carrying her sherry glass."

"You asked me that before, and I've thought about it, but I honestly can't remember if she was or not. Sorry."

"Well, thank you for your help."

Nancy's expression was one of surprise. "Have I helped?"

"A great deal." And, although he said it as a matter of courtesy, as he thought about it, he realized it was true. Now he knew from one more source the accuracy of Mrs. Cunningham's notations in her date book and also just how Mrs. Cunningham operated; she hinted – with Nancy and Linda and Sandy and the Alexanders – about what she knew and let her victims sweat.

Then he frowned, aware he was thinking about those people as victims, and that compromised his role as Mrs. Cunningham's advocate. And if not him, then no one.

CHAPTER FIFTEEN

Gwen Cunningham at Home

But I know thy abode...
2 Kings 19:27

Dawson did not have a firm picture in mind of what Gwen Cunningham's home would look like, but he was not prepared for the half-timbered mansion sitting well back from the road on tended lawns. "Oh My God!" he muttered, stopping by the front door. "So this was hers. I'd seen it before, but I didn't know who it belonged to."

Eggleton, sitting in the back seat (and a bit irritated he was not up front where he usually sat), was less restrained. "Holy sh . . ." he started but modified to "cow!" in deference to Marjorie Meyerson who now sat in the passenger seat. "That's really something!"

Marjorie turned to Eggleton, a tiny smile on her face, her eyes twinkling. "It is rather magnificent, isn't it? It was the Fischer estate. Gwen had it completely renovated."

"She lived here alone?" Dawson asked.

"Yes. She used a cleaning service twice a month. Other than that, she managed by herself."

"Even when she was ill?"

"I think she canceled the cleaning service when she wasn't feeling well – anyway that's what I heard. She pretty much holed up, and she probably didn't want people in the house."

"Do you know the name of the service?"

"As a matter of fact, I do," Marjorie said. "It's the same service we use at the store.

"If you will give me the name, Mrs. Meyerson, I'll make a note of it," Eggleton said, pulling his pad from his pocket.

Dawson stretched as he got out of the car. Looking around at the grounds, he said, "I suppose she employed a gardening service."

"Several times a week, I think. Last I heard she was using a service connected with Tyler Nursery."

Eggleton, who was looking about in amazement at the gardens and house, stumbled slightly as they climbed the stairs to the front door.

"Easy Sergeant," Dawson said, grabbing Eggleton's elbow.

"Sorry. I was gawking."

Dawson bit back a comment about falling down on the job and pulled a ring of keys from a manila envelope. "These were in her purse," he said, selecting one and easing it into the lock. "I'm probably going to activate an alarm system," he added as he stepped through the door. But all was silent.

The furnishings Dawson could see from the entry-way resembled a display in a furniture store: coordinated and unused. "It doesn't take long for a house to feel empty," he commented to Marjorie.

"It was always like this," she said, wrapping her arms around herself and shivering slightly. "I never really liked coming here, because it never felt like a home. I got the feeling Gwen resided here, but she didn't live here." She looked at Dawson, her eyes sad. "I wonder if she really ever lived any place."

"Perhaps for those few days when you helped her decorate her dorm room," Dawson said, his eyes holding hers.

Marjorie turned away. "I don't know what you want me to do while we're here, Jake," she said. "I'm not sure how my being here will help you solve a death that occurred someplace else."

Dawson noticed she did not say 'murder' and he looked at Eggleton, but Eggleton was studying the crown moldings and rolling her use of *Jake* around in his mind.

"Sergeant Eggleton and I will be going through drawers and cupboards, desks, closets, anyplace where she might have kept papers or documents or substances which could pertain to her death. I want you here in case we have questions about anything we find."

Right, Eggleton thought. He had seen the way Dawson's eyes followed every move Marjorie made. And he had to admit they were nice moves. *An economy of grace.* He smiled as he marveled at his own poetry.

Marjorie looked skeptical.

"Did she use a desk?"

"I think there's one in her den," Marjorie said, leading the way down the hall.

The desk revealed a drawer of canceled checks, filed by number and dating back seven years, a drawer of large envelopes containing tax returns, a drawer with daily planners from 2010 to 2014, and still another drawer with information on investments, statements, and correspondence with a brokerage firm. On the desktop, a brass coil held current bills. An expandable folder– the pockets labeled medical, utilities, house repair/upkeep, food, entertainment and donations – contained paid receipts. Dawson noted the entertainment pocket was empty. The center desk drawer, like all the others, was scrupulously neat; not a pencil, paper, or paper clip out of alignment. There was no evidence of personal correspondence.

Beyond the diaries, except to gather insight into the fastidious nature of Gwen Cunningham, the search of the desk had been unrewarding, and Dawson decided the bedroom closet was next.

It was with a sense of awe the three had stood in the doorway viewing Gwen Cunningham's clothes and accessories. "*Precise* takes on a whole new meaning," Eggleton muttered, peering over Dawson's shoulder.

"OCD crosses my mind," Marjorie said.

"Was she like this in college?"

Marjorie shook her head. "Not this bad. Oh, maybe lining up the silverware just so – but she would do that when we lunched together here. I didn't think much of it."

Gwen Cunningham's dresses hung on a rod across the far end of the closet. They were sorted according to length, the longest being on the far left, ascending toward the right. A half inch difference in hem length determined the dress's location on the rod. The right side of the closet was comprised of shelves. One held sweaters, meticulously folded and stacked by color. Shoes, positioned by heel height, stood on a low shelf. Scarves, neatly folded and arranged by color, took up much of one shelf while a satin box holding tightly coiled belts sat on the end of the scarf shelf. On the left side of the closet were two rods; the upper held blouses and jackets, again arranged according to length while the bottom rod was for skirts, their position also determined by length.

"I don't see slacks," Dawson said.

"I never saw her wear them," Marjorie said. "Not even in college."

The spread on the double bed was as taut as a military cot, and Dawson resisted the temptation to bounce a quarter off it. Bureau drawers revealed hose, rolled into nylon balls and sorted by color: beige, navy, black. In another drawer were rigid garments, apparently designed to support and minimize Gwen Cunningham's girth. Dawson recognized only slips, panties and bras. The bras, too, were neatly folded into squares.

Marjorie pointed to the bras and shook her head. "That's not easy to do," she said.

"What?"

"Fold them like that. Women aren't exactly flat, you know."

Dawson laughed.

Eggleton blushed.

A large jewelry box on the dresser contained costume jewelry: in the bottom drawer of the box were necklaces and beads arranged serpentine fashion in a single layer, in the middle drawer earrings – sorted by size and carefully clipped to the velvet dividers; brooches lay in the top drawer along with several sets of massive silver and gold bracelets. A small key with a safe deposit box number lay in the corner of the top drawer. "That must be where she keeps the real jewelry," Marjorie said. "She had some lovely pieces."

"Any chance of a safe here in the house?" Dawson asked.

Marjorie shrugged. "I wouldn't know."

Dawson looked at Eggleton who nodded and left the room.

Gwen Cunningham's medicine cabinet rivaled a drugstore in Dawson's estimation. Shelves of prescription drugs, mingled with over-the-counter drugs, began with Advil and ended with Zylocaine. Dawson made a note of the prescription drugs, including Ativan, Ambien, and Halcion. He would call Hench as soon as he got back to the office. Or home, he amended, glancing at his watch.

The kitchen revealed little. By that time, Dawson was not surprised to find the spices in alphabetical order. There were frozen dinners, arranged by contents and neatly stacked, ice cream, and frozen cheesecakes in the freezer, while the refrigerator contained a pound of butter, a quart of milk, various cheeses, and a half empty bottle of Fume Blanc. A wine rack on the counter held more wines. Eggleton, who had joined them following his search for a safe, peered at the labels. "My God!" he exclaimed. "Even the wines are alphabetized!"

"Find anything?" Dawson asked.

Eggleton shook his head. "I looked behind all the pictures. Also checked the bookcases. Nothing." He looked around. "Which doesn't rule out some sort of hiding place—an old house like this – but I didn't find anything."

"I'll take the key," Dawson said, "And get an order to open the safe deposit box." He turned to Marjorie. "Could you identify her jewelry?"

"You mean, go to the bank with you?"

"Yes."

"I . . . I don't know," she said. "I suppose so. Some of

it, anyway."

"What I'm thinking is, if you remember a piece of jewelry we don't find in the safe deposit box, or if I don't find the documents I'm looking for, it might indicate there is another safe on the premises – or hiding place as my sergeant suggested. If that's the case, I can bring in a search crew, and we can go over things more thoroughly." He pointed to the bookshelves. "I notice she had a number of books on genealogy. Was this a hobby of hers?"

"Oh, yes. She was always offering to look up somebody's relatives for them." She laughed. "Some people panicked; they didn't want Gwen Cunningham looking up relatives."

"Uh-huh," Dawson muttered. He was remembering Doctor Glasco's comment about Gwen offering to do a family tree for Mavis Dillon's daughter.

It was nearly six o'clock when Dawson, Eggleton, and Marjorie Meyerson got back into the car. Eggleton carried a laptop computer; Dawson carried a manila envelope containing small, black daily planners – one for each of the previous five years. In riffling through the pages, Dawson had noted cryptic entries such as he had read in the current diary. He planned to make them his evening's reading; perhaps study would make them more illuminating.

"I'll drop you off at the station, Bill," Dawson said, closing the car door, "and then I'll take Mrs. Meyerson back to the store." He turned to Marjorie. "Your car is there?"

"Yes," she said. "That would be fine."

Eggleton started to speak but changed his mind. He had something he wanted to tell Dawson but decided it could wait.

"Bill?"

Eggleton shook his head. "Nothing. Just thinking out loud." He settled into the back seat. Scowling.

Marjorie Meyerson was silent as they began the ride back to town. It was turning to dusk, and shadows fell across her face. Dawson glanced at her from time to time. In the back seat, Eggleton sat erect, drumming a tattoo on his knee with his fingers.

"She was very precise about things," Dawson said finally, as much to break the silence as anything.

Marjorie nodded. She turned to Dawson. "I've been thinking about that, Inspector."

What happened to Jake? Eggleton wondered.

She paused, as though unsure of how to continue. "I don't know if I can explain what I mean, but it seems, since she was so careful about everything, well, if she was planning to commit suicide, would she have left food in her refrigerator, or bills unpaid? Wouldn't it be more likely she'd tidy up everything?"

In the back seat, Eggleton stopped drumming his fingers; Marjorie Meyerson had just posed the question Eggleton had been waiting to ask.

"Unless . . ." Marjorie continued, ". . . like we talked about this morning, she did it deliberately . . . to implicate the others . . ." Her voice trailed off, and she shook her head. "It's too complicated. I can't get in her mind." She turned away, looking out the window. "I don't even want to," she said.

Eggleton's fingers resumed their beat, and for several miles the occupants of the car were silent. Then Marjorie spoke again. "Did you notice there were no pictures of people in the whole house?"

"I noticed," Dawson said.

"Just scenery. Landscapes."

Another point Eggleton, who was starting to feel redundant, had planned to make.

"I didn't notice if you found documents like a birth certificate or marriage license." Marjorie said.

"I'm hoping to find those in the safe deposit box," Dawson said. "They weren't in the house. At least that I found."

"Did you see any sign of Mr. Cunningham?"

"No."

"Maybe he never existed," Eggleton said – if for no other reason than to assert his presence.

"I think you're right, Sergeant," Marjorie said.

At the station Dawson jumped out of the car, saying to Marjorie. "I'll just get my briefcase and be right back." He ran to catch up with Eggleton who was already sprinting up the stairs. "You wanted to say something to me, Bill? Back when we were getting in the car?"

"Yeah. Well," Eggleton said, "I was going to point out to you just what Mrs. Meyerson said. About leaving things undone – not like her, her wanting everything to be just so."

"Unless . . .?"

"Right. Unless she did it deliberately to place the blame . . ." Eggleton stopped on the landing and turned to Dawson. "We're not one bit ahead of where we ever were, are we?"

"Oh, I don't know," Dawson said. "We've got the diaries. Besides, we know a lot more about Gwen Cunningham."

"Yeah. Well, that and three dollars will buy you a cup of coffee. Sir!"

"Goodnight, Sunshine," Dawson said, racing ahead up the remaining stairs. He wondered if he should offer to take Marjorie to dinner. Gwen Cunningham's daily planners and the phone call to Hench could wait.

CHAPTER SIXTEEN

Tuesday

For in much wisdom is much grief,
and he that increaseth knowledge increaseth sorrow.
Ecc. 1:18

June 9

After leaving Eggleton at the station, Dawson had taken Marjorie to dinner at Gino's Italian restaurant, then back to the jewelry store where her car was parked. Once home, he fell into bed, satiated with good food and wine, Marjorie's excellent company, and, after having gone through Gwen Cunningham's house in the afternoon, more questions than he had started the morning with. He wondered briefly if he should call Marjorie and thank her for joining him for dinner, but quickly abandoned the idea. *Creepy,* he thought, and went to sleep.

When he arrived at his desk Tuesday morning, he found several pages, copied from a medical text, on the disease: *Amyotrophic lateral sclerosis*. A yellow post-it, positioned precisely in the top center of the first page, read, 'I hope this helps. It's from: <u>A Textbook of Clinical Neurology</u> by Nielsen. Doctor H.' Naturally Henchcombe would underline the title – with a ruler. *Henchcombe and Cunningham have much in common,* Dawson thought as he leaned back in his chair, put his feet on his desk, and began to read.

He had just finished the report when Eggleton pushed the door open with his hip. He carried two Styrofoam coffee cups. "Morning," he mumbled though teeth clenched on a greasy white bag. "Brought doughnuts."

"Urban legend," Dawson said as Eggleton set the coffee and the bag on the side of Dawson's desk.

"Huh?"

"That all cops like doughnuts."

"You don't? Thought you did."

"Didn't say I didn't. Lots of legends have their roots in fact."

"What's the matter? She refuse your dinner invitation?"

"As a matter of fact, she accepted. How'd you know I invited her to dinner?

"I'm a detective."

"So you are. Detect what you can about the deaths of Margaret Billings and Danny Resnick."

"Glasco."

"Just do it, Bill. OK? Start with the death certificates. And Bill . . ."

"I know. Don't ask questions. Want a doughnut?" Eggleton asked, holding out the bag.

"Thanks," Dawson said, selecting an old-fashioned. He took a bite. "This report," he said, jabbing his finger at the pages on his desk as though angry with the report itself, "says the duration of the disease is usually about two years, but many patients live longer, some much longer – some less. The symptoms described are horrible and progressively debilitating. Finally they can't even swallow." He shook his head and set the report aside, laying his partially eaten doughnut on top of it.

Henchcombe would have a stroke if he saw that, Eggleton thought.

"I'm going to work on Cunningham's daily planners," Dawson continued. "It's got to be less depressing. What'd you find out about Mrs. Alexander's first husband?"

"Just as she said. Alcoholic. Died in the ambulance on the way to the hospital. Aneurism." He grabbed a doughnut from the bag, looked at it and reached in for another. Then he left the room.

It was two o'clock in the afternoon when Eggleton returned to Dawson's office. Dawson had spent the day combing Gwen Cunningham's daily planners, trying to decipher the cryptic notations she had made next to people's names, gazing at his motive chart, and avoiding phone calls from the Commissioner. The doughnut, partially eaten, lay where Dawson had put it that morning. A large grease stain spread on Henchcombe's neat report. The greasy white bag still sat on the edge of Dawson's desk.

"You been out at all?" Eggleton asked.

Dawson shook his head.

"You need to eat something."

"Had a sandwich sent in, Mother. What'd you find out?"

Eggleton pulled a chair up to the desk, reached across, picked up the half-eaten doughnut, and tossed it in the wastebasket.

"The death certificates were signed by Doctor Glasco. I also checked the obituaries in the newspapers. A lot of bio material, but that was all. Although, Resnick's bio did say he'd been diagnosed with Lou Gehrig's Disease about a year ago. So, if your article is correct about the progression of the disease, Danny died a little earlier than would be expected." He looked at Dawson, waiting for a comment. When nothing was forthcoming, he continued. "Both asked for donations to be made in their name. Danny Resnick specified the ALS Foundation, and Margaret Billings listed the Cancer Society and the local Hospice. I'm assuming she was under Hospice care when she died, but that would have me contacting the Hospice nurse or nurses, and I didn't think you would want me to go too far with something that could point to Doctor Glasco unless we had more information." He made it a statement, but his eyes hinted it was a question.

"You're right, Bill. There is no point in stirring the pot until we have something to put in it."

"Great analogy," Eggleton said, pulling a doughnut from the bag. "I think."

The two men were silent for a while, Eggleton quietly munching the stale doughnut while Dawson stared at the article Henchcombe had sent him.

Finally Eggleton said, "Are you thinking what I'm thinking?"

"How would I know what you're thinking, Bill?"

"You're evading the question. You know what I'm talking about."

"Do I think Doctor Glasco had something to do with the death of these two people? He may have, although I know him well enough to know it would be at their request. However, assisted suicide is still illegal in California, and if news got out, he would have his license revoked. At the least. Given Gwen Cunningham's notes in her planner, I'm suspecting she talked to him at some point during the party, probably hinting she hadn't realized Danny and Margaret had been so near death." He paused. "Although if Hospice was actually involved with Margaret, it's a pretty good sign."

"How would it have been done? These deaths?"

"I can only surmise. But I suspect, knowing what was coming his way, Danny Resnick asked for . . .," he paused, taking a deep breath, "probably a pill or pills he could take himself while he still had the use of his arms and hands and the capability to swallow." Again, Dawson stabbed his finger at Henchcombe's report. "According to this, patients lose the ability to speak intelligibly, motor control, and finally swallowing. The only thing they have left is their intellect. In most cases, the brain is not significantly impaired. They can't move, they can't speak, they can't control bodily functions, and they are fed through a tube – all the time knowing full well what is happening to them. If I'm right, Danny Resnick probably asked Doctor Glasco for help so he could make the decision while he still had the capacity to carry it out."

"Whew!" Eggleton said. "Can't say I blame him."

"Who? Glasco or Danny?"

"Either."

"Good Presbyterian?"

"I can't believe in a God who would condemn such a decision."

Dawson raised his eyebrows but said nothing.

"What about Margaret Billings? What do you think

happened there?"

"Again, I'd be guessing, but Hospice care can stretch out over a long period of time – or it might seem a long time if you're in constant pain. Perhaps she was on a low-dosage morphine drip. Self administered. She might have asked Doctor Glasco to hurry things along. If he increased the dosage – well – again the patient would have control over how much to deliver to herself." Dawson, his eyes brimming, slapped the desk. "Damn!" he said.

Eggleton jumped.

"Sorry. It's all conjecture, Bill. I don't have anything solid to go on. Maybe they died a natural death, and Cunningham's notations meant something else." He shook his head. "I don't know. And I can't start asking around – or have you asking around – without jeopardizing Doctor Glasco's reputation. He's a good doctor, a compassionate doctor. You don't find many of those around anymore."

Eggleton stood and walked to the window. "You could ask him," he said, his back to Dawson, his gaze fixed on a vintage Mustang parked near the entrance of the station.

"No I can't. Not yet. When I get all the information about the other notations, maybe then."

"I did check to see if there had been an autopsy in either case," Eggleton said, returning to his seat. "There wasn't."

"I didn't expect there would have been. They were both terminally ill. Unless some family member got suspicious. But, frankly, I would imagine family members would be relieved and not question what was inevitable anyway." He picked up a post-it from a pile of papers on his desk. "We have a memorial service to attend tomorrow afternoon."

"Cunningham?"

"Uh huh. Father Gifford called me just before you got here."

"That didn't take long to set up. I only called him yesterday to tell him the body was ready to be released."

"Probably wants the whole business out of the way."

"Can't say I blame him," Eggleton said. "Speaking of Mrs. Gifford . . ."

"Were we?"

"We were. Did you give her a motive number?"

"Very low," Dawson said. "She shoplifted the necklace she was wearing at the party – the one she was twisting when we interviewed her – from Meyerson's around Christmas time. She returned it – put it in an envelope and slipped it through the mail slot at Meyerson's Saturday night. After Cunningham was dead." He shoved the planners in his briefcase and stood up.

"So Cunningham's notation of 'Nancy-slash-Meyersons' was accurate. Another one explained."

"I'll tell you all about it later – it's a long story." Glancing at the white bag still on his desk, he made a face, as though he had just realized it was there, and swept it into the waste basket. "Let's pretend we're sleuthing and go home."

"Alright by me," Eggleton said. He gestured toward the stack of daily planners. "Did you find anything in those?" he asked.

"Not much. I'll go over them with you tomorrow – see what you come up with. There's a few more instances of this *sec.* stuff, but I can't tie it to anything. Several *r-l-n-s-p* notes. But we know what that means."

"Well, we know it's an abbreviation – the others have been. I'm thinking secret, second, secretary, Seconal," Eggleton said. "That's all I can come up with. Anything on the medicine you found in her cabinet? Any Seconal there?"

"No. By the way, I found the *sec.* notation in the daily planner in her purse next to *Mayor.*"

"No way!"

"Still don't know what it means – well I have an idea, but . . ."

"Yeah. So do I."

". . . back to Mrs. Cunningham. I checked with Abernathy – doctor who prescribed the Ativan. He was furious when he heard she'd been taking Ativan and Ambien – said it was a bad combination." Dawson pushed some papers into a pile. "I didn't tell him who prescribed the Ambien."

Eggleton walked to the door. There he turned back for a moment, looking at Dawson who was still at his desk. "I thought we were pretending we were sleuthing," he said.

"You go on. I'll just be a minute," Dawson said and pulled his motive sheet from the pile on the desk. He penciled in a '5' by Charles Glasco's name, stared at it for a while, and then erased the '5' and penciled a '7.' His heart felt heavy, as if it weighed too much.

CHAPTER SEVENTEEN

Requiem Aeternam

…thou takest away their breath, they die,
and return to their dust.
Psalm 104:29

June 10

When Dawson and Eggleton entered St. Francis, the organist was playing Bach. They stood for a moment at the back of the sanctuary.

"*Sheep and Lambs May Safely Graze,*" Dawson said.

"Huh?"

"What the organist is playing."

"How do you know this stuff?" Eggleton asked.

"Another life."

"Music major turned cop? That piano of yours?"

"Something like that," Dawson said.

"How come you don't sing?" Eggleton asked.

"Keyboard," Dawson said, as though that explained everything. He was amused by the organist's choice. The sprightly melody seemed incongruous for a memorial service. Was the organist subtly saying this was a time of joy? Or was he likening the residents of the town to the sheep and lambs who would now be safe from the lupine cunning of Cunningham? Had the organist fallen victim to Mrs. Cunningham's innuendos? Questions to which Dawson knew he would never have the answer.

Two vases of flowers stood on a shelf behind the altar, but otherwise there were no bouquets or funeral arrangements. Dawson wondered if this was because no one sent flowers or if it was the custom of the church. He made a mental note to ask Father Gifford.

Members of the vestry sat in one pew near the front of the church, while another pew consisted of middle-aged men and women, one of whom was Mrs. Marlin Goering, wife of Castlemont's Mayor.

"Probably Historical Society," Dawson whispered.

Across the aisle from the Historical Society sat four women. Eggleton looked inquiringly at Dawson. Dawson shrugged. "Friends of the Library maybe?"

"Works to me," Eggleton muttered.

"Let's find a seat."

"Looks like we pretty much have our choice."

Toward the back in the sanctuary, Marjorie Meyerson sat by herself. Dawson stopped beside her. "May we join you?" he whispered.

"Of course," she said, smiling as she shifted down the pew. Dawson sat beside her with Eggleton next to him on the aisle.

Dolores Alexander, who had just taken her seat next to George, spotted Dawson and Eggleton; the whisper of their presence slipped down the pew. George Alexander raised a hand in greeting, and Mavis Dillon gave a small smile. Mrs. Liske and Mrs. Gentry kept their eyes to the front, while Nancy Gifford, her hair piled high, started to turn but apparently thought better of it. Dawson could see the pearl necklace around her slender neck.

"Where's Doctor Glasco," Eggleton said in a low voice.

Dawson looked over his shoulder. "He's just coming in."

Charles Glasco stopped at their pew, and again Dawson felt the heaviness on his heart. Glasco shook hands with the two police officers, looking closely at Dawson for a long moment before nodding to Marjorie Meyerson. Dawson watched him as he took his place with the rest of the vestry, wondering if he knew – or sensed – Eggleton had been checking the death notices of the two people mentioned in Gwen Cunningham's daily planner. *But how would he?* Dawson thought, chiding himself. *My own paranoia.*

"They're all here," Eggleton whispered.

"Except the Bishop and Andrew."

"You can't possibly think Andrew . . ."

"I am the resurrection and the life, saith the Lord . . ." came a voice from the back of the church, and as a body, the vestry stood. The Historical Society and the four women Dawson had earmarked Friends of the Library followed their example, as did Marjorie Meyerson, Dawson and Eggleton.

Father Gifford came slowly down the aisle, holding the Book of Common Prayer, reading as he walked. He was dressed in a black cassock over which he wore a white cotta; around his neck was a narrow black stole.

". . . he that believeth in me, though he were dead, yet shall he live."

When he reached the front of the church, Father Gifford directed their attention to the pages in the Prayer

Book, reading aloud the beautiful words, meant to comfort the grieving, in clear, resonant tones.

Dawson wondered if any there grieved.

The eulogy, delivered by Father Gifford, consisted of enumerating her many generous gifts of time, intellect and treasure for the benefit of church and community. No one else spoke.

The service was brief, little more than fifteen minutes long, and Dawson reflected on the barrenness of Gwen Cunningham's life, that it could be marked complete in so short a span of time. At the end of the service, Father Gifford said, "Into Thy hands, Oh Lord, we commit Thy servant, Gwendolyn." The organist began the Postlude – something Dawson didn't recognize – and Father Gifford walked up the aisle and out of the church. Slowly, the small group of attendees fell in behind him.

Outside, the assemblage gathered, as they had in the church, into their respective groups, as though to disperse and intermingle might upset the delicate balance of the occasion. Eggleton, Dawson and Marjorie Meyerson remained together.

"Was it as she would have wanted?" Dawson asked Marjorie, more for something to say then from any need to know.

"I expect, knowing Gwen. I'm sure she gave Father Gifford directions for her service a long time ago. She would want to have control over even that."

Dawson looked at her in surprise.

"Sorry." She gave a small smile. "That wasn't very kind of me, was it?"

"Maybe not," Dawson said with a shrug, "but you're

probably right."

"Yes. Well, I need to get back to the store."

"Could we give you a lift?" Dawson asked.

"No thank you. I have my car."

"Oh . . ." Dawson hesitated, glancing at Eggleton, willing him to walk away, but Eggleton failed to get Dawson's message – or got it and ignored it.

"I'll . . . I'll call you," Dawson said finally. "If I may?"

"Of course you may," she said. "Inspector, Sergeant." She shook their hands and walked off in the direction of the parking lot. Dawson's eyes followed.

Eggleton pursed his lips thoughtfully, and was just about to make a comment, when Father Gifford joined them. "Is this out of respect, Inspector, or are you observing?"

"I didn't know Mrs. Cunningham, Father Gifford."

"I guess that answers my question."

"Who are the four ladies?" Eggleton asked, gesturing to where the women stood, chatting now with the Historical Society.

"Garden Club," Father Gifford said. "She was very active."

"Not many members," Dawson observed.

"Oh, there are quite a few, I think. They just . . ." He didn't complete his thought, but Dawson interpreted his silence as a reluctance to suggest most had elected not to attend.

"The bishop didn't come."

"No. He didn't know her well. I wouldn't expect him," Father Gifford said.

Dawson filed the bishop's absence away in his mind

283

as something to think about. "I noticed there were no flowers," he said. "Is that customary or . . . ." He stopped, not knowing how to tactfully phrase his question.

"It's customary at St. Francis. We discourage any ostentatious display of wreathes and arrangements. If it's a burial service, the mortuary takes the flowers to the grave site."

"Ah," Dawson said. "Will there be a burial service?"

"No. Gwen requested cremation, which I ordered as soon as your Sergeant called to tell me the body was ready to be picked up. The ashes will be placed in an urn and put in a niche at the Castlemont Cemetery Mausoleum."

"It sounds like she left explicit instructions for you."

Father Gifford laughed - a short, tight laugh. "She was one of the first people to greet me when I came to Castlemont. She arrived at my office with typed instructions regarding her memorial service. She wanted to be sure she had control of the situation, I guess."

Remembering Marjorie Meyerson's comments, Dawson smiled. "You managed to put this together rather quickly," he said.

Father Gifford looked at him, perhaps sensing an element of criticism in Dawson's comment. "I did. With her instructions, and the fact I'm not exactly a novice to this type of event, it didn't take long. But to answer your underlying question, Inspector – and there was an underlying question – I am anxious to have this whole incident behind us as quickly as possible. You'll let me know if I can be of help, won't you?" Gifford said. He shook both officers' hands and walked away.

"Inspector?" It was Mavis Dillon. She was wearing a blue suit; her hair styled in a severe bun at the nape of her neck. A heavy gold necklace and earrings were her only jewelry. "We're meeting at George and Dolores's house for refreshment. They asked me to invite you and Sergeant Eggleton to join us." She laughed nervously. "I think it's an old custom – gathering to eat the funeral meats."

"I'm sorry. We have to get back to the station," Dawson said, wondering why Marjorie Meyerson hadn't been included.

As though reading his thoughts, Mavis said, "That's too bad. Marjorie couldn't make it either. I talked to her before the service. Really, she was probably the one closest to Gwen." She turned to go. "Well," she said over her shoulder, "if you change your mind . . ."

"Thank you anyway, Mrs. Dillon," Dawson said.

"We'd be specters at the feast!" Eggleton said when they reached their car. "They keep inviting us to things, don't they? Like it was a social event or something."

"I've noticed. Maybe it's just good breeding. Or maybe they're anxious to appear innocent."

"If they're so innocent, why'd they all handle the bottle?"

"Exactly."

"Just what did we get out of this? You know . . . this funeral service."

"Well, murderers frequently turn up at the funeral or the gravesite. Or so we're led to believe."

"Come on! We knew they'd all be here! Were you hoping one of them would break down with sobs of remorse?"

"Hardly. I was watching for some subtle behavior, that's all."

"And did you see any?"

"Not really," Dawson said with a small shrug. "Maybe Charles. He seemed . . . I don't know . . . sort of questioning. The teachers and Mrs. Gifford ignored us. Alexander, who apparently doesn't have a care in the world, waved at us. Mrs. Dillon invited us to a party. Bishop didn't show. Interesting bunch of people."

"Huh! What's on for the rest of the afternoon?"

"I'm going to try to get some information about Stephen Dillon from Harvard University. I have a feeling . . ." He stopped, his thoughts apparently far away.

"About Dillon?"

"What?"

"Dillon. You have a feeling."

"Oh, yeah." Dawson shrugged. "Probably nothing. I'll know more when I talk with Harvard." He glanced at his watch. "Oh-oh. It's nearly four. They're several hours ahead of us, so they'll be closed. I'll call them in the morning."

"Anything you want me to do today regarding Cunningham. Because if not, I'll go back to the station and finish some paperwork on a couple other cases."

"Fine. Tomorrow I want you to go to the Social Security office and check on Mavis Dillon. See Mac McConnell. He's a friend. I talked to him – he knows you're coming. Also, he owes me big time."

Eggleton looked a question at Dawson.

"I saved his dog. Pulled it out of the way of a speeding car. Tell him I'm cashing in my chips on this one. I want date of application, maiden name, any cards issued under the maiden name, date of birth, place of birth, any surviving parents, any records of work history."

"And if he's not there?"

"He'll be there. It's a nine-to-five for him."

"Social Security's not going to know about surviving parents."

"You'll have their names. Try to trace them. Oh, and tell Mac now I'll owe him."

Eggleton smiled, marveling at the machinations of a small town.

CHAPTER EIGHTEEN

Dawson Attends Evening Prayer

...confess your faults one to another...
Jas. 5:16

June 11

"Have I got gossip!" Eggleton exclaimed, plopping himself into the chair by Dawson's desk.

Charts, graphs, sketches of Mavis Dillon's house, some scrunched balls of paper Dawson had neglected to throw in the waste basket, and a half-eaten ham sandwich littered the desktop. Dawson didn't look up. "So did Mrs. Cunningham," he muttered finally, making a notation in the margin of one of the charts and taking a bite from his sandwich.

Eggleton hiked the chair closer. He pushed aside a stack of papers – clearing a place for his elbows to rest – and leaned toward Dawson. "I had lunch with Laura," he said, his voice eager with the news he carried.

"I know," Dawson said through a mouthful of sandwich.

Laura Eggleton had called at nine-thirty that morning. "Is Bill there, Jake?" she asked. "I tried his cell, but he forgets to check his messages."

"He's at the lab picking up a report, Laura. He should

be back soon. I can have him call you."

"Just tell him he's taking me to lunch."

"Aw, Laura, " Dawson began, "I want him to go to Social Secur . . ."

"I won't keep him long, Jake," she interrupted. "I think you'll be happy with what I have to tell him."

"Cryptic," Dawson said dryly. "Are congratulations in order?"

Laura laughed. "Don't I wish! No. I'm helping you with your case. You'll tell him?"

"Laura …" Dawson began, but she interrupted again.

"I'll make it up to you, Jake. Dinner next week – pot roast."

"Well. . . "

"The Feed Store. Twelve o'clock. Thanks Jake." And she hung up.

Dawson made a face at the phone and put down the receiver.

"So what was her big news?"

"She had coffee with Diane Ricardt this morning. Diane's Laura's best friend. They are like that!" Eggleton said, crossing his fingers.

"And?"

"Diane is the City Manager's assistant. You know, Buzz Halpern. . . ."

"Bill!" Dawson's voice held a warning.

". . . at the City Offices."

"I don't have time to pry this story out of you word by word, Bill. I need you to get to Social Security. Also I have to get back to Harvard about Stephen Dillon."

"Anyway," Eggleton continued, apparently unconcerned by Dawson's impatience, "it seems Mrs. Cunningham paid a call to His Honor, the mayor, last week. Turns out, at least according to the office grapevine at the City Offices, His Honor is having a wee bit of the nasty with his secretary, Ruth. Or was."

"Is that what we call it now? A wee bit of the nasty?"

Eggleton waved a dismissive hand. "I guess they all suspected it, but this day, when Mrs. Cunningham comes, she's in with His Honor for quite a while. Well, they didn't think too much of it; she's come in before – all the committees she's on – but later Diane and several other of the staff went out to lunch, except Diane forgot her purse, so she went back to the office. Mrs. Cunningham had left by then, but Diane heard His Honor talking with Ruth, and he was saying something about it being over, and Ruth was crying, and he says, 'For God's sake! If my wife ever found out . . .' and then something like '. . . that Cunningham woman'll spread it all over town."

"And this has what to do with our case, Sergeant?"

"Well, Diane told Laura the mayor found out about Mrs. Cunningham's daily planner . . ."

"Shit! Who?"

Eggleton shrugged. "Search me. But it's all over – seems everybody knows about it. Laura's in the DA's office, and they know about it. No reason to think the mayor's office wouldn't know about it."

Dawson shook his head. "Damn!"

"You can't unring the bell, Jake."

"If I find out who leaked it, they'll be job hunting." He slammed his fist on the desk. "Damn! Ouch!" He shook his hand. "Go on . . . about the mayor and the 'wee bit of the nasty.' "

"Well, one thing, Ruth hasn't been to work for about a week, since Cunningham was in, – and nobody knows if she resigned or if she's coming back – they've got a temp. And . . ." Eggleton paused as though to add drama to his story, ". . . and, Mayor Marlin Goering has been trying to get hold of the chief, except the chief's been out of town, so His Honor hasn't been able to reach him. And he's called the commissioner. Probably wants to see if Cunningham made some notes in her little book about her meeting with him." Eggleton sat back, smiling.

"How come His Honor didn't call me?"

"Probably doesn't want anybody to know – especially you, out there looking for motives."

"Since he wasn't at the party . . . "

"Still. Probably thought his little secret – which isn't much of a secret – would be better with the chief or the commissioner – since they're political buddies. Anyway, seems Cunningham served on the Historical Society with His Honor's wife – well, we saw Mrs. Mayor at the funeral yesterday," he added as Dawson rummaged under the stack of papers on his desk and came up with the daily planner. "Upon whom he is dependent for his green fees and his yacht."

"Huh?"

"Mayor – dependent on his wife's money – need I add campaign funds?"

"Oh, Yeah. I know," Dawson said, already engrossed in the diary.

"He's back in town," Eggleton said, twirling a pencil

in his fingers.

"Mayor?"

"The chief. Just now. Met him as I was coming in."

Dawson was leafing through the pages. "Last week?"

"Yep."

"Here it is. June second. *M.G.sec.*. Damn it, Bill! Here's that goddamned *sec.* It crops up a couple of times in her diaries, but I didn't know what . . ." He threw the book down. "Marlin Goering secretary. Shit!"

Eggleton was surprised; Dawson didn't usually swear much, but he was doing a lot of it now.

"So *sec.* means 'secretary,'"

"Seems so, Sir."

"Then the notation by the bishop's name meant . . ." The phone rang.

"Probably the chief," Eggleton said, glancing at his watch. "He's had just enough time to get His Honor's message – or the commissioner's."

Dawson rolled his chair back and jumped to his feet. "I'm not here," he said, heading for the door. "He's going to pull the case, you know," he said over his shoulder. "Call it suicide."

Eggleton picked up the phone. "Inspector Dawson's desk," he said.

The voice on the phone crackled, and Eggleton, holding it away from his ear, nodded at Dawson who stood just outside the door watching.

"He's not in his office right now, Sir," Eggleton said, grinning. The phone crackled some more and Eggleton said, "No, Sir. He didn't say." He paused, listening. "The diary from the Cunningham case?" He picked up the diary and tossed it to Dawson who was still standing in the doorway. "No, Sir. I don't see it on his desk." There was more squawking from the phone. "Yes, Sir. As soon as I see him. Yes, Sir. I'll tell him. Yes, Sir. I do enjoy the title of Detective." He hung up the phone. "Asshole!" he said, rubbing his ear.

Dawson came back into the room. "Call the bishop, Bill. See if he's in. Tell him we're on our way."

"That's nearly a three hour drive," Eggleton protested as he flipped through his notebook to the list of addresses and phone numbers of Mavis Dillon's guests. "It'll be. . ." He glanced at his watch again. "It'll be nearly five o'clock before we even get there. What about the chief?"

"I'll call him once we're on the road."

"Right! What if the bishop's not in?"

"Then find out where he is," Dawson said, grabbing his briefcase and putting the diary in it. "I'll be in my car."

"Assuming he's available."

"If he's not, we'll drive around. Better than a conversation with the chief," Dawson said, and hurried down the hall toward the door and the parking lot.

"She said he'll see us, but he attends Evening Prayer at five." Eggleton said, as he dropped into the seat beside Dawson and adjusted the seat belt. "Without fail," he added.

"She being?"

"His secretary – as in *sec.* – I would assume. Or Executive Assistant as they prefer to be called. You were going to tell me about your conversation with Nancy Gifford," he said, as Dawson pulled into traffic.

And so Dawson talked, and Eggleton listened.

"She returned the necklace on the evening of the day Cunningham died," Dawson said, finishing his tale of tears and pearls.

"Coincidence you were there just when Mrs. Meyerson opened the envelope."

"A word I've heard in this context before, Sergeant. Nancy Gifford was quick to make that point. As though, save for *coincidence*, she would never have been found out."

"You don't think much of her, do you?"

"Does it matter?"

"Not in the least," Eggleton said as he rummaged through Dawson's collection of CDs. "You got anything that's not so . . . ?" He rocked his hand back and forth.

"No, Sergeant, I don't have anything that's not so . . ." Dawson responded, mimicking Eggleton's gesture.

"Huh!" Eggleton snorted, selecting a disk of Chopin *Nocturnes*. He slumped in his seat and closed his eyes. The CD was nearly halfway through when he turned to Dawson. "I suppose we'll find out what *sec. son* means today."

"I hope so."

"What I'm getting at is, will we know more than we know now if we do?"

"You mean, will what we learn be relevant?"

Eggleton nodded.

Dawson continued. "I don't know. Maybe to motive but probably not evidence. So far we've learned what the notations about Alexander, Gifford, Liske and Gentry, and probably Glasco meant – all issues that might be a motive for wanting Cunningham dead – leading this detective to the deduction the notation by the bishop's name has something to do with his secretary's son."

"Are any of those issues, the ones we know about already, motive enough?" Eggleton asked, his expression doubtful.

"One man's trash is another man's treasure," Dawson said.

"I think that's an analogy for garage sales. Sir!"

"Whatever. You know what I mean. It might not seem like a big deal to us, but to the person . . ." He stopped speaking and looked at Eggleton. "Which one would you have us not track down?"

"I didn't mean that. It's just knowing what she had on these people doesn't seem to provide us with evidence. And we're going to need evidence – like somebody seeing somebody pour the nicotine into her glass would be the optimum evidence. Especially if you think the chief is going to pull the case on us . . . speaking of which, weren't you going to call him?"

"You're right. I should. You drive for a while, and I'll call." He pulled the car to the side of the road and slipped it into 'park.'

"If I drive, does it mean I get to choose the music?" Eggleton asked as he slid into the driver's seat.

Dawson gestured to his small box of CDs. "Help yourself."

"I had in mind a radio station."

"Just drive," Dawson said and hit his contact number for the chief.

Dawson's contribution to the call was limited. Eggleton could hear the chief shouting on the other end.

"Yes. Eggleton did tell me you called . . . Yes. I interviewed him that day. . . Yes. I interviewed everyone that day. . . I have new information – that's why we're . . . No. I don't think the case is . . . Sir. I think we're breaking . . ." Dawson tapped the end of his pen on the phone. "I'm sorry . . . . can't . . . 'morrow." And he hit 'end call.'

"You weren't breaking up," Eggleton said with a huge grin.

"Sergeant! That would be devious."

"It would."

"If the reference is to his secretary's son, what is the relevance to the bishop?"

"Maybe he's helped the kid out of some scrape or other," Dawson said. "Although that is hardly something to hold over the man's head."

"Maybe she didn't have anything to hold over his head," Eggleton said. "Maybe she was just complimenting him on a charitable deed."

"So why didn't the bishop tell us what it meant? He must have known *sec.* referred to *secretary*."

"Maybe he didn't think of it."

"Oh, come on, Sergeant."

Eggleton turned to Dawson. "How come you use my rank to address me whenever I say something you think is stupid?"

"Just so, Sergeant. Watch the road."

Eggleton made a rude noise, and Dawson grinned. "Maybe the secretary's son was an altar boy, and the bishop was playing naughty games with him," he continued.

"Don't see it," Eggleton said.

Dawson shook his head. "I don't either," he admitted. "Still, you can't judge by appearances. I'll talk to the bishop. You stay in the office – chat up the secretary. Find out about her son if you can."

"OK," Eggleton said, and they rode, without speaking, the rest of the way, listening this time to *Pachelbel's Canon*.

The stone walls of the cathedral echoed their footsteps as they followed the signs leading to offices. Tapestries hung from the walls, and small niches held icons and plaques. "Like a bloody mausoleum," Eggleton muttered, his eyes taking in the lofty ceilings and marbled floors.

"Yeah," Dawson said, stopping before a heavy wooden door with a plaque reading 'OFFICE OF THE BISHOP.' As they stepped inside, Dawson was struck by the warmth of the room. Bright carpets lay scattered across the hardwood floor, bookshelves lined the walls, overstuffed chairs and a large sofa furnished the area, and, behind an antique oak desk, sat a lovely, auburn-haired woman. Her computer monitor seemed out of place.

She smiled at them. "You must be Inspector Dawson and Sergeant Eggleton. The bishop will be right with you." She gestured toward the sofa.

Dawson had scarcely time to set his briefcase at his feet when a door opened, and the bishop beckoned to them. "Come on in," he said. Turning to the young woman, he smiled. "Hold my calls for a while, Susan."

"Sergeant Eggleton needs to use your phone," Dawson said as he walked past the desk. "Cell went dead." He turned to Eggleton. "I'll call you if I need you to take notes." And with that, the bishop and Dawson disappeared into the bishop's office, the bishop closing the door softly behind them.

"I will use your phone if I may," Eggleton said, walking to the desk.

"Of course. I'm always forgetting to charge my cell, too."

"I'm pretty bad about it," Eggleton said, and, leaning against the side of her desk, called Laura.

"Hi, Hon," he said to the answering machine. "Jake and I are travelling – I won't be home until late. I'll get Jake to buy dinner. Kiss Beth. Explain later. Love you." As he hung up, he gestured toward the silver-framed picture on her desk. "Cute," he said. "Yours?"

"Yes," she said. "Michael. Eighteen months and full of it."

"I have one. A little older." He removed his wallet and pulled out a picture of Beth.

"Oh!" Susan said. "She's gorgeous!"

Eggleton couldn't help but agree. "She was constant motion at that age," he said, gesturing to the picture of Michael. "Still is, but at least now she understands what 'no' means – sometimes she understands. He your only one?"

"Yes. Actually, my husband will be in to pick me up a little after five. He brings the baby when he comes, so you may get to meet him." She glanced at her watch. "If you're still here."

"Oh, I expect we will be. You said something about the bishop going to a service."

"Evening Prayer. If he's here, nothing stops him. Not even the police, I should imagine – although it's the first time we've had the police visit." She looked questioningly at Eggleton. "I expect it's about the death in Castlemont last weekend."

Eggleton nodded. "Every evening?"

"Every evening. It's only a half-hour service, and the bishop says he much prefers it, even to the Holy Communion service. Frankly, I think the reason he prefers it is because he rarely has to officiate. Here at the Cathedral it's Canon Yarnell's duty to do Evening Prayer. It's a sung service, and Canon Yarnell has a beautiful voice, so it's a treat to attend."

"The bishop doesn't sing?"

She laughed. "Oh, he sings alright. With gusto and not much accuracy." Her expression changed, her eyes softening. "He's truly a holy man, Sergeant. I think an anomaly among the hierarchy of the church."

"How so?"

She paused, frowning slightly. "He is totally committed to the church and what it stands for," she said finally. "Fund raising, long meetings, banquets, and squabbling congregations make him angry. He feels that loses sight of what the church really is all about." Her tone became brisk and she said, "Unfortunately, being a Bishop means fund raising, long meetings, banquets and squabbling congregations."

"Did he ever have a church of his own?"

"Yes. Two parishes before he became a Canon and

then was elected Bishop. From what I hear, he was an excellent parish priest, too." She turned off her computer and tidied her desk top. "Anyway," she continued, "I think that's why he is so adamant about attending Evening Prayer. He says it refreshes his commitment, sweeps away the cobwebs of politics."

"You're very fond of the bishop," Eggleton said.

* * *

Fond, but was she in love with the bishop? She was married to the devoted Mike and, although they had never been able to conceive, they were a moderately happy couple. Doctors said this inability to conceive probably dated back to the removal of an ovary as a teenager, and Susan took full responsibility for their failure to have a child. She found solace in her job; she had worked for the bishop for nearly five years – the best five years of her life, she reasoned – admiring the grace and wisdom he brought to the office he held. She found a much-needed intellectual stimulus in the demands of her position as well as in the man himself.

But was she in love with him? Of course she was. Would she act on it? Of course she wouldn't.

But she did. Just once.

* * *

"Yes," she said. "I am fond of him."

"Do you go?"

She looked puzzled.

"To Evening Prayer?"

"Not with Michael," she said. "He's too squirmy. We used to, when he was in his little car seat with a bottle." She shook her head. "Can't get by with that now." She paused. "It really is a beautiful service, Sergeant. You don't have to be an Episcopalian to find it moving."

The door of the bishop's office opened and the bishop, ushering Dawson ahead of him, emerged. "I think I made it quite clear when you asked for time this afternoon that I attend services at five, Inspector," he said, nodding to Eggleton and placing a thin folder on Susan's desk. "I'll need this tomorrow afternoon, Susan," he added.

Scowling, Dawson stopped in front of the bishop and turned to him. "I have one question left, Bishop Kindermann. It won't take much time."

Like hell it won't, Eggleton thought as he watched the two men: one with the power of the law, the other with the power of the church.

"Depends on the question, doesn't it, Inspector?" Then, smiling, the bishop put his hand on Dawson's shoulder. "Walk with me," he said, his voice softening. "Join me at Evening Prayer, and then I will give you all the time you want and answer your question. Fair enough?"

Dawson, who had had more than enough church recently to last him for a very long time, shrugged. "Why not? You want to come, Sergeant?"

"I think I'll stay here," Eggleton said. He wanted to see the secretary's son.

It was 6:30 when Dawson and the bishop returned to the bishop's office. Eggleton, who, after Susan and her family left, had spent the time leafing through back issues of *The Episcopalian,* was sullen and hungry as he slipped into the driver's seat of Dawson's car.

"When you're over your little snit, Sergeant, I'll buy you dinner."

"I know. I already told Laura you would."

"Huh!" Dawson snorted. "What did you get out of the fair Susan?"

"Well, we talked about her son." He looked at Dawson. "That's what you wanted isn't it? He's eighteen months old. His dad works swing, so he takes care of the baby during the day. Except she told me she was quitting in two weeks, because her husband got a promotion and he'll have regular hours. Also, the new job is someplace in Nevada, so they're moving. She's happy she's going to be able to stay home with the kid. Real nice lady. And she thinks the world of the bishop."

"Oh, yeah!" Dawson said, nodding.

Eggleton shot him a glance, but Dawson was leaning back in his seat, his eyes closed. Eggleton turned on the radio and found the classic rock station. "I deserve this," he said.

Dawson said nothing.

"And it's nearly seven. I could stand something to eat."

"What a surprise," Dawson said. "Stop any place that looks good to you. Now, tell me more about this Administrative Assistant," he prompted.

"Not much more to tell. About five minutes after you and the bishop left for Evening Prayer, her husband came in with the kid. Cute little bugger, but I didn't see anything unusual about him." Eggleton was watching the roadside, looking for a restaurant. He was quiet for a while. Then he continued. "Seems real bright – the kid – into everything, talking a mile a minute. Not that he made much sense." He swung the car into the parking lot of a restaurant called Swiss Chalet Steak and Keg. "This OK?"

"Red meat, beer and yodelers. Should meet our most basic needs, Bill."

The host, dressed in lederhosen, showed them to a booth. Soft music piped through the P.A. system. Polkas. Dawson grimaced; Eggleton studied the menu.

A waitress, dressed in a short dirndl skirt and peasant blouse that revealed fleshy shoulders and a spectacular cleavage, stopped at their table. "Can I get you gentlemen anything from the bar?" she asked as she deposited a basket of warm bread and a ramekin of butter on the table.

"I'll have a glass of house Merlot," Dawson said.

"Heinekens," Eggleton muttered, reaching for the bread while still engrossed in the menu.

As she walked away, the many layers of petticoat swished in time to her step. Dawson watched, his lips pursed. Then he turned back to Eggleton. "Any more to tell me about the bishop's secretary? Or her kid?"

Frowning, Eggleton closed the menu. "Such as?"

"Whatever you might have noticed."

"Why do I feel like you know something I don't?"

"Because I do," Dawson said. "Tell me about the kid."

"There didn't seem to be anything wrong. He's obviously too young to be an altar boy so scratch any idea of the bishop messing with him." He scowled at Dawson. "I never did buy that idea in the first place," he added. "Husband seems a nice enough guy. Real friendly. A big, sandy-haired fellow. Bright blue eyes, lots of freckles, outgoing – you know the type. Kid's got dark hair. Sort of strange, with one parent sort of blond and the other a redhead. But you never know."

Eggleton paused, nodding to the waitress as she set a bottle of beer and a frosty mug in front of him and a glass of wine in front of Dawson. Tipping the mug on its side, he poured the beer. "Actually," he continued, the scowl returning to his face, "the kid doesn't look much like either one of them. Although, you can see some of her – shape of the face – eyes. Big brown eyes." He sipped his beer. "But kids always seem to have big eyes, don't they?"

"Umm."

"Maybe the kid's adopted." He wiped some foam from his upper lip and thumped his mug on the table. "I'm through with the guessing game, Jake. What's up?"

"You're so damned close," Dawson said, shaking his head. "I don't know if I'd have seen it. Oh, I would have after I talked with the bishop, but you didn't even have to talk to him, and you almost nailed it."

"I don't have the faintest idea what you're talking about."

"Let me tell you about my interview," Dawson said, sipping his wine. "I found out what *sec.son* means."

"I think that was the purpose."

Dawson ignored Eggleton's sarcasm. "You were right-on when you described the kid, Bill. You just didn't take it far enough."

Eggleton raised his eyebrows at Dawson and took another swig of the beer, draining the mug.

"May I take your order now?"

Startled, Dawson jumped. "Huh? Oh, yeah. I'll have a steak, New York, rare, baked potato, and salad bar," Dawson said, handing her the menu. "And another Merlot."

"And you, sir?"

"The same," Eggleton said. "And a side of onion rings." He held up the empty beer bottle. "And another one of these."

"Help yourself to the salad bar anytime," she said, taking the empty bottle and turning to go.

"Oh, miss?"

She turned back, her petticoats quivering.

"Make it two baked potatoes," Eggleton said. Then to Dawson, "Sometimes the ones they give you are so damned puny. So, tell me about the bishop."

"Well, we attended Evening Prayer. It was a beautiful service, by the way. If you're into that sort of thing."

"Not really."

"Neither am I, but the liturgy is sheer poetry – gorgeous music – it was worth it just to hear that guy sing. Not the bishop – the other guy."

"Umm."

"After the service, the bishop said, 'We might as well talk here as anyplace.' I was surprised, figuring he'd want to go back to his office, but I thought, *what the hell?* The place emptied in a hurry. I think most of the people who attend are either employees of the cathedral or people who work nearby and stop in on their way home from work. It was a strictly professional crowd." He sipped his wine. "I shouldn't say 'crowd,' but the place was about half full. It's a small chapel off to the side of the main sanctuary. So, the bishop makes himself comfortable, sits sideways in this padded pew, pulls one leg up on the seat, very much at ease, and proceeds to tell me his tale." Dawson leaned across the table to Eggleton. "After I reminded him of our initial interview when I had asked if he had a son, and how he didn't answer the question, just said he had two daughters."

"Did you tell him about Mrs. Cunningham's daily planner."

"I did. While we were still in his office. I think that's probably what prompted him to tell me his story. Anyway, he said he did remember I had asked him if he had a son, and no, he had not answered me fully, and yes, he does have a son."

"Hold it right there!" Eggleton said. "You want salad?" he added, sliding out of the booth.

"Sure."

While they ate their salads, Dawson related what the bishop had told him – that he had long been in love with Susan and apparently she with him and about their singular 'encounter.' Here Dawson paused to drain his wine glass as the waitress set another glass of Merlot in front of him and a bottle of beer and fresh mug in front of Eggleton. When she moved away, he continued. "He said Susan has resigned, and he will miss her terribly, but it will be better, now the baby is getting older, not to have him around so much, since he does bear some resemblance to the bishop. He said Susan's husband has a new position, and the time just seemed right."

"Nevada."

"Huh?"

"New job's in Nevada."

"Oh."

"Maybe they should have each gotten a divorce."

"I suggested that, but he said it would have caused too much pain to too many people. Also wouldn't be great for his job – that's me talking – he didn't mention it. Besides, he said, Susan never told him the baby was his. Maybe she wasn't sure."

"She never told him! She's never had a kid – has a one-off with the bishop – nine months later has a kid that is starting to look like the bishop. It's not rocket science! I'm thinking a few years from now; they've got a kid that looks a whole lot like the guy mama used to work for."

"A bridge to cross when they get to it. Apparently Susan's husband had an Armenian grandfather, and he, the husband, credits the kid's dark hair to those genes. The Bishop says Mike Senior calls the baby their *miracle baby*."

"Lipstick on a pig if you ask me."

"I didn't ask you. The bishop smiled when he told me that – a real tight smile, I might add. He said 'God moves in a mysterious way.' "

"God! Huh! Sounds to they're lucky to have Grandpa in the family album," Eggleton said and poured some beer into his glass. "Or maybe the kid is the husband's."

"Maybe."

"Or it could be the husband has already figured it out, and that's why he's taken a job in Nevada. Getting the hell out of Dodge, so to speak. He's bonded with the kid, wants to keep the family intact.'

"Could be."

"Did you promise the bishop confidentiality?"

"I promised a 'qualified' confidentiality, but that seemed to satisfy him. If he proves to be responsible for Cunningham's death, the secret is out. Otherwise, it stays with the principal investigators."

"Which would be us."

"Which would."

The waitress arrived with two large platters of sizzling steaks, baked potatoes, several limp asparagus spears – the restaurant's token nod to a healthy meal – and onion rings on Eggleton's.

"Anybody else know about this?" Eggleton asked as he cut into his steak.

"Apparently Cunningham suspected. The bishop told me she said something to him at the party about his secretary's kid and his dark, curly hair – wondered if he might be adopted. He figured she was letting him know her suspicions."

"So he's probably pretty happy she's dead."

"Well, he's not grieving."

"Hummm. You know, it seems everybody's having sex with everybody," Eggleton said, shaking his head. "Even the bishop and his secretary."

"People do, Bill. Even Bishops. Even mayors. Even sweet schoolteachers who remind you of your Aunt Pearl or whatever her name was."

"Is."

"Is what?"

"My aunt. She is – not was. Besides her name is Sarah."

Dawson nodded. "Right."

"So," Eggleton said, leaning back in the booth.

"Now we know his dirty little secret. Does it put us any further ahead?"

"I didn't feel it was a 'dirty little secret' as you so succinctly put it, Sergeant."

Eggleton winced.

"Besides, don't you have any secrets you wouldn't want anybody to know?"

Eggleton thought for a moment and then shook his head. "No," he said.

"Not even a few backseat fumbles or candy bars filched from the local Seven-Eleven?"

Eggleton frowned. "I stole a matchbox car from Sprouse Ritz when I was six," he said at last. "My mother made me take it back and tell them what I'd done– hardly counts as a secret, does it?"

Dawson put his face in his hands.

"And I never had a car to fumble in."

Dawson's shoulders were shaking.

"What's so funny?" Eggleton demanded.

"Nothing, " Dawson said, wiping his eyes with the back of his hand. "Nothing at all."

"You're laughing because I'm so damned pure, aren't you?"

"Actually, that may make you a better detective than I could ever dream of being."

Eggleton blushed. "How so?"

"People are going to be more open with you. You even look pure, sort of a cross between an ex-football player and a Baptist minister." Dawson glanced at his reflection in the darkened window. "Me, I look like a fox in the hen house."

Eggleton followed Dawson's gaze. "Yeah, actually you

do," he agreed. "Although I'd say you're getting your fair share of secrets with this case. Anyway, I asked you if this information from the bishop puts us any further ahead."

Dawson played with his glass. "I honestly don't know," he said finally. "As a motive, it's a damned good one. Cunningham's death protects Susan. The bishop's got his position and, from what he says, a suitable marriage."

Eggleton's eyebrows shot up. "Suitable."

"My word. Not his. But underlying what he said, about her poise, elegance, demeanor being so appropriate for a bishop's wife, I gathered warmth is not one of her qualities. And warmth is obviously what he found with Susan."

"You're sure it was only once?"

"That's all it takes, Sergeant. But yes, I believe it was only once, and they both felt guilty about what they had done." Dawson took a sip of his wine. "Watching him at the Evening Prayer service, I think I saw a truly devout man, without artifice. And I think murder would be contrary to everything he believes in."

"And infidelity?"

"Doesn't quite equate with murder. Anyway, he's carrying a huge burden about it."

"You said anybody's capable . . ."

"I know what I said. I just have a feeling is all – he's not the one – even after our first interview with him, I didn't buy him for it." Dawson sipped again. "Besides, nobody at the party saw him leave – or admits to seeing him leave – not even to go to the bathroom. Since he was the guest of honor, you'd think somebody would have noticed if he left."

"So why did we chase all the way here if you'd already eliminated him?"

"I didn't actually say I'd eliminated him – I just said I had a feeling. Nobody admits to having seen him leave the party – which doesn't mean he didn't." Dawson sighed. "We'll just have to stack his motive up against the other motives. Give it a number on my chart."

"Your chart. Subjective," Eggleton muttered.

Dawson ignored the comment. "His motive is fairly high, I would say, but my gut is telling me otherwise.

"Do you have a chart for your gut?"

"Go to hell, Sergeant," Dawson said and switched the subject to Mavis Dillon. "I was hoping you could get to Social Security this afternoon and see Mac, but since we got sidetracked, first thing tomorrow."

"Do you like her for it? Dillon? Couldn't we just ask her about her background?"

"Can't say if I like her for it or not. But I think you were right about her having been a dancer. You remember how she tried to put her carriage off as deportment lessons. Deportment lessons are practically last century."

"Which was fifteen years ago."

"You know what I mean. It didn't ring true with me at the time. Her response sounded practiced – too quick. I think she was lying."

"Your gut again?"

"That – and experience. I think unless we're armed with a little more, she won't tell us the truth."

"We've got motives coming out the ying-yang, Jake."

"Way too visual, Bill."

Eggleton ignored him. "But evidence? What would

312

you consider evidence?"

"Well, like you said, an eyewitness. But since they all seem to be covering for each other, I guess my other choice for evidence would be an extra glass."

"Someone filled it with nicotine and sherry in the kitchen and . . .?"

"Put it on the hall table – switched with the one she placed on the table when she went into the bathroom. Or, maybe this person had been carrying around the doctored drink for a long time, just waiting for Cunningham to set hers down, made a switch. In that case, there wouldn't be an extra."

"Assuming she did set hers down."

"Assuming."

"Did we find one? An extra one? Because I don't think I've heard about it if we did."

Again, Dawson ignored Eggleton's sarcasm. "No."

"Then it's rather a moot point, don't you think?"

Dawson rolled his eyes. "How long have you been waiting to use that, Sergeant?"

"Since Sunday," Eggleton said, grinning. He stared at the wall behind Dawson's head. "What'd she get out of this?" he asked finally. "Mrs. Cunningham, I mean. All this stuff she had on people. It was a form of blackmail, wasn't it?"

"It is. Except she never gave anybody a chance to pay up. Want some dessert?"

"Of course."

CHAPTER NINETEEN

Dawson and the Chief

...men of corrupt minds and destitute of the truth...
1 Tim. 6:5

June 12

There were two messages on Dawson's phone when he got home that evening, both from Chief of Police Moynahan. The first was, "Please call me as soon as you get in," the second, "Where the hell are you, Dawson?" Dawson sighed. The clock on the stove said it was 11:00. *Much too late to call the chief – it would be downright rude,* Dawson thought – and went to bed.

The next morning, after fixing himself a breakfast of oatmeal, whole-wheat toast, and orange juice, and feeling smugly virtuous for having such a nourishing meal, he left his house, closing the door on Moynahan's first phone call of the day.

When he got to the station, the red light on his phone was blinking.

Dawson made a face and dialed.

The voice that answered Dawson's call was icy. "Good morning, Inspector. I will expect you in my office in five minutes – with the Cunningham woman's file and her diary. And Inspector, you might want to have the telephone company *and* your cell provider check your land-line *and* your cell service. Seems they are both out of commission." The receiver clicked in Dawson's ear. Sighing, he picked up his briefcase. He knew what was ahead.

Dawson considered Chief Moynahan to be as corrupt as it was possible to be in a relatively small place. He was sure, given a larger location, Moynahan could easily rise to the height of greater corruption. That morning Moynahan sat behind a desk cluttered with papers, an empty coffee cup, books, a computer screen and the artifacts of cases two years old. A tall, heavy set man, he managed to look untidy despite the excellent cut and quality of his clothes. His features were large: thick lips, moist and purplish in color, a soft, spreading nose, and large protruding eyes with heavy lids that closed slowly – seemingly challenged to cover the eyeballs. His neck was short, giving his head the appearance of sitting directly on his shoulders; turning his head necessitated rotating his upper body. Dawson had once heard Moynahan kept a large pet turtle, and he could think of nothing more apt. Moynahan's speaking range had two levels: a whisper and a shout.

He chose to shout. "Goddammit Dawson! Don't you ever respond to a message?"

"I called you yesterday when I was on my way to an interview," Dawson reminded him. "Follow-up on the . . ."

"Siddown!" Moynahan interrupted, stabbing a thick finger in the direction of a chair. "Now!" This reminded Dawson of people he'd seen trying to train their dogs; he was not pleased with the image.

Moynahan's voice dropped to a raspy whisper. "Tell

me what you've got so far, and give me Cunningham's diary."

Dawson, knowing the chief was about to pull him off the investigation, slowly and reluctantly removed the folder from his briefcase. Pushing aside the detritus on the desktop, he spread his notes over the cleared space and proceeded to bring the chief up to date.

"You don't even know it was murder!" Moynahan said, a smile of satisfaction on his face, said when Dawson finished his report.

"It was," Dawson retorted with more confidence than he felt.

"Prove it! Show me one piece of concrete evidence it was murder."

"All the people at the party had a motive. At least so far. I still have one to go, but those I have . . ." he stopped for a moment and then continued. ". . . besides, it was an extremely painful way to die, Sir." He put a strong emphasis on 'Sir.' "Suicides don't usually pick such painful ways." Dawson, hearing his own words, knew how weak they sounded.

Moynahan's response was scathing. "Usually, Inspector? Usually? Can I take 'usually' to the DA? Can I hand him a suspect and say, "Well, sir, we think this is the guilty party because he has a motive and because suicides don't 'usually' seek such a painful method. Get real, Dawson. Show me some fingerprints. Show me somebody putting the nicotine in her glass."

Dawson said nothing.

"You can't, can you?"

"No. Just the motives. I believe they all had a motive

of one degree or another for wanting the woman dead."

"You believe! Something else I can take to the DA!" The chief's tone became soft and soothing. "Jake, I have too much respect for you as an investigator to think you haven't turned every possible stone in an attempt to find concrete evidence. But if there is none – and as I said, if it was there to be found, you would have found it – then we have to look at the alternative: suicide."

Dawson's fingers gripped the sides of his chair at the chief's patronizing tone and words – he preferred it when the chief shouted. "I have not *turned every stone* yet," he said, his voice taut with anger.

From someplace in the depths of the clutter on his desk, Moynahan drew a document Dawson recognized as the autopsy report. "Dr. Henchcombe found evidence of a previous suicide attempt," the chief said, pointing out the relevant paragraph.

"Years ago. When she was in college."

"We don't know it was the only one."

"We don't know it wasn't either."

The chief's smile was benign. "Jake, I think you've taken this case too much to heart."

Here it comes, thought Dawson.

"The case is closed. It was suicide, nothing more."

Dawson was on his feet. "You're telling me to cover up a murder," he said, his face flushed with anger.

The chief's smile hardened in place. "Can you prove it was murder?"

"Not yet."

"Then I'm not telling you to cover one up, am I?"

"For Christ's sake, give me time! It hasn't even been a

318

week! What's the hurry?"

"I like things tidy."

Dawson, looking at the chief's desk, wondered if one could call that an oxymoron. "Murder is seldom tidy," he said, scooping his notes from the desk and placing them in his folder.

"Besides," the chief continued, ignoring Dawson's comment, "you have a woman with a history of suicidal behavior, depression, taking a drug that produces suicidal thoughts . . ."

"*May* produce suicidal thoughts."

The chief dipped his head. " . . . *may* produce suicidal thoughts, Inspector. Access to a lethal poison, and no suspects." He stood, leaning across his desk.

His face was close enough to Dawson's that Dawson could smell the coffee the chief had been drinking.

"The case is *closed,* Inspector Dawson. End of conversation. Now, if you will give me the diary, I'll make sure it's filed with the rest of the case materials."

Dawson skimmed the evidence envelope with Gwen Cunningham's daily planner across the desk. "You'll notice I've signed it out to you," he said. At the door, he turned, "By the way, what you're looking for is on June second," he added and closed the door gently behind himself.

He didn't wait to see Moynahan's face turn red with anger.

Dawson spent the remainder of the day at his desk. What he accomplished, he could not have said. At 4:00 he left.

"What the hell?" Lieberman muttered when the doorbell rang. He lifted himself out of the leather chair, scowling as he made his way to the front door.

Dawson, slouched on the sofa, heard Lieberman greet Eggleton. "Sergeant! Come on in. We were just discussing the merits of beautiful women."

"Like hell we were," Dawson grunted, taking a healthy gulp from the highball glass he held in his hand. "We were discussing the best way to off Moynahan."

"I lied about the women," Lieberman said. "We considered strangulation, but he doesn't have a neck."

"How about nicotine?" Eggleton suggested.

Dawson ignored them both.

"Sit down, Sergeant," Lieberman said, gesturing toward the sofa. "What can I get you?"

"Beer if you have it."

Lieberman nodded and left the room.

Unlike Dawson, Lieberman had decided to make a home of his dwelling. Floor to ceiling bookcases lined the walls, faded Orientals, a legacy from the doting aunt, covered the hardwood floors, complementing a tasteful mixture of leather and upholstered furniture. It was a warm room, strangely at odds with the foul-mouthed, abrasive Lieberman who headed the Crime Scene Division.

"Thanks," Eggleton said as Lieberman handed him a bottle and a frosted mug.

"I'm sorry to break in on you like this, but I figured I'd find him here." He nodded toward Dawson.

Dawson stared at the glass in his hand. "Come to the wake, have you Bill?" he asked, his enunciation hinting he might have had more to drink than was prudent.

Eggleton shook his head. "No. After you left today, I got some information you asked me to check on, so I thought I'd let you know."

"The case is closed."

"Somehow I doubt that," Eggleton said, sipping his beer.

Dawson's eyebrows asked the unspoken question.

"Look," Eggleton said, turning sideways on the sofa and addressing Dawson. "You think it was murder. I think it was murder. For all my hassling you about us getting no place, I don't think she killed herself."

"Moynahan won't give a damn about what you think, Sergeant."

"Let me give you what I've got," Eggleton said, ignoring the interruption. His face was shining, like a small child with a good secret. "By the way, your friend at Social Security says you owe him," he added pulling his notebook from his pocket. "Big time."

Then he read: "Mavis Jennings Dillon. Birthplace, Seattle, June sixteenth, 1967. I got that from Social Security. So right away I called King County Vital Statistics office, asked for birth records. It took some time for them to find it; I suspect their records that far back aren't computerized. Anyway, they called just after you left today. She was born at Swedish Hospital, parents Colin and Estelle Jennings, address at the time of birth, 4002 50th N.E., mother's maiden name, Reardon."

Dawson sat up.

Eggleton's grin threatened to break into a full-blown smile. "I checked with information. There's a Colin Jennings still living at that address."

"Her father!" Dawson said, slapping Eggleton on the knee. "Damn, you're good, Bill! Hot damn! Hot damn!"

"When did she apply for this Social Security?" Lieberman asked.

Eggleton glanced at his notebook. "1990," he said.

"Twenty-three. Interesting she was that old when she registered with Social Security."

"Just about the time her daughter was born," Dawson said.

The three men were silent for a few moments, and then Lieberman spoke. "So, Jake, does this new information help?"

"I don't know. But if past history with Mrs. Cunningham's diary notations is anything, there is something in Dillon's past she doesn't want known, and I figure her father is a good place to start."

"Moynahan says the case is closed," Lieberman reminded Dawson.

"Stuff Moynahan!" Dawson said, smiling for the first time that evening.

"He's going to know if you pursue this," Lieberman cautioned.

"No he's not. I've got a lot of vacation coming, and I've just decided to spend some of it in Seattle."

"Hot damn!" Eggleton said, raising his beer mug in salute.

CHAPTER TWENTY

Dawson Visits Colin Jennings and Then Takes a Long Vacation

I have been young, and now am old…
Ps. 37:25

June 15

The elderly man who answered the door seemed lost in his baggy trousers and cardigan sweater. His white hair was thin and stuck up in tufts at the back of his head, as though he had been caught napping in his favorite chair. Rimless glasses sat low on his nose, and he peered at Dawson over the glasses with eyes as bright as some woodland creature. "Yes?" he said.

"Mr. Jennings? Mr. Colin Jennings?" Dawson asked, flipping open his identification. The old man nodded and, pushing the glasses up with his forefinger, peered closely, checking the man at the door against the picture. Dawson sensed a strength emanating from the man that belied what Dawson calculated to be his eighty-plus years.

"Detective Inspector, huh? From California? What would you be wanting with me?"

Dawson's experience had been most people reacted to the police on their doorstep with either apprehension or fear, sometimes, both, but Jennings showed neither. His gaze was as direct as his question. *Perhaps,* Dawson thought, *when one reaches this man's age, there is little to fear: not even death – or the police.*

"May I come in, Mr. Jennings? I've come a long way to see you."

Jennings stepped aside, gesturing toward a large room furnished during another era. Dawson, seating himself on a sofa, recognized a style of furniture from the 1960s, old but of excellent quality.

Jennings stood, his eyes wandering to the clock on the mantel that spoke with a gentle, low-throated tick. "It's late in the afternoon," he said. "Since you've come such a long way, it seems only right you should join me in a glass of something. Or are you on duty?"

"Whatever you're having would be fine," Dawson said. Jennings left the room, his slippers making soft slapping sounds. His gait was slow, but there was no evidence of a shuffle. Dawson leaned back and surveyed the room. The house itself was circa 1920, as were most of the large homes in the area. Ornate crown molding provided an elegant demarcation between the walls and the high ceilings. The only untidy element Dawson noticed in the otherwise spotlessly-clean room was the random stacks of books sitting precariously on tables and on the numerous bookshelves. The afternoon sun shone brightly, and through the window Dawson could see a magnificent view of Lake Washington. Jennings was sitting on a valuable piece of property; perhaps not all of Mavis's money came from the Dillons, Dawson speculated.

The slap of slippers announced Mr. Jennings' return. He was carrying a tray on which were two highball glasses with ice cubes, a bottle of Scotch, and a bottle of soda water. He set the tray on a coffee table in front of the sofa where Dawson sat. "I'll let you fix your own," Jennings said, pouring a splash of whiskey into a glass and retreating to his chair, an overstuffed recliner bearing the impression of long use.

Dawson took his time preparing the drink. He had thought of many approaches on the plane ride from San Francisco. Yet now, as he faced Mavis's father, he found himself without a plan. How could he tell this man his daughter was one of a number of people suspected of murder? He returned to the sofa and leaned back. "This is a lovely house," he said, gesturing around the room.

"My parents built it," Mr. Jennings answered. "Now, how can I help you?"

So much for stalling, Dawson thought. "I'm here about your daughter, Mavis," he said.

"Mavis?" Jennings' hand jerked convulsively, his eyes widened in surprise. He set his glass on a small table beside his chair.

"She is your daughter, isn't she?"

"She was my daughter, Inspector," he said.

Disowned, Dawson thought. "Was?"

Jennings pulled a handkerchief from his pocket and blew his nose. "We lost Mavis when she was just a baby, Inspector. Two years old."

"I – I must have the wrong . . . " Dawson stammered. "I'm so sorry. . ."

But Jennings continued as though Dawson hadn't spoken. "They told us when she was born she wouldn't live long." He wiped at his nose and stuffed the handkerchief back in his pocket. "In fact, they suggested we put her in an institution right away – not take her home – but we couldn't do that." He shook his head, as though remembering a long-ago picture. "We couldn't do that."

"I'm sorry," Dawson said again. "I didn't mean . . ."

Jennings waved his hand, dismissing Dawson's discomfort. "When I was a kid, the term for these children was 'mongoloid,' but now it's . . ."

"Down's Syndrome."

"Yes, that's what they call it now. We brought her home. I think it was the best two years of our lives, those years we had Mavis." He shook his head again. "She was a happy little person. Laughing, giggling. We never compared her to other children; it would have been unfair – we were just grateful for whatever she did." Dawson could see a hint of moisture in Jennings' eyes. "She gave us such pleasure," he added, turning his face away from Dawson.

"And she died when she was two?"

"Pneumonia. Her lungs were just too frail." Jennings pushed himself from the chair, the handkerchief a white flag sticking out of his pocket. He took a small framed picture from a bookshelf. The picture, nearly fifty years old, was faded. "This is Mavis and Estelle," he said, handing it to Dawson. Dawson saw a pretty woman holding a child on her lap; the child bore the unmistakable features of Down's Syndrome. The baby was laughing, patting her mother's cheek. His mind registered the mother's name: Estelle.

He regarded the picture for several moments, then handed it back. "Mr. Jennings, I'm afraid I owe you an apology. I've brought up painful memories for you, and I'm not sure I've furthered my investigation. I'm not even sure I'm in the right place."

Jennings replaced the picture on the book shelf and returned to his chair. "On the contrary, Inspector," he said "The memories are happy memories, and you have nothing to apologize for. But perhaps you could tell me a bit of what you're investigating – how is my daughter your concern?" Jennings picked up his glass and sipped at the whiskey.

Not wanting to discuss the case, but feeling he owed Jennings something, Dawson gave a brief account of the events, beginning with the death of Gwen Cunningham. "One of the women present at the gathering is named Mavis," he said. "We have reason to be interested in her background, so my sergeant checked with Social Security and found her birthplace listed as Seattle, and her parents were a Colin and Estelle Jennings." He pulled his notebook from his pocket and read. "She was born on June sixteenth, nineteen-sixty-seven at Swedish Hospital. Her mother's maiden name was Reardon." He looked at Jennings. "Was your wife's maiden name Reardon?"

Jennings nodded. When he spoke again, his voice shook, his tone was bitter, and he looked every one of his advanced years. "I would say you have furthered your investigation a great deal, Inspector. It seems to me this woman found the obituary of my daughter's death in an old newspaper or perhaps was walking through the cemetery and saw the stone, copied down the information, and found the birth record at the County Offices." He paused, composing himself. "Then she stole my daughter's identity," he said.

Dawson realized there was nothing he could say at this point.

"That makes me angry," Jennings said, his voice was stronger now, but his hands were shaking, and he set his glass on the table beside his chair. "My daughter's life was complete, if short, Inspector. She lacked for nothing. It was not possible to have more love or care than our Mavis had. When she died, her life was finished. It was not there to be *stolen* by some woman seeking a new identity."

"I agree."

For a moment, Jennings stared out the window. Then he turned back to Dawson. "Well, what do you intend to do with your new information?"

"I'm not sure," Dawson admitted. "I'm here on vacation time. My chief has closed the case; he's calling it suicide."

"And you don't buy the suicide theory." It was a statement, not a question.

Dawson shook his head.

"Did you check with the shrinks about suicide?"

"I called the expert witness the prosecution uses. But she said many suicides act perfectly normal just before the act."

"And I suppose everybody at the event thought she was acting normally?"

"Yes."

"How long have you been working on this?"

"About a week."

"Then I suspect your chief has closed it for purposes of his own," Jennings said, again pushing himself out of the chair.

Dawson, startled by Jennings' keen grasp of the situation, rose to his feet. "Thank you," he said. "I'm sorry to have. . ."

Jennings made a brusque gesture with his hand. "Sit

down. I'm gonna put our dinner in the oven and use the bathroom - at my age a little Scotch . . ." He left the sentence unfinished.

"I couldn't possibly impose on you."

"Nonsense! You owe me more than you've given me. Besides, my housekeeper leaves me gargantuan meals which I usually end up feeding to Caruso. It will be a pleasure to have a guest. Help yourself to the Scotch." And with that, Jennings left the room.

The housekeeper had left a large casserole. Dawson put together a green salad while Jennings rummaged in his basement for a bottle of wine. "I know I've got a wonderful old Merlot down here," he called up to Dawson. "Just can't remember where I put it."

Dawson chuckled.

"Ah!" came a shout of satisfaction, and Jennings appeared at the top of the stairs, clutching a dusty bottle. He went to the kitchen door, letting in a cocker spaniel. "This is Caruso," he said. "He likes to be present at dinner preparation."

Dawson stooped to pet Caruso. The dog gave him a suspicious glance, and took a place close to Jennings' side. "He's extremely protective," Jennings said, scratching the dog's ears.

"Why Caruso?"

Jennings threw back his head, belting *Vesti la giubbi*. The thin voice wavered and cracked. The dog lifted his nose and sang along, a cross between a howl, a whine and a yelp.

Momentarily taken aback, Dawson began to laugh. "You seem to take very good care of yourself Mr. Jennings," he observed when he got his composure back.

"Colin, please. I have a niece, Inspector. She's made it quite clear when I stop eating well and the house starts to smell, she'll ship me off to one of those god-awful retirement places where you get a schedule of god-awful activities at the beginning of every week along with the god-awful menu. It behooves me to pay a housekeeper. Comes in a few hours every week day – cleans, cooks, does my laundry."

"What did you do before you retired?" Dawson asked, still smiling over the brief concert.

"I was with the police department," Jennings replied.

Dawson raised an eyebrow.

"A Detective Inspector."

Over dinner Jennings said, "I figured you were here about some old case of mine. I am sort of 'emeritus' with my department, and they frequently come by to pick my memory about an old case. Or – sometimes – even a new one. So I was surprised when you started talking about Mavis."

"I should have guessed. You certainly didn't react like the average citizen when I showed you my ID."

Jennings laughed. "Most people have some guilty secret," he said.

Dawson helped himself to a second serving of stew. "Are you busy tomorrow?" he asked.

Jennings snorted. "People my age are seldom 'busy.' Usually our social life consists of trips to the doctor. What's on your mind?"

"I was wondering – would you take me to Mavis's grave?"

Jennings pursed his lips. After a moment he said, "All right. If you want. I haven't been in a while. Do you mind if I take some tools and do some cleanup while we're there?" He picked up the wine bottle, tipping it to pour for Dawson.

"Not at all. We'll both work," Dawson said, putting his hand over his wine glass. "I still have to drive tonight," he added.

"Just out of curiosity, why do you want to see the grave?"

Dawson shook his head and put down his fork. "It's – it's just this case has gotten to me like no other case ever has," he said finally. And, having developed a feel for Jennings' professionalism, made the decision to share some of the details of the case and Moynahan's subsequent closing of the same.

When he finished bringing Jennings up to date, he said. "Perhaps it's the people involved, the suspects, or the dead woman, a woman with no friends," he said in summary. "I can't put a finger on it. I just want to experience every aspect of the case, is all."

"I had a few cases like that," Jennings said, and the evening passed as the two men shared their stories.

Dawson woke the next morning to find Seattle enjoying a light drizzle, enough to keep the windshield wipers on his rented car at a low speed. "We can go another day," Dawson said when he arrived at Jennings' house. "I've got plenty of time."

Jennings looked at the sky. "It'll pass. By the time we

get up there, it'll be over." He picked up a small tool bag by the front door. "Anyway, this'll loosen the weeds – make 'em easier to pull. Just let me pick some roses, and we'll get going."

"I – uh – brought some flowers," Dawson said. He had stopped at a florist stand on his way to pick up Jennings.

Jennings' eyes filled with tears. "That was kind of you."

The cemetery where Mavis and Estelle Jennings lay was high on a hill overlooking Seattle and Puget Sound; in the far distance, Mt. Rainier, a shadow behind heavy clouds, stood as sentinel. Three stones stood on the small plot: a tiny stone engraved *Mavis Jennings 1967 – 1969*, flanked by two larger stones. One of the larger stones bore the name *Estelle Reardon Jennings;* one was still blank. Dawson regretted his intrusion on this little family.

The lawns of the cemetery were neatly trimmed, and Dawson could not see much that needed care, but Jennings dropped his kneeling pad on the ground and, easing himself down, began to pull small weeds from the white rock covering the graves. While Jennings weeded, Dawson took the containers from the base of the stones and went to find a faucet. Returning the filled containers to their receptacles, Dawson divided the flowers between the two graves. Then he squatted beside Jennings, and silently the two men weeded.

As Jennings had promised, the drizzle stopped, and the sun made a feeble appearance. The morning passed quickly. When Dawson invited Jennings to have lunch with him, the old man readily accepted. "If you'd stand me to a Big Mac, I'd be very grateful. My niece, my doctor, and my housekeeper – they're all in league against me, so whenever I get the chance, I sneak one." His eyes twinkled as he grinned at Dawson. "With French fries," he added.

Dawson stopped the car in front of Jennings' house and popped the trunk. Jennings collected his tools and then stuck his head through the passenger's window. "What are you gonna do now?" he asked. There was a small splotch of ketchup on his sweater.

"I thought I'd take a few days and wander up the Strait of Juan de Fuca. Then maybe I'll go to Victoria. I was there once when I was a little kid. I'd like to go back."

"Huh! Tourist trap."

"I'm a tourist," Dawson said with a shrug. "I'll call you when I get back to town. Meanwhile, give this case some thought. I would welcome your wisdom."

Jennings nodded. "See you around."

"You might want to get the ketchup off your sweater before your housekeeper sees it."

Jennings laughed and swiped his finger at the offending condiment. "You're a good man, Inspector Dawson." Then he turned and made his way slowly up the walk to his house.

And Dawson, with an afternoon ahead of him and remembering the disdain in Jennings' voice, parked his vehicle at the Monorail station and rode out to the Space Needle. Although he'd seen it many times, he had never been to the top. *Just a tourist, Jennings,* he said to himself as the elevator rose. *Just a tourist.*

That evening, following a solitary meal at Anthony's

Home Port, a seafood restaurant on the waterfront, he returned to his motel and made two phone calls.

Laura Eggleton answered the first. "Jake," she exclaimed. "Where are you?"

"Seattle."

"Bill's got ants in his pants waiting to hear from you."

"He could have called."

"He said you'd call when you had news. Do you?"

"I do."

"He's giving Beth her bath. I'll take the phone to him."

Dawson could hear Eggleton singing about an eensy weensy spider and Beth giggling, then Laura saying, "It's Jake. I'll take over."

"It's about time. Sir! I've been going crazy."

"Guess your cell doesn't work, huh?"

"Never mind. What did you find out from Mavis's father?"

"She stole her identity from a dead baby."

"Holy shit!"

"You put it so succinctly, Bill," Dawson said and relayed his visit with Jennings, including the trip to the cemetery and the trip to MacDonalds.

"Sounds like quite a guy."

"He is. I'll speak with Mrs. Dillon when I get back. Unofficially. We still don't have any proof, but this is one hell of a motive. I'll at least make her uncomfortable."

"Oh, yeah you will. Moynahan'll accuse you of harassing her."

"No he won't, because she won't complain."

"You're right. When are you coming back?"

"I'm going to do the tourist thing for a while, Bill. There's no hurry on this. Officially, it's not going anywhere."

"Call me when you finish being a tourist."

"I will."

Dawson's second call was to his daughter, Virginia. Their relationship, since he and his wife had divorced, had been fragile and their contact infrequent. But Dawson's mind was filled with thoughts of much-loved daughters that evening: Mavis Jennings who died at two and Beth Eggleton, the same age, who was giggling with her father as he sang and bathed her. Had he ever sung to Ginny? But then, he reminded himself, he didn't sing. For all his musical training, he had never sung. Would a two-year old have minded if he didn't sound good? His thoughts skittered like a mouse on ice.

"Dad?"

"Hi, Gin. I just thought I'd give a call."

"Something wrong?"

"No, actually I'm in Seattle." He started to say, 're-search on a case,' but thought better of it. "Just some vacation time – take a few days, go up the Straits –maybe go to Victoria for a day. Would it be OK if I came down to Portland for a quick visit?"

There was just a brief moment of silence, and then she said, "I'd love to see you, Dad. But instead of you coming to Portland – well, actually, Victoria sounds like fun. Could I tag along?"

"Absolutely! I'd love it."

"How soon were you planning to go?"

"Up to you. I've got another two weeks."

"Why don't you do your trip up the Straits, and I'll make arrangements here at the clinic and give you a call. I could probably meet you in Port Angeles and we could take the ferry from there."

"Perfect," he said, his voice thick – his eyes watering a bit.

"You got a cold, Dad?"

"I'm fine. I'll hear from you. Love you," he said as he ended the call – and grabbed some tissues from a box in the bathroom.

CHAPTER TWENTY-ONE

Shall I Be Mother?

...to undo the heavy burdens...
Isaiah 58:6

Dawson's trip up the Strait of Juan de Fuca was leisurely. As the boats that took him from island to island plowed through the choppy waters, he tried to push the case to the back of his mind.

Stopping in at quaint bed-and-breakfasts, he asked about walks, beaches, and where he might rent a bicycle; he concentrated on his next meal and his next destination, his slight sunburn and the sand in his shoes, his upcoming visit with Ginny. Yet his time with Colin Jennings kept creeping in. Whatever the results of his new information, the old man and his story would stay with him long after he moved on to other cases.

When Ginny called with a time and place to meet in Port Angeles, he set off for the Olympic Peninsula with a light-heartedness he hadn't felt in years. "Four o'clock, Wednesday, Red Lion Inn," she had said. "It's walking distance to the ferry. We'll catch the eight-twenty Thursday morning."

Eager to see Ginny, Dawson arrived in Port Angeles several hours early and killed time roaming the little shops that lined the streets of town. But as four o'clock approached and he pulled his car into the parking lot of the Red Lion, he found he was nervous. *She's my daughter, for God's sake*, he thought. *"I'm scared,"* he thought, realizing he hadn't seen her since his father's funeral. And then she pulled in next to him.

"Dad!" she said as she stepped from the car and opened her arms. For a moment, her smile was too bright, his voice too loud, her body a bit stiff when he hugged her, his body a bit stiff when she hugged him. But just for a moment. Then they softened to each other and he whispered, "Hi, Gin."

They chose to have an early dinner at a seafood restaurant on the waterfront, but later Dawson could not have said what they ate. All he would remember was that time and wine loosened their tongues and memories.

"So, what brought you to Seattle?" Ginny asked as the waiter set a basket of warm sourdough bread on the table. She reached across and took a piece.

"It seems a person of interest – that's what we call it now - in my investigation has stolen the identity of a baby born in Seattle nearly fifty years ago. I talked with that baby's father last week. The baby was two years old when she died."

"That's awful, Dad. How'd the father take it?" she asked, spreading butter on the bread.

"As you might imagine. Angry."

Ginny nodded. "Yes. He should be. Does this information help your case any?"

"Oh, yes. Except it isn't my case anymore. The chief closed it down. He's ruled it a suicide – purely for political reasons. Too messy, too much dirty laundry in high places if he doesn't just tuck it away. Anyway, I had time coming, so I'm here on my own dime, spending my vacation days.

"So what are you going to do with your information?"

"My plan is to confront her with my findings and see what she does."

"And if she refuses to respond?"

Dawson shrugged. "The case is closed. Not much I can do. Moynahan – that's the chief – won't be interested in what I have. His mind is made up. But if she refuses, I think I will have solved the case – at least in my mind."

"No arrest?"

"No. But she'll always know I know. There will be some small satisfaction in that," he said, helping himself to the bread and butter.

"Be hard for her to live with, I would imagine – you knowing."

"Yep! At least the average person would find it difficult to live with. But she's not the average person, Gin. Far from it."

"Do you ever wish you weren't a cop?" Ginny asked, as she took a bite of the bread. "Do you ever wish you'd made music your career?"

"Not really. I would have ended up in academia, maybe doing solo work with small orchestras. I would have been bored to death – and terribly frustrated. So, no. I like what I do."

"Do you still play?"

"Huh?"

"The piano."

"Just for myself."

Ginny smiled. "I loved it when you played. Sometimes when you got in late, you'd go to the piano. You thought you were playing softly – and you were - but I could just barely hear it. And I'd go to sleep."

His throat tightened, and he couldn't speak– so he didn't.

Ginny didn't seem to notice his hesitation. "Maybe I'll come for a visit, and you can play for me."

"Yes," he said, his voice little more than a croak. "Yes."

Eventually the conversation turned to the divorce – it was Ginny who started it. "I was devastated when you and Mom broke up – I mean high school's hard enough on a kid. But I was glad when a job opened up for you in the wine country, and you went to live with Grandpa. It had to be a blessing for him to have you there, especially when he got so ill."

"About us breaking up . . . " Dawson said.

Ginny put her hand up. "At the time, I blamed you. Every case seemed more important than we were. That was hard on me, even harder on Mom. And then you nearly got shot."

"Actually, I did get shot."

"Right– but at least you didn't get killed. Anyway, later, when I got over being mad – which, incidentally, took me a long time– and stopped to think about it, I realized, hey! Mom knew you were a cop when she married you; she knew cop hours weren't nine to five; she knew you could get shot at any time. She just wasn't prepared for the reality of what she knew." She stopped and took another piece of sourdough from the basket. "Anyway, Dad, Mom's OK now," she continued." She's got Claude, two dogs, and a house in the country. And Claude's underfoot all the time. So, for her things have worked out."

The waiter placed their salads in front of them. *Perfect timing* Dawson thought, since he didn't want to talk about his ex-wife's happiness. "And things have worked out well for me, too," Ginny went on, as she poured extra dressing on her salad. "I love where I am. Gary wants to branch out and concentrate on large animal care, so Mark and I get the dogs and cats and birds and lizards and hamsters. Good all around. And I appreciate your support through my license— you and grandpa. Most of the students at Davis had huge loans when they got out. I didn't have any."

"The money was from your grandpa. He was so proud of you going to vet school," Dawson said, pushing his salad around on his plate.

"I know. But you were cheering me on all the time." She looked at him closely. "How are things with you, Dad? After the divorce and losing Grandpa and all?"

Dawson thought of his sterile condo, a freezer of frozen dinners, a single-ticket symphony subscription, of days off spent listening to CDs or reading, the fact that he had free time now that he hadn't had when he worked in Southern California, the fact that his boss was more crooked than many of the criminals he had dealt with. "I'm fine," he lied. "I'm fine."

Ginny pursed her lips.

"My boss is an asshole, but I have a great partner, Sergeant Eggleton," he continued. "And I like being up in the vineyards." He paused, nodding his head. "I'm good. I really am."

"Any ladies?"

"Maybe."

"Maybe?"

"I'm still leasing out your grandfather's vineyards," he said, changing the subject. "Mostly we're growing Chardonny – that's a large market – but we have a few acres of Merlots, too. I'm a hands-off landlord. The wineries handle all the work. I just collect the rent."

"Right!"

"No, really."

"Do you ever think of selling the vineyards?"

Dawson shook his head. "Not yet. I've had offers, but I'm just not ready to let them go. Maybe someday. I had an excellent offer several months ago from . . ." but at that moment the waiter arrived with their dinners, and he never did finish what he had started to say.

"Would you like another?" the waiter asked, gesturing to their wine glasses.

"Yes," they both said, and the evening– and heavy subjects– passed.

Morning found them at the ferry slip. Thick fog and the smell of salt air lay over the town; righteously-angry gulls squawked, fog horns alerted. Ginny wore a tee shirt, jeans and a matching jean jacket, her blond hair pulled into a ponytail, a large, soft leather pouch over her shoulder. Dawson wore khakis, a long-sleeved checked shirt and a wind-breaker.

"Looks like we're dressed for any weather," Ginny said.

"We'll probably end up carrying the jackets."

"Might be glad we have them while we're on the boat."

And they were.

Upon disembarking in Victoria, their jackets tied around their waists, Dawson and Ginny strolled the streets of Victoria, enjoying the hanging baskets of flowers, the horse-drawn Tally Ho carriages.

"You want to take a ride?" Dawson asked.

Ginny shook her head. "I'm away from animals today."

"Mom and Dad brought me here when I was just a little kid," Dawson said. "We took a Tally Ho ride, and the driver asked everyone to lean forward to help the horses up the hill." He stopped to laugh. "So I did; I leaned forward. Your grandpa got the biggest kick out of that."

Ginny slipped her arm through his.

"That was the same trip when I tried to drink the water in the finger bowl – right there in the dining room at the Empress."

"Dad!"

"He never let me forget that one either."

"Memories."

"Good ones. That's why I wanted to come again." He stopped at a window display. "I'm going to pop in here for just a minute."

"A china shop?"

But he was already through the door.

Remembering Marjorie's offer to fix dinner when he got back from his trip to Seattle and remembering his mother's admonition to never arrive for dinner without a

343

hostess gift, he– after much deliberation– selected a cup and saucer, cream colored and of such delicate china he could see the shadow of his hand when he held it to the light. *Belleek*, it said on the bottom. Ginny watched the transaction with a slight smile.

Dawson was carrying two bags when they arrived at the Empress for their two o'clock Afternoon Tea. One bag was large and held a green and black gift box of Glenfiddish Single Malt Whiskey: the smaller, a beautifully wrapped package containing a china cup and saucer. The lobby of the hotel was scattered with small tables arranged for tea. Oriental carpets, faded with the passage of decades and the footsteps of guests, covered the floors. Comfortable wing-back chairs invited lingering, antique tapestries hung from the walls. In one corner of the room, a pianist played the grand piano; gentle music from a gentler era.

Their waiter, crisp in his blazer and tie, appeared, seemingly out of nowhere, bearing a large tray which held a teapot and cups crafted of delicate china, and a tower of tiny scones, sandwiches and desserts. Dawson and Ginny made small talk about the weather as the waiter organized their table, then disappeared as silently as he had arrived.

"Shall I be mother?" Dawson asked, picking up the tea pot.

"Dad! I think you're getting a bit carried away with this high tea thing," Ginny said, laughing as Dawson filled her cup.

I don't think I could be any more carried away then I am right now, Dawson thought, but didn't say. What he did say was, "Usually I get my tea in a chipped mug at the police station."

"Cop!"

"That I am."

Ginny pointed to the small bag Dawson had set on the floor at his feet. "Maybe?"

He smiled. "Maybe."

Their ferry docked in Port Angeles at five-thirty.

When they arrived at their cars, still parked at the Red Lion, Ginny reached in her bag and pulled out what looked like a wad of bubble wrap. "A souvenir," she said, handing it to Dawson.

"What's this?"

"Open it."

Unrolling the bubble wrap, he found a mug with 'VICTORIA' on it and a small picture of a horse-drawn Tally Ho.

"For your tea at work," Ginny said, "I tried to find a finger-bowl, but they didn't have one," she added, straight-faced, her voice flat.

Dawson rolled his eyes. "You're as bad as your grandpa," he said, and kissed her cheek. "When did you get this? You didn't go in any of the shops."

"Gift shop on the ferry. When you were snoozing. Did you know you snore? Just a tiny bit."

Dawson ignored her observation. "Thanks, Gin," he said. "Are you sure you don't want to stay over? I think I will. It's a long drive."

"I'm going to spend the night with a friend in Olympia," she said, not quite meeting his eye. It was a mannerism Dawson remembered from her high school days.

"Maybe?" Dawson asked, his eyebrows high.

"Maybe," she said and laughed.

A brusque-sounding woman answered the phone when Dawson called Jennings the next day.

"Is Mr. Jennings there?" he asked.

"Who's calling?"

"Tell him Jake Dawson."

Jennings voice was strong and eager when he came to the phone. "Where are you?"

"I just checked into my motel. Can I take you out to dinner? "

"You come here. I'll get Judy to whip up her chicken casserole."

"I feel like I'm imposing again."

"Don't. I'm an old man, and I don't really like to eat out that much anymore." His voice dropped to a whisper. "Unless it's MacDonalds."

Dawson laughed. "I'll bring the wine."

"You do that. I've been making some notes. Five-thirty OK?"

"I'll be there," Dawson said and closed his phone.

Colin Jennings accepted Dawson's gift of Glenfiddish with due appreciation. "That's the real stuff," he said.

"Got it up there in that tourist trap," Dawson said, not meeting Jennings' eyes. He held up a bottle of California chardonnay. "I'll put this in the refrigerator. Where's Caruso?"

"Outside."

When Dawson opened the door, the dog looked at him skeptically and hurried to Jennings' side. "Well?" Dawson said.

Jennings' eyebrows asked the question.

"A song. From the two of you."

"Oh," Jennings said. "What shall we sing today, Caruso?" Then he threw his head back; this time it was *La donna e mobile.*

Again, Caruso raised his head in his combination howl, whine and yelp.

"Does he sing the same song every time?" Dawson asked, wiping tears of laughter from his eyes.

"Limited repertoire."

Judy's excellent casserole and the chilled wine received only cursory attention as the two men discussed Dawson's case. Jennings had filled several sheets of yellow legal pad with a scrawl only he could read, and the sheets littered the table where they ate. Jennings scribbled notes and crossed out questions as they talked.

"It seems to me," Jennings said, pointing his fork at Dawson, "that even though you've found out about this Mavis's. . ." and his voice put quotes around the name, ". . . identity – which, as I mentioned before, she stole– there's another layer that you have to penetrate to find out her real motive."

"Don't you mean real secret? I think her motive is her daughter. Dr. Glasco, who was one of the . . . uh," Dawson paused, ". . . one of the people at the party, said *'that girl is her life.'* So, whatever she's hiding about her background, she's done because of the girl, to protect her. The next layer would be the secret she has to keep from her daughter."

Jennings picked up his wine glass, and, taking a sip, looked at Dawson, his eyes narrowed. "Do you realize you're not able to say 'suspect' when it comes to your doctor friend? Your chief was right about one thing, Jake: you're too close to this case." He set his glass down and said, "But I digress. What's the secret the girl can't know? Tell me again, when did this Mavis person apply to Social Security?"

"Nineteen-ninety."

"You told me earlier that the girl is in her mid-twenties. So Mavis established her new identity about the same time the child was born."

"Uh huh."

"And you said something about a family tree . . ."

"Apparently at the sherry party Mrs. Cunningham offered to do a family tree for the girl's wedding. She dabbled in genealogy."

"That's right," Jennings said, nodding. "Background."

"The notation in Cunningham's diary: *b-k-g-d.*"

"So she offered the family tree which would mean a genealogy check. That certainly would have rattled Mavis! Answers another one of my questions," he added, crossing out a portion of his scribbles on the legal pad. "She would have come up empty, wouldn't she? Mrs. Cunningham, I mean."

"She would."

"She wouldn't have access to records like you do," Jennings continued. "Social Security and all that. And when she submitted the name to whatever sources those genealogy people submit to – zilch." He flipped one of the yellow sheets. "Would she have had the knowledge about the nicotine?" He ran his finger, crooked with arthritis, down a list. "Mavis? Your doctor friend might, and the landscape guy, of course. Also the gardener. If you're including him as a suspect. But would Mavis?"

"She's certainly knowledgeable about gardening," Dawson said. "But would she specifically have information about nicotine? I don't know. Apparently, when Alexander – that's the landscape gardener -– arrived at the party, he said something about bringing the nicotine and he would show Andrew how to dilute it. So anybody could have overheard him."

"She's marrying well . . . the daughter. You mentioned a symphony conductor when you were here before."

"Yes. A maestro. He's Russian – serving as a long-term guest conductor with the San Francisco Symphony." Dawson shrugged.

"Quite a coup, from her point of view."

"Certainly a reason to want to keep any secrets secret."

Jennings looked at Dawson. Again his eyes narrowed. "Do you think that Mavis is the one who killed your Mrs. Cunningham?"

Dawson was silent for a few moments. "I honestly don't know," he said at last. "But it's one hell of a motive. Still, could she actually commit murder? Could any of these people?"

Jennings made a derisive noise.

"I know, I know," Dawson said, as he remembered being on the opposite side of the same conversation recently with Eggleton.

But Jennings went right on. "Anybody, given sufficient motive, is capable of murder!"

"You're right," Dawson said.

"Of course I'm right. But motives are purely subjective." Again Jennings pointed his fork at Dawson. "Take your doctor friend. I think you see his maybe giving some assistance to terminal patients as a fairly strong motive for keeping Mrs. Cunningham quiet" He took a mouthful of chicken and washed it down with wine. "Even though you don't want to admit he could do such a thing," he added with a twinkle in his eye. "Now me, I don't see it as such a big deal. I expect we'd be surprised to find out just how many doctors do it. Who's to question? The families are just delighted their loved one is out of their misery– or they're delighted they don't have to take care of them anymore. If it was me – which it probably won't be because it looks like my terminal disease is old age – but if it was, I'd welcome a doctor like your friend."

"His license to practice would be revoked."

"If it became public."

"True. Still, information like that in the hands of a woman like Mrs. Cunningham . . ."

"Now this Bishop fellow," Jennings interrupted. "That's a powerful motive if I ever heard one – prominent position in the hierarchy of the church."

"After talking to him, I felt he was most concerned about the woman and her husband – their marriage, the well-being of the little boy. That doesn't mean he didn't care about his position and his own family. He definitely did. But I got the impression of a highly moral man."

"Who slept with his secretary."

"He's a man, Colin. First, he's a man. We're all fallible."

Jennings folded his arms on the table and leaned across to Dawson. "Well, anyway. You just proved my point. One man's motive is not necessarily another's."

Dawson nodded.

"Incidentally, I happen to agree with you about this landscape fellow," Jennings said, looking back at his notes. "I don't think he has much of a motive. Did you check his story?"

"I spoke with the warden of the prison where he did time. Model prisoner, nice guy, said their grounds at the prison are a show place, thanks to Alexander."

"What about his wife?"

"His wife? At the time, I wondered if her candor about her husband's prison record might be a smoke screen. But, no. I don't think so," he said, shaking his head. "We checked her out – her story. Seems she was married to a scum who passed out and died of an aneurysm on the way to the hospital. Pretty much what she told us – nothing suspicious about his death. Besides, there was no cryptic notation by her name."

"Still, if holding her head up in the community meant a lot to her, having it found out that her husband had been in prison . . ." Jennings shrugged his shoulders and slid his chair back. "It's just something to consider. You want some dessert? It's ice cream."

"Sure," Dawson said, standing. He began to clear the dishes from the table.

"Just stack 'em," Jennings said. "Judy'll put 'em in the dishwasher in the morning." He took a carton from the freezer and began scooping ice cream into two small dishes. "You know, Jake, you're gonna have to ask this Mavis person why she took on the phony identity." He licked the spoon and dropped it in the sink. "If she tells you, you can judge just how strong her motive really was. If she admits the false identity but refuses to tell you why she took it, you'll probably have your murderer." He set the dishes on the table. "You follow me?"

"I was thinking the same. But she'll know Moynahan has closed the case and will probably refuse to talk. So I won't ask her – I'll tell her what I know. See what she does with it."

The old man nodded. "Yes. It's difficult to solve a case based on motive. I know. I've tried it. It doesn't stick."

Dawson took a bite of ice cream. "Maybe I can get a confession," he said, grinning at Jennings.

Jennings laughed. "Yeah! And I've got a bridge you're gonna want to buy."

CHAPTER TWENTY-TWO

A Vase Cracks – A Petal Falls

Why askest thou thus after my name, seeing it is secret?
Judg. 13:18

July 10

It was early Friday afternoon, and Mavis Dillon was tending her borders. Several weeks had passed since the wedding, and the weeds were popping up. Mavis, who enjoyed gardening, had told Andrew not to worry about that section; she would take care of it.

As she worked, her thoughts, as they had so often in the past weeks, turned to the wedding. She felt it had been as perfect as such an occasion could be. St. Francis, decorated with flowers echoing the rose, gold and purple tones of the stained glass windows, was filled with dignitaries, famous musicians, personal friends of the young couple, the vestry of St. Francis and other Castlemont acquaintances.

Carole Anne, on the arm of Dr. Charles Glasco, and stunningly beautiful in her dress – a creamy satin sheath with a chapel train – had drawn gasps from the assembled well-wishers as she walked slowly down the aisle to *Purcell's Trumpet Voluntary*, the clear tones, played by the first chair trumpet player of the San Francisco Symphony Orchestra, cutting through the deep-throated voice of the accompanying organ.

Following the exchange of vows, the symphony concert master played Massenet's *Meditation from Thais*. A string quartet, made up of symphony members, performed for the reception in Mavis's garden, which, thanks to Andrew's hard work, was meticulously groomed. A team of caterers served the gourmet luncheon with efficiency and near invisibility.

There had been no mention of Gwen Cunningham or the recent tragedy.

"I see you've recovered from the wedding."

Startled, Mavis jumped. "Inspector!" Pulling off her gardening gloves, she wiped her cheek with the back of one hand, leaving a small smudge of dirt. Her fair hair escaped in wisps from under her gardening hat, and again Dawson was struck by her beauty. Struck and unmoved.

"I'm just finishing up here." she said, placing her tools and gloves in a small basket. "I didn't know anything could be so much work. As a wedding, I meant. Not pulling weeds."

"It went well?"

"It did. Very well." She looked around. "Your sergeant isn't with you?"

Dawson shook his head. "I have a few small things I want to go over with you regarding Mrs. Cunningham's death."

"I thought it was suicide."

"Officially. Just a few loose ends, and we can file it away. Anything of this nature generates a great deal of paperwork. I won't keep you long."

"I see," she said, clearly not pleased. "Well, in that

case, can I offer you a glass of wine? Or are you on duty?" And without waiting for Dawson's response, she led the way to the front door.

"I'm not on duty and a glass of wine would be a treat," Dawson said as he followed her.

Once inside, she turned to Dawson. "You'll excuse me for a moment – I'll wash up." With a vague gesture, she motioned toward the morning room and then went up the stairs, leaving Dawson alone in the entry hall.

Dawson dismissed the suggestion of the morning room, and when Mavis, dressed in jeans and a blue chambray western shirt, came downstairs, she found him seated at the big oak table in the kitchen. "I hope this is all right with you," she said, holding a bottle of wine for Dawson's inspection. He recognized a vintage Merlot and remembered his first visit with Colin Jennings.

"You have a cellar?"

"A climate controlled closet under the staircase. Not exactly a cellar." Moving aside a vase of roses, she placed some small paper napkins, embossed with 'D', on the table.

"Charles called me last week," she said, turning away from Dawson to a cupboard where Dawson could see an array of crystal stemware. "He told me Gwen's death has been determined a suicide."

"I've been instructed to consider it a suicide," Dawson countered.

"Instructed?" Her hand trembled slightly as she set two goblets on the table. One started to tip and Dawson caught it before it fell on its side.

"Officially, the case is closed."

"And unofficially?"

"Unofficially, I still think it was murder. For one thing, nobody saw Mrs. Cunningham going to the kitchen. The only time she left the party was to use the bathroom – upstairs – which you deflected to the downstairs one."

There was a pause as she took a corkscrew from a drawer. "Maybe she went into the kitchen after she came out of the bathroom. After all, I had several decanters of sherry on the counter for replacements in the drawing room."

"Perhaps. Can I help you?" He held out his hand as though to take the corkscrew.

She shook her head.

"You realize whoever killed her left all the other guests at the party to take the rap as suspects." He shifted in his chair. "Something that could hang over them the rest of their lives. Including you."

"Assuming it was murder. Will you pursue your theory?"

"I'd rather get a confession."

Her laugh was strained as she poured Dawson's wine. "As in good for the soul, Inspector?"

Dawson nodded, raising his glass toward her in a toasting gesture

Mavis frowned. "Confession is more a tenet of the Catholic Church than the Episcopal, I should think, and your suspects are Episcopalians, so I wouldn't hold out a lot of hope," she said, sipping her wine as she took a chair opposite Dawson. "Do you have proof of murder? Or just your personal feeling?"

"Right now, my personal feeling."

"Well, then. That just about takes care of it, doesn't it?"

Dawson turned sideways in his chair, crossing his legs. "Maybe. Of course, there's no statute of limitations on murder." He took a small taste of the wine, appreciating the velvety smoothness of a good Merlot, and then set the glass on the table. "Let me tell you what I think. You see, I wasn't able to approach this from the angle of evidence, since no one saw the nicotine added to her glass– or, I should say, no one *admitted* seeing it added to her glass– and fingerprints would not be relevant since all the glasses and decanters were heavily faceted crystal, and the nicotine bottle was handled by everyone. Also, means and opportunity were out, because everyone there had means and opportunity, which makes everyone present at the sherry party a suspect. I had eight suspects, nine if you count Andrew.

"Andrew?" Mavis gasped.

He ignored her interruption. "So I was forced to look at motive. Now, one member of the party was very forth-coming with motive from the beginning, and that person, having admitted to motive, gave credence to the datebook we found in Mrs. Cunningham's purse." He paused, sipping his wine. "She had written 'Sherry with the bishop' by the date. Then she listed the names of everyone attending the party, including you, with an abbreviated notation by each name."

"I see," Mavis said, looking at him over the rim of her glass. "And just what did she write by my name?"

Dawson picked up his glass. "In a minute," he said. "My sergeant and I spent a lot of time tracking down those notations, trying to decipher what they meant. Since the first one proved to be so accurate, we had reason to believe the subsequent ones had at least an element of truth in them."

"And did they?" she asked, setting aside her glass and tracing the 'D' on her napkin with her fingernail.

Moving the wine glass out of the way, Dawson leaned toward Mavis, his arms folded on the table. "They did."

"Mine?"

"The notation by your name was '*b-k-g-d* period' which we interpreted to mean 'background.' Let me show you," and taking a pencil from his pocket, he wrote on one of the napkins. "Obviously," and here Dawson made a sweep of his arm as though to include the entire house, "obviously there is money in your background, and, from just talking with you, one assumes education. Also, a glance at your bookshelves indicates an educated woman. We know your daughter is a violinist with the San Francisco Symphony. I've read the newspaper accounts of her wedding and find she was educated in private schools and even studied music abroad. All this says money: for schools and private music lessons . . ."

Mavis interrupted. "Inspector! You only had to ask!"

"And what would you have told me, Mrs. Dillon? About the husband who died shortly after – or maybe shortly before – your daughter was born? About his family, that they had been very wealthy, you were well provided for, and the family was all dead now?"

"It's all true," she said. "But how did you know all that?"

"Some of it I picked up in conversation with other people who know you," he said, "and some of it I guessed.

Now, I would expect if we were to peruse your personal documents, we would find your birth certificate, maybe a diploma from a prestigious university, a marriage certificate, a death certificate for your husband, your daughter's birth certificate. Am I right?"

Mavis's tone was defensive. "Surely that's not a crime," she said.

"No. And I imagine, when you die, those documents will satisfy your daughter. However, when I had my sergeant run a check on Stephen Dillon, he came up blank."

"A check on Stephen?"

"Stephen Dillon, Harvard University, 1980."

"The library books," she said under her breath.

"Yes. The trouble is, Harvard University has no record of Stephen Dillon. We even tried S-t-e-f-a-n and S-t-e-v-e-n. Then we thought perhaps it was a middle name, so we had them search for 'blank Stephen Dillon'." He took a sip of wine. "Mrs. Dillon," he said, "there was no Stephen Dillon enrolled at Harvard University from 1960 to 1995 – dates well beyond the parameters of your husband's possible attendance."

"I'm sure it was just a glitch in the computer," she said, looking at Dawson sternly, as one might look at a naughty child who had been spinning stories. "Of course Stephen was a student there."

Dawson continued as though she had not spoken. "At the same time, I had Sergeant Eggleton checking with Social Security, which gave me even more interesting information."

Mavis pulled the napkin up around the footed glass, making a type of paper cup. "Oh?"

Although Dawson knew the information by heart, he withdrew a small notebook from his pocket and began flipping the pages. "Your maiden name was Jennings?"

"Yes."

"Birthplace, Swedish Hospital, Seattle," he read. "June sixteenth, 1967, parents, Estelle and Colin Jennings, mother's maiden name, Reardon?"

She nodded.

He returned the notebook to his pocket. "Are your parents living?"

For the first time in many years, Mavis thought about her family, the little group of people she had left so many years before. Her sisters were probably replicas of their mother now – faded women bending to the yoke of their husbands' demands. She assumed her parents were dead. They would be in their late seventies if they were alive, but medical care was something her father had scorned. "The body is the temple of the Lord!" he would thunder whenever his wife suggested calling a doctor for one of the girls. "If it is His will she be sick, or taken from us, so be it!" Mavis had long since put her family out of her mind. "No," she said in answer to Dawson's question. "They're not living."

"Hummmm. ." Dawson murmured as he picked up his wine glass and took a sip. "I should tell you that up there in Seattle we found a Colin Jennings. Now, Mr. Jennings is in his eighties, but he's very sharp. In fact, I visited him while I was in Seattle recently."

"You went to Seattle?" Mavis 's face turned hard for a moment, and Dawson caught a glimpse of the woman beneath the façade, rather like an exquisite vase which has cracked, exposing the humble clay foundation.

In a low, unemotional voice, Dawson related his visits with Mr. Jennings. "The last thing Mr. Jennings said to me was, 'I hope it was someone else who murdered your Mrs. Cunningham – I'd hate to have my daughter's name sullied any further.'"

When he finished, Mavis was silent, her face impassive but very pale.

Dawson continued. "You, or someone acting for you, obtained a false identity. It's not unheard of – take the name of an infant off the gravestone, go to the county offices and newspapers, find all the particulars about the birth, then get a Social Security number in the child's name. For Social Security purposes – which you had to have for income tax. Then Mavis Jennings marries, becomes Mavis Dillon, is widowed." He took a sip of wine. "And constructs a whole new life with counterfeit documents."

"I think you missed your calling, Inspector. You should write for the reality shows."

Again, Dawson ignored her interruption. "When I talked with Charles about the party for the bishop, and what conversation he had with Mrs. Cunningham, he mentioned, when he joined you and Mrs. Cunningham, she was talking about a family tree as a gift for your daughter's wedding. Then, when I was at her house, I found an extensive library on the subject of genealogy as well as a sophisticated genealogy program on her computer." Dawson began folding his napkin, as though for some elaborate origami bird, concentrating on the folding as he spoke. "I also learned from Mrs. Meyerson that Mrs. Cunningham was more than willing to poke into someone's family history. I suspect she offered to look up your family for you – trace your ancestors – or your husband's. So when I discovered Mavis Jennings had died at the age of two, I asked myself, what would Mrs. Dillon think about Gwen Cunningham planning a genealogy search?" He looked up from his paper folding, meeting Mavis's eyes. "And I answered myself that Mrs. Dillon might find it very threatening."

Mavis's face was stony.

"She would have asked you for names," he continued. "Would you have stonewalled her? If you did, she could have spread it about you had something to hide, which couldn't have been good for you or for your daughter's upcoming wedding. You couldn't risk giving her names, because she would have run into the same kind of problems we did when we checked with Harvard University. No such person."

"I'm sure it was just a computer . . ."

"Then perhaps you can give me the years he was enrolled, and I can have them run it again."

"What possible connection does my husband's college . . .?" She stopped and stared into her empty wine glass, her lips pursed. Out in the hall a clock struck, ponderous, deep-throated chimes: one-two-three-four. When she spoke again, her voice was flat, emotionless. "That won't be necessary, Inspector."

Dawson leaned across the table. "Why don't you tell me about it," he said softly.

Mavis was silent for a long time. She was recalling the letter she had received from Felipe's lawyer two years before. In it, he had told her of Felipe's death. *The trust remains unchanged unless you violate your agreement of total confidentiality. Should you do so, the trust will be immediately*

revoked. We have followed you closely since the implementa-
tion of the trust and find you have honored your agreement to
date. The death of Mr. Contraras does not alter the agreement,
and we will continue to monitor. Upon your death, the entire
principal, as coming from the estate of Stephen Dillon, will be
made available to your daughter.

When Mavis spoke, it was to refuse Dawson. "You
came to discover a motive for me wanting Gwen dead; you
have it. You don't need anything else. It would serve no
purpose in your investigation."

Dawson reflected on his conversation with Colin
Jennings. *If she admits the false identity, but refuses to tell*
you why she took it, you'll probably have your murderer.
"Shouldn't I be the judge of that, Mrs. Dillon?" he asked.

"No." she said, her voice biting. Outside the window,
a bird was singing, a happy trill going on and on in marked
contrast to Mavis's tone. "No. I should be judge of that.
Except to borrow a name I had no right to borrow, I've hurt
no one with the identity I've chosen. I've raised a daughter
of whom I am extremely proud. My first concern has always
been she be protected, and I will continue to do that."

"And a mother protecting her child is an extremely
strong motive for murder," Dawson countered.

"You said you have no firm evidence it even was
murder. I hardly think you can get a conviction based on
my motive. Or the motives of any of the other guests for
that matter." She poured herself a small amount of wine.
"Besides," she smiled – a smile that did not reach her eyes.
"if you really thought you had a case against me, you'd be
advising me about my rights and telling me to call a lawyer."

Dawson did not respond. Instead he said, "Let me

tell you what I think happened to Mrs. Cunningham on Saturday afternoon. Actually, I have several scenarios about what happened. Now this is still conjecture, but I think she said something to someone . . ."

"A hypothetical someone," Mavis interrupted.

Dawson tipped his head in acknowledgement. ". . . something that frightened that person into thinking Gwen Cunningham had to die. So here's my first scenario. Suppose my suspect took his or her own glass into the kitchen, added the nicotine, and carried it back to the party, naturally never drinking from the glass. He or she waited for a time when Mrs. Cunningham put her own glass down, then made a quick switch."

"And your next scenario?"

"A variation of the first," Dawson said with a shrug. "Mrs. Cunningham left the room to go upstairs – an attempt you thwarted," he added, "so she set her glass on the table in the hallway and went into the downstairs bathroom. Then my hypothetical suspect picked up Mrs. Cunningham's glass, nipped into the kitchen, added a few drops of nicotine to the sherry remaining in the glass, and returned the glass to the hall table."

"And since I was in the hallway about then, you think I might have 'nipped into the kitchen'."

Dawson spread his hands in a you're right, 'what-can-I-say' gesture?

"And no one saw this suspect of yours pick up the glass? Assuming Gwen did set it on the hall table."

Dawson thought back to his conversation with Nancy Gifford. *"When I came out of the kitchen, Gwen was headed down the hall toward the downstairs bathroom, and Mavis* was gone. I guess she was back in the drawing room."

"Did you see Mrs. Dillon back in the drawing room, Mrs. Gifford?"

"No. But I wasn't looking for her either."

"This person could have slipped into any one of the rooms along the hallway if someone else came along – or the wine closet."

"Suppose someone else came along and picked up the glass after the poison was in it, thinking it was theirs." Mavis said.

"A possibility if the poisoned glass was set down in the drawing room, but very unlikely someone would mistake a lone glass on a table in the hallway for their own."

"That would have cut it awfully close, wouldn't it?" Mavis asked. "I mean for this suspect of yours – this hypothetical suspect of yours – to take the glass off the table and go out into the kitchen. Suppose Gwen came out and found her glass gone?"

"I'd thought of that. It's possible my suspect got a clean glass from the cabinet," Dawson said, gestured toward the cupboard containing Mavis's collection of crystal stemware, "put the nicotine and some sherry in right here at the sink, and carried it out into the hallway, maybe intending to carry it around until a switch could be made, but Mrs. Cunningham's glass was still sitting on the hall table, so this person made the switch right then.

Mavis frowned. When at last she spoke, her voice was faintly mocking. "This last version of yours, Inspector – the fresh-glass-from-the cabinet version –would mean there was an extra glass floating around. Was there?"

"An extra glass could have been washed and put back

in the cupboard."

"And do you have any evidence that is what happened? Did anybody witness this?"

Dawson said nothing, but the expression on his face conceded the point.

"Well, then," she said, dismissively, plucking a dead petal from a rose in the vase and setting it on the table. "Besides, I must say I prefer your first version," she continued. "At least it broadens your range of suspects."

"Actually, all versions call for someone to leave the party – something that would be fairly obvious to the other guests." He paused and took a sip of his wine. "Unless it was you."

"Me? Why wouldn't it be equally obvious if I left the party?"

"I'm sure you've heard the murder story about the mailman. He was the guilty party, but no one saw him because he was there every day and as such had become virtually invisible."

"Probably an urban legend. Besides, I'm hardly invisible, Inspector."

Dawson's smile was small. "No, you're not. But it's the same concept. As hostess, if you left the party to go into another room, you would do so with impunity. No one would think anything of it and would, in fact, put it right out of their mind. On the other hand, if one of the other guests – the bishop would be an extreme example – were to leave, it would be noticed and remembered."

"Well, I'm certainly glad to hear you think the bishop is innocent."

"And there's the time element. She drank the sherry

just after she returned from using the bathroom."

"Gwen did not sip at sherry, Inspector. I'm sure you've heard from other people present. She carried it around for a while, and then tossed it back like someone might a shot of whiskey. She could have been carrying the poisoned glass around for some time before she drank."

Dawson said nothing, and Mavis continued. "This is all just conjecture, Inspector. No one saw the nicotine added to the glass, no one saw the glasses switched, there was no extra glass found. So none of these little scenarios can you take to the prosecutor, am I right?"

Dawson drained his glass. "You're right."

"Well then, it seems the verdict of suicide will stand."

"Unless I can convince the DA to reopen."

"Without evidence," Mavis said. She reached for the wine bottle as though to pour some into her glass, then stopped. "I mustn't have any more." She stood and went to the sink. "I think I'll continue with water. Would you like some?"

"No thanks,"

"I'm driving into the city tonight," she said over her shoulder. "Symphony, you know. Sergio's conducting."

"Ah," Dawson said as he slipped the rose petal into a small evidence bag in his pocket. Fingerprints from organic material were difficult to lift, but worth a try–might give a clue as to *bkgd.* Lieberman claimed he had a tech that could get a print off water.

"I attended last Sunday's matinée." He didn't mention it had been a date with Marjorie Meyerson.

Mavis turned from the sink. She was holding a glass of water. "Did you enjoy the concert?"

"Excellent concert – probably the program you'll be hearing this evening."

"A Chopin piano concerto. It doesn't get much better than that."

"No, indeed it doesn't." He stood. "I won't keep you," he said, placing his glass on the counter. At the front door, he turned back to Mavis. "The Catholics may have something – about confession, I mean."

"Goodbye, Inspector," Mavis said. She closed the door firmly behind him and returned to the kitchen table where she sat with her head in her hands, thinking of what Dawson could find if he pursued it hard enough – and then what Carol Anne would know: that she was the illegitimate daughter of a major crime boss, that Stephen Dillon was fiction, that her mother had killed a woman.

She picked up the origami bird Dawson had fashioned and crushed it, then gathered her own napkin and plucked another drooping petal from the rose. She looked around for the first one, but couldn't find it – not on the seat of one of the chairs, not on the floor. Suddenly, she remembered the time in Las Vegas, almost thirty years ago. She had been fingerprinted in an under-cover sting when she was working as an escort. Her face burned with anger – and fear. If Dawson took it, it was for a purpose. *This man is so dangerous on so many levels,* she thought. And knew what she had to do.

When Dawson reached the station, he called Eggleton into his office.

"Jesus man!" Eggleton exclaimed when Dawson had finished relating his time with Mavis. "You need to watch your back. She's killed once to save her secret. She won't hesitate another time."

Dawson waved a dismissive hand. "She gets me, she still has you, because she'll know I've told you. Then she would have to get Jennings for the same reason. I don't think she's going to start that fall of dominoes. "

"You don't *think*! Wisdom from an experienced cop if I've ever heard it!" Eggleton said, his voice heavy with scorn, and walked out the door. When he got to his desk, he phoned Laura. "I won't be home tonight. I'm going to sit outside Jake's place. I'll explain later."

Dawson heard much the same when he called Jennings. "Be very vigilant," Jennings said. "She won't hesitate."

"You sound like my Sergeant," Dawson said.

"Then he's a wise man," Jennings responded and hung up before Dawson could say more.

Dawson shrugged and walked down the hall to Lieberman's office to deliver a rose petal.

CHAPTER TWENTY-THREE

The Night Watch

...what shall a man give in exchange for his soul?
Matt: 16:26

July 11

Dawson's cell rang at 3 a.m..

"What the . . .?" he snapped, his voice thick with sleep and anger.

"Sorry to wake you, Inspector. This is Officer Brady."

"Yeah?"

"I'm at the scene of an accident, Sir. Car went off the road and hit a tree. Single car accident. Anyway, I thought you'd be interested, given the case you were working on a while ago – the Cunningham death."

Dawson was suddenly wide awake. "And?"

"Well, the car and the victim are pretty well banged up, but I'm pretty sure the victim is Mavis Dillon."

"Shit!"

"I called it in as soon as I got here, and then I ran the plates. I couldn't get in the car to check registration or her purse. Front end too smashed. Anyway, plates say it's her car, and there's a blonde woman in the car. No question she's dead."

"Shit! You sure it's her?"

"Yeah. I remember her from the Cunningham scene.

I was assigned to stay with the suspects while you were interviewing, so I got a good look at her. Like I said, she's pretty messed up now, but let's say I'm ninety-nine percent sure it's her."

Dawson shook his head as though to clear the image.

"I called you when I learned whose car it is. I thought you might want to come out."

"Where are you?"

"About a mile off the highway on Vintner Lane." He paused. "Sir, I didn't see any evidence of evasive action."

"Huh?"

"Skid marks, Sir."

"Ummm. Call Doctor Henchcombe and Doctor Lieberman."

"Sir!"

"All right. You call Doctor Henchcombe, and I'll call Doctor Lieberman."

"Thank you, Sir."

"How come you're there?"

"I was just getting off duty and on my way home. Vintner's a shortcut."

"You were right to call me; I'll see you in a few minutes," Dawson said and hung up.

Marty Lieberman was even less happy to be awakened than Dawson had been.

"What the fuck?" he shouted.

Dawson held his phone away from his ear. "Yeah, Marty. It's Jake. We've got an accident on Vintner Lane. Seems Mavis Dillon wrapped her car around a tree out there. She's dead."

"Shit!"

"A lot of that going around," Dawson said. "Can you meet me out there? Officer on the scene's calling Hench."

"Oh, he'll be delighted," Lieberman said and ended the call.

Dawson's next call was to Eggleton's cell. "Wake up, Sunshine."

Eggleton, who had fallen asleep in his car outside Dawson's condo, said, "Huh?"

"We're going detecting."

"Uh . . . where . . . where should I meet you?"

"You should just stay where you are. Outside my place."

"How did you . . . ?"

"I know many things, Sergeant. I'll be out as soon as I get dressed."

"I'm going to need a bathroom."

Dawson sighed. "I'll unlock the front door."

By the time Dawson and Eggleton arrived, the scene was one of flashing lights and emergency vehicles. If the responders were surprised to see a Detective Inspector, his Sergeant, the Coroner, and the head of Forensics on the scene, they made no mention, but their eyes asked questions. Henchcombe was, as usual, immaculate in an overall garment with pant legs and sleeves creased to military perfection. Lieberman's overall gave credence to the department rumor about him sleeping in his clothes.

It was the head of the Emergency Response Team who approached Dawson. "Is this a crime scene, Sir?"

"It doesn't appear to be," Dawson said. "But I wanted it checked out. The victim was a person of interest in a previous crime. Her death, if not an accident, could have some bearing on that case." *(Which is now closed due to Moynahan's corrupt nature,* he thought, but decided not to say.) "So I wanted Doctor Henchcombe and Doctor Lieberman here at the scene."

"Yes, Sir."

"Have you found anything to indicate this was not an accident?"

"No, Sir. Not really. Except – I think Officer Brady already told you – there's no evidence of skid marks, so if she swerved – like a deer or something - we would've found skids. Also, the tracks run directly across the dirt on the side of the road without hesitation, like she just drove straight through. The big guy over there, he's taking a real close look."

"Doctor Lieberman."

"Huh?"

"The big guy."

"Oh. And it looks like she wasn't wearing her seat belt. Anyway, your shop'll check for mechanical failure – brakes went out maybe . . ." He shrugged. "I figure you'll have your answers in a few days." Then, turning back to look at the demolished car, he said, "If it's OK with you, Sir, I'll order the body removed to the ambulance and get the tow truck started pulling the car."

"Go ahead."

Dawson stood for a moment, looking at the demolished car. Then he walked slowly toward where Eggleton was waiting. "She didn't need to do that, Bill," he said.

"What if I was wrong? I couldn't prove anything."

She didn't know that, Eggleton thought.

She probably figured you'd worry it like a dog with a bone, Eggleton thought.

But, being a kind man, all he said was, "Probably couldn't live with her conscience."

EPILOGUE

"Lord, let me know mine end, and the number of my days...
Psalm 39: 4

July 14

It was just a few weeks after her wedding that Carole Anne Dillon Sokolov again entered St. Francis Episcopal Church and made her way slowly down the aisle. This time she was on the arm of her husband. This time she slipped into a front pew. This time she wore black.

Next to Carole Anne sat the tiny figure of Andrew's wife, Fiona. Fiona cried softly into a linen handkerchief, accepting the comforting pats of her equally distraught husband who sat on her other side.

For the prelude, the organist chose Bach's *Jesu, Joy of Man's Desiring*. Dawson approved. Unlike the service for Gwen Cunningham, St. Francis was filled to capacity, and when Dawson and Eggleton arrived, they had to take a standing position along the back wall. Like the service for Gwen Cunningham, two simple bouquets of roses stood behind the altar. Seeing the roses, Dawson swallowed deeply.

He had received a call that morning regarding the rose petal he had taken to the lab.

"Pain in the ass to process a print on a rose petal," the forensic technician said without preamble. "Very difficult. However, I'm extremely good at what I do. Extremely. How

377

come Lieberman was in such a flap to get this done?"

Dawson ignored the question. Instead he said, "It's a moot point. She's dead. Sorry. I should have called you."

"Huh! All my excellent work for nothing! However, just for your information, your subject – now dead – was a hooker in Vegas nearly thirty years ago. Got busted in a sting operation – some *escort service.*" His voice and his words were heavy with disdain. *"Escort!"* he said again. Dawson thanked him and was glad to hang up. *Too much information,* he thought.

The procession began at the back of the church. The Bishop, dressed in a white cope and miter, and reading from The Book of Common Prayer, entered. *"I am the resurrection and the life, saith the Lord."* The congregation stood. *"He that believeth in me . . ."* and so the small procession, led by a crucifer and followed immediately by the Bishop and Father Gifford, made its way to the front of the church where a beautiful hardwood casket sat on a draped bier – a closed casket. It was a short service which began with prayers and scripture readings. Charles Glasco, his eyes brimming with unshed tears, read from the 39th Psalm. *"Lord, let me know mine end, and the number of my days,"* he began – then stopped. He cleared his throat and continued in a stronger voice. *"That I may be certified how long I have to live."*

Father Gifford stood to give the eulogy. He began with the words, "A tragic accident," but Dawson and Eggleton knew it was no accident. A report they received shortly after the crash confirmed the response officer's observation that Mavis had not been wearing a seatbelt at the time of the crash, and the brakes were in good condition, underscoring their belief the incident was deliberate. Dawson had asked that the information not be released to the news media or given to Carole Anne. He knew his request was probably futile.

There were the final prayers, and then the Bishop spoke the same words he had recently said over Gwen Cunningham's body where it lay on the oriental carpet in Mavis's drawing room: *"Into thy hands, O merciful Savior, we commend thy servant, Mavis . . . ."*

Dawson, struck with the irony that neither Mavis Dillon nor Gwen Cunningham had gone to their graves with their real names, for one nearly hysterical moment pictured St. Peter with his roll sheet denying access to the two women.

And then it was over. The organist began Franck's *Chorale in A Minor* as the Bishop, followed by Father Gifford, began a slow walk down the aisle. The casket, borne by Andrew MacBride, Charles Glasco, George Alexander, Sergio Sokolov and two dark-suited men from the funeral home, followed the small procession. Carole Anne and Fiona, each supporting the other, came last.

Outside the crowd milled, shaking their heads as people do after an event they cannot understand. Dawson and Eggleton skirted the crowd, making for the parking lot.

"I notice nobody's asking us to a party," Eggleton said.

"Ah, Inspector, Sergeant!" George Alexander, accompanied by Dolores, came toward the two policemen, his hand outstretched. "A tragedy," he said, gripping first

Dawson's hand and then Eggleton's. "A terrible tragedy." He, too, shook his head, his eyes fixed on Carole Anne where she stood beside her husband. "I overheard her husband say that when she got the news of her mother's accident, she just picked up her violin and began playing." He made a small "tch, tch" behind his teeth. "So sudden – we never know how to act." Dolores looked at him, a faintly quizzical expression on her face, and he put his hand on her arm. "I was just telling Dolores about when my father died. It was like that," he said, snapping his fingers, "and he was gone. And my mother ironed. She just kept ironing." He shrugged. "Even Mavis – after Gwen's suicide," and if he gave a particular inflection to the word 'suicide' neither policeman heard it, "there's Mavis, in the kitchen – before your guys got there . . ." he made a sweeping gesture to include Dawson and Eggleton ". . . and I was on my way down the hall to the bathroom. Anyway, I glanced into the kitchen, and there's Mavis washing one of the sherry glasses. Sherry glasses all over the place, and she washes one." He shook his head again, in puzzlement perhaps, at the vagaries of human nature. "Go figure." And, with another "tch, tch," he took Dolores's arm. As the couple walked away, Dolores's words drifted back. "George, what on earth was all. . .?"

Eggleton, who had been watching Dawson carefully during the exchange, could see the lines of tension on Dawson's face relax slightly.

"He knew," Eggleton said. "All the time, he knew."

Dawson nodded.

"And now he wanted you to know."

Dawson nodded again.

380

"Go figure," Eggleton said.

"Jake!"

It was Marjorie Meyerson.

"I didn't see you," Dawson said.

"Lost in the crowd. I saw you at the back of the church. I hadn't realized you were coming." She slipped her arm through his. "You look like a cup of tea would be a good thing. We'll go to my house. I have a beautiful new cup you can use."

Dawson smiled – just a small one – but the first Eggleton had seen in many days. "That's your cup," Dawson said.

"Perhaps we could share," she said. She turned to Eggleton. "If you could spare him for a few hours, Sergeant?"

"I could," Eggleton said.

And Marjorie led Dawson to the parking lot.

"Go figure," Eggleton said again, this time to himself.

That night, when he and Laura lay spooned in bed, and he was telling her about the funeral, he said, "And then they went off to share a stupid cup of tea! Who shares a stupid cup of tea?"

"Ummm," Laura said, turning and pulling him to her. "Would you like to share a stupid cup of tea?"

"You think they . . .?"

"Oh, yeh."

ABOUT THE AUTHOR

Carol Biederman is a writer, storyteller, musician, and, when time allows, quilter. She is the author of *The Oldest Inhabitant,* a collection of short stories about the Gold Country. Her work has appeared in a number of literary publications, as well as *Ellery Queen Mystery Magazine.* She holds a Bachelor of Music degree with an emphasis on liturgical music, a California Teaching Credential, and a Master of Science in Counseling Psychology. Carol leads Ghost Tours in Columbia State Historic Park, volunteers in the Education Department at a nearby prison, serves as Director of Music at St. Clare Episcopal Church in Avery, California, and is a member of the St. James Concert Series Board in Sonora, California. Carol is a twenty-year student of Tai Chi. She lives in the Sierra foothills with her husband, Gordon, and their psychotic miniature golden doodle, Jodi.

30992414R10215

Made in the USA
San Bernardino, CA
29 February 2016